A LIFE GIVEN TO ME

PART TWO: 1982-2019 LOWELL MASSACHUSETTS

PART ONE: A CHILDHOOD TRAGEDY UNDER A MOTHER'S WATCH
1975-1982 LOWELL MASSACHUSETTS

Catherine Mellen

NFB Publishing
Buffalo, New York

Copyright © 2022 Catherine Mellen
Printed in the United States of America

A Life Given to Me, Part Two: 1982-2019 Lowell Massachusetts/Mellen- 1st Edition

ISBN: 978-1-953610-38-6

1.Title. 2. Memoir/Autobiography. 3. Childhood Trauma/Abuse. 4. Survivor. 5. Nonfiction.

No part of this book may be reproduced or transmitted in any form by any means, electronic or mechanical, including photocopying, recording, or by any information storage and retrieval system without permission in writing by the author.

NFB
<<<>>>
NFB Publishing/Amelia Press
119 Dorchester Road
Buffalo, New York 14213

For more information visit
Nfbpublishing.com

Dedicated to all the statistics in a world full of abused children and the voices left silent in the wake of a horrifying reality.

If you suffer from child rape or suspect a child is being abused, please call 1-800-387-5437 to report a concern to a Child Intervention caseworker. They are available in multiple languages, 24 hours a day. You can report anonymously or give your name and telephone number.

Trigger Warning

This book consists of graphic material content involving childhood, mental and emotional abuse. Please read with caution.

If you suffer from child rape or suspect a child is being abused, please call 1-800-387-5437 to report a concern to a Child Intervention caseworker. They are available in multiple languages, 24 hours a day.

Contents

Introduction	11
A Little Bit of Confusion	15
A Teenage Promise and a Road Unknown	59
A Life Given To Me: Under God's Watch	135
Moving Forward on a Path Called Life	167
A Search for Answers and The Horrifying Reality	217
An Abused Child (Poem)	241
About the Author	243

Introduction

How could I possibly have known I would grow up to be smack dab in the middle of repressed memories, unsolved murders and a horrifying reality? I grew up in a world when the library was our google and smoke signals were the 911 for emergencies. It was also a time when family secrets were kept secrets and child abuse was a silenced matter. For six years of my childhood I was a trophy in a child predator's sick world where I was raised to believe family secrets were a part of life and admitting you're being abused also meant you would be looked down upon by society.

From late 1975 until the last attack on me in 1981, I was abused by a man who continued to rape and terrorize my childhood because he was allowed to by a mother who continued to defend his actions towards her own daughter. I told her about the cloth he made me smell to put me asleep on Fletcher Street and a jug of blue liquid she found tucked under her bed on Pleasant Street. Throughout the years of 1975-1981, I went to my birth mother about things her boyfriend Dave was doing to me.

Growing up I was often told how it was my responsibility to forgive my birth mother and I did try, but all it did was drown me. It took me many years to forgive myself for what happened to me when I was a child. A helpless and defenseless child who my mother allowed to be viciously abused by the same man she slept next to every night

In hopes to be part of the only family I knew to be mine, I stayed quiet to avoid the many confrontations as I was always worried what they would say, what they would think and how they would feel about me bringing up my childhood again. Though I was not to blame for what happened to me when I was a child, I blamed myself for always remembering. It was easier to believe it was my fault than it was to believe my own family didn't love me. A painful truth I would one day have to face. In order to forget my abuse I had to forget my childhood, yet I wanted the people from my childhood to be in my adult life. It was a confusing scenario I replayed over and over again for twenty plus years. An emotional roller coaster of reconnections, distancing and the lasting effects of being a grown up abused child.

My story starts one year after my childhood tragedy was over and months after what would become Lowell, Massachusetts second unsolved murder in a year. In hopes millions like myself who suffer from childhood trauma and family secrets know they are not alone, bringing awareness about the little girl in photos buried in a cellar wall and the unsolved murders in my hometown of Lowell, Massachusetts. My name is Catherine Alice Mellen and this is my continuing life story, a life given to me.

A Little Bit of Confusion

I found myself at age twelve years old standing on a sidewalk looking at the front door of 33 Butler Ave as I thought about the people who were inside. They were my family and I was so unwanted by them, but why? Why did they hate me so much? They all knew I was living next door with the Landry family who were complete strangers to me. They all knew I suffered a severe physical beating on Pleasant Street. They all knew I was missing from the home.

I was just a kid feeling an empty gut wrenching, heart tearing and hurting sadness.

With all the inhumane things done to me, forced to do and left to feel for a lifetime, what hurt me to the core was the lack of support, acknowledgement and accountability from my own family. Dave was going to kill me, bury me in that cellar hole and I lost my family because I didn't let him. All I was to my mother in the summer of 1982 was a reminder of the man she lost because I ran to my friend's house that Saturday morning a year earlier.

They could never understand how much emotional pain I felt that day as I stood on the sidewalk looking at the front door my family lived in. Like a slice ripped open in my heart with mounds of burning blood dripping one drop at a time. My eyes burnt as I tried so hard to not cry. Before tears could fall, Sandi's family pulled up and I headed off for the weekend back at Sandi's house where I had lived for ten months the year before. As always I had a lot of fun being a kid at her house. I assumed I was going to live with Sandi again but her parents thought I was only staying the weekend.

When the weekend was over I was questioned if my mother was coming to pick me up. So I called my mother and when she answered I told her I was at Sandi's house and she had to come get me. My mother snapped at me, asking why she had to pick me up? "Because I'm your daughter," I answered her. Then my mother questioned me, "Is there anyone else you can stay with?" I started screaming into the phone, "Yes there's my dad," I yelled as I started getting upset over my mother's unloving ways. "He moved out of state," she snapped as I went on naming my uncle and her neighbors. But she had excuses for every name I said until finally stating, "I'm on my way." Sandi and I were dumbfounded as we wondered why my mother was so mean to me. We went upstairs to get my duffle bag, I thanked her mom and stepdad for letting me stay over and then we went to sit on the outside front steps as we waited for my mother to pick me up. Her neighbors Tammy and Jimmy came over to hang out with us also. We are all around the same age, give or take a year apart at the most.

Moments later my mother pulled up in her car. I grabbed my duffle bag, said goodbye to my friends and headed to the passenger side of my mother's car. I was about to open her passenger side door when I heard her voice outside of the car. So I turned around to where my friends were standing and there was my mother outside her car asking them all a question.

"Will your mother let Cathy stay with you?" I heard her question Sandi whose mother already raised me for almost a year. My mother then questioned my friend Tammy who she didn't even know. "Are you kidding me," I yelled at my mother as I stood there so embarrassed, humiliated and pissed off. My mother acted as if I wasn't even there. Then she questioned Jimmy, "Will your mother let her stay?" I was beyond baffled as Jimmy said to me, "Don't worry Cathy I got this." My mother walked right by me and followed Jimmy to his house. She never went inside his house as she talked to Jimmy's mom through an open window. Less than a minute later my mother walked right by me. Looking at me with a smirk as she got in her car and didn't say one word to me. My friend's and I were all flabbergasted over my mother's actions.

I met Jimmy's mom from hanging in the neighborhood when I lived at Sandi's the year before but my mother didn't know her. All my mother cared about was that I didn't go home with her and leaving me feeling so very beyond abandoned. There I was by seven o'clock that night living with a new family, my friend Sandi's neighbors. I stayed out of school the first week I lived with them because I led them to believe I was still going to the Moody School as I was the year before when I lived with Sandi's family. Jimmy's mother Rosie was very nice, understanding and motherly as she could tell I was having an emotionally hard time dealing with why I was living with them and not my own family. All I did was cry and cry. She was just as shocked over my mother's approach to her through her living room window. She explained to me that no matter the situation at home, no mother should ever abandon their child as my own mother did to me.

It wasn't long until Rosie confronted me about going to the Butler School which was walking distance and I went back to school. I would walk to the corner of Sandi's house, turn down Barrington St, cross Andrews St, down to Otis St and cut through to an open field of train tracks that was once home to the prince spaghetti company, then I'd walk the back way up to the Butler School. I also had the same rules at the Sullivan home as I did at my mother's cousin, my friend Sandi and the Landry homes which was to clean up after myself, do my homework and be a kid. But all I did was cry because I couldn't understand why? All those times Dave told me he would kill my family. All those times I kept his secret so he didn't kill them.

So many times, for so many years he threatened of killing my brothers and baby sister and there I was without them. I couldn't understand why my family never called the police. All I wanted was not to be attacked, raped, abused or terrorized again. No one stopped Dave from raping me, from abusing me, from terrorizing me and no one protected me.

There was no reason why my mother hated me the way she did. I didn't want to be raped or killed by Dave and that is no reason to hate your child. It didn't change the fact that I was just a twelve-year-old kid in 1982 who wanted to be home with her family.

I stayed living with the Sullivan family for almost two months and they even offered me the choice to be adopted by them. As much as I tried to stay strong, I cried a lot while I lived with them. I called my mother a few times but every phone call left me crying until Rosie convinced me that the calls weren't worth the heartache and I knew she was right. I was a little bit of an explorer and tried all different ways of walking to the Butler Jr High School from Agawam Street. Some days I walked down Lawrence Street and cut through the old mills. Some days I cut through the old Prince spaghetti factory and some days I walked straight down Moore Street and stopped at Cunningham's variety store for snacks on Gorham Street.

Sandi's mother found out my mother abandoned me again and told Sandi to call me over at Jimmy's to let me know I was welcomed to live with them again. I gathered my clothes and I thanked the Sullivan family for all they did for me. Especially Rosie for all her motherly talks with me. But Sandi's family was the closest I had to a family and by November 1982, I was back living with Sandi and her family. I continued going to school at the Butler School while Sandi and her sister went to a catholic school on Gorham Street.

Soon it was my thirteenth birthday December 15, 1982 where there was cake for me and Christmas was a lot less awkward for me as Sandi's family continued to make me feel at home. The same rules applied as when I lived with them before. Of course, being older meant we all had chores to do. From dusting, mopping floors, vacuuming or laundry, we all took turns with the chores and sometimes we would make money off of Sandi's older sister by doing her chores for her. I was always included in all their family gatherings. From a holiday get together, Portuguese festivals, trips out to dinner, for ice cream, ice skating at Janas Skating Rink on Douglas Road or on a frozen pond. Always paying my way so I could get a snack at the local variety store Quelly's on South Whipple Street, paying my way at the High-hat roller rink or a Friday night school dance which was held at the Sacred Heart school hall on Andrews Street. I felt my safest when I lived with my friend Sandi and her family. I felt the most comfortable not only in the home but also in my life.

I felt it was ok to be a kid and I learned to not feel scared about wanting to be a kid. Moving back in with Sandi again made for a safe and fun ending to one year, and a promising start to the next.

As 1983 started off, life for me was once again back to being a more normal one. I was getting to know more of the kids in Sandi's neighborhood and I was learning to live with stability being a teenager in Lowell, Massachusetts. Sandi's family always encouraged me no matter how many times I needed to hear it. My favorite memory was taking long walks after dinner with Sandi, her mom and her siblings throughout Lowell's Cemetery on Lawrence Street and exploring all the very amazing and very old tombstones. Some of Lowell's most famous people and tombstones are in that cemetery of narrow pathways and beautiful trees, flowers and landscape. Making a walk through the cemetery in any season a pure serenity experience.

When springtime came, we learned how easy it was to skip school and how easy it was to get caught by her stepfather who would sometimes come home for his lunch break from work. The phone calls to my mother stopped as she never bothered to call me either and some days it hurt more than others. Sandi's mother Honoria hated to see me cry. One day she knew I was upset and sat me down at the dining room table. "This is not your fault," she said as she explained how wrong my mother was for her actions towards me as a mother. "No one is hurting you anymore," she continued to reassure me and I knew she was very much right.

Sandi's mom and stepfather would go out sometimes and leave us to watch over the younger siblings. With no internet or cell phones invented yet, we entertained ourselves the best we could. From turning the volume to high on the television as the latest music video aired on the MTV music channel, dressing up in her mom's clothes or taking a mattress off a bed and using it to slide down the stairs. We were ordering food to be delivered across the street to the mayor's house. (Mayor M Brendan Fleming, Lowell's Mayor 1982-1984) Something we started doing when I lived with Sandi the year before. The mayor's sons would pay for the food when it got delivered as we would crack up laughing peeking through a shade out the window from a room with the lights off. Until one day an older brother opened his door, paid for the food we ordered and then waved to me and Sandi as we peaked out the window.

We never ordered take-out food to the mayor's home again.

As the school year was coming to a close, we were taking risks more often and skipping school more. I would pretend to walk to school while Sandi and her sister would do the same. Then we'd turn around and go back home. Hiding in the closets when her mother or stepfather came home for lunch and answering the phone when their school called to report they had been absent from school. I was off the hook on that as my school never called my friend's house when I skipped with them. Like my 6th grade diploma, my absence from school phone calls also went to my mother. One day when we all skipped school Sandi and I had a mattress off a bed and was sliding with it down the inside stairs. We had done it plenty of times before only this time we weren't expecting her stepfather to come home early that day and we all got caught skipping school, me included and we all got grounded.

Running errands with Sandi and her stepfather one day, we drove by a place that looked very familiar to me. As we were driving back, I was looking out the window of the truck when I noticed cobblestones. If I could have spun my head in full circle I would have as I focused solely on where the cobblestones led too; the rows of brick apartments my dad and stepmother lived in. I stared out the truck window and watched as we drove by. Heading straight down the street to a gas station called Haffeners and onto the cobblestone street of downtown Lowell. I knew right away how close my dad actually lived to the downtown area. Then my eyes focused on the drive from those cobblestones to Sandi's home on Agawam Street. I started to question myself, 'Where has my dad been?' I last saw him when he was expecting me to stay over his place in January of 1981, it was now June 1983. I don't know why I didn't think to find my dad's phone number or where he lived or if he really did move out of state, but I knew I was going to find out.

It was the first Friday in June when I left my friend's house in the morning and pretended I was heading to school. Without telling Sandi, I decided I wasn't going to school when I went to bed the night before. Knowing the school department called my mother's house when I missed school and not Sandi's house, I knew I wouldn't get caught. I hid outside by the prince spaghetti factory and waited a while in the morning before heading down Lawrence Street. I walked until I got to the end at Zayre's department store and I continued walking through the downtown area until I found the gas station Haffeners which had a neon sign with a donkey that kicks hanging high above the building and the streets of cobblestones below.

I knew my dad was up the street from there so I continued walking until I saw the rows of brick apartment buildings. When I saw the street, sign read Garin Terrace, I ran as fast as I could until I reached my dad's door. I opened the screen door and pounded on the main door. A woman opened the door and told me she had just moved in a few weeks earlier. I questioned if she knew where my dad moved to but she didn't know where the previous tenants moved. I looked at the other doors in the row of apartments, but I knew I had the right door. I felt so alone as I sat on the sidewalk and cried.

A boy about my age came over to me while riding his bike. He questioned me, "Why are you so sad?" I told him my dad used to live there but moved and I didn't know where to. "You mean Miller?" the boy questioned me as he sat on his bike. I knew that was my dad's nickname from when I stayed with him before so I nodded my head yes. "I know where he moved to," he said to me, "follow me," he continued as he pedaled his bike away. I got up from the sidewalk and followed him. I ran across Adam's Street and over to the Market Street brick apartments. I followed him to a door he stopped at. "Your dad moved here on the first floor to your right," he said to me as he explained, "I helped him and his wife move." I thanked him and headed inside the hallway of the brick apartment.

I walked to the door I was told was my dad's and I knocked on it. My stepmother opened the door and I was swallowed into the apartment by the huge hug she gave me. My dad was sitting on a chair looking at me with an ear-to-ear smile and looking frail as he reached his arms out to hug me. He questioned me, "Where have you been?" As I looked at him, "Where have you been?" I questioned him in return.

Seeing my dad for the first time in two years, I had mixed emotions. I was glad to see him again and glad I found him again but upset he moved without telling me as I wondered where he had been. My dad told me how he was calling me for the past two years. "Your mother moves without telling me and she always has a story about how you're too busy or don't want to see us," my dad said to me in a disgusted attitude while talking about my mother. "You've been calling me?" I questioned him as he informed me, "We waited two years for you." He continued to explain he had to move because he wasn't able to make the stairs to his bedroom anymore. "We needed a one floor apartment," "We waited for you and I told your mother," he continued saying to me. Then he leaned over reaching for another hug from me. I told my dad that I never knew he was calling and how I thought he moved out of state. My dad was so upset over the loss of time he should have had with me. He called my mother a selfish woman and then mumbled about her not being a woman at all.

My dad and I talked a lot that day. He was not happy to hear I was living with friends and not family. (I think I could see the steam coming from his ears) I told him I was very happy living where I was with Sandi's family and even happier that I found him again. He explained how the state only allowed him to get a one-bedroom apartment because he couldn't find me and he was out of work due to being sick. He looked more skinny, frail and old since I last saw him in January 1981 but I assumed it was just because he was sick like he told me. I ate lunch with my dad and stepmother. We talked about my friends, where I was living and my upcoming 8th grade graduation. They told me my dad would still be too sick to attend my graduation. I didn't understand how he knew he'd still be sick in two weeks but I noticed the time and I had to get back to Sandi's house. I got his phone number, another hug and headed back to Sandi's where I started talking to my dad on an everyday basis.

Whenever we talked, my dad would ask so many questions about my friends, school, the places I lived and if I wanted to go live with my uncle; his brother. He questioned how my days were, what I was wearing, my schoolwork and even gave me money to go places with Sandi so her mother didn't have to always pay. I assured my dad I was very happy living at Sandi's house.

Shortly after reconnecting with my dad and talking with him every day on the phone, my mother called me. I wasn't happy when she called me as I answered her call, "What do you want?" I snapped. My mother insisted she just wanted to talk. She began with a question, "How's school going?" I told her I was passing 8th grade and my graduation was soon. She informed me she would go to it but I wasn't interested in listening to her talk at all until she informed me, "We moved again." I shook my head in disbelief as I said into the telephone "Again, where to this time?" I questioned my mother. "Right down the street from Sandi's house," she answered me as she continued talking and letting me know she didn't have a man living with her anymore. That's when she questioned me, "Want to move back home?" I stood there in Sandi's kitchen staring at the phone in my hand and then I hung it up. It was the first time I said out loud, 'My mother is whacked.'

I continued living with Sandi's family, talking to my dad on the phone every day and when my 8th grade graduation came, I didn't go to it. Instead, Sandi and I walked to where my mother had moved which was literally right down the street and one street over from Sandi's house. My mother wasn't home because she went to my graduation and it didn't bother me, she went there. It would have bothered me if I had gone to my graduation and I saw her there. Sandi and I just really wanted to see where my mother had moved to. Like my 6th grade diploma and my absence from school phone calls, my 8th grade diploma also got sent to my mother's address.

I grew up fast in the two years since I first ran to Sandi's house in June 1981. Being thirteen years old in June 1983 seemed like my horrible childhood was a million years behind me. That monster was out of my life and that's all that mattered to me. I guess I cried myself out when it came to being unwanted by my family. I had no more tears to cry over being unwanted, unloved or unworthy by them anymore. When I first ran in 1981, I was a scared confused kid. Now 1983, I was a steadfastly determined never to be touched or hurt again teenager. I spent the summer living at Sandi's house, dodging my mother's phone calls and walking to my dad's when I could. As summer went on, my mother's phone calls to Sandi's house became more persistent. She was constantly asking me to move back home and informing me she talks to my father and she knows I talk to him. I informed my mother of all the lies she told me about my dad, asking why she kept me from him and hanging up the telephone before I could hear her answer. I guess I knew her answer would more than likely be another lie. One day when I walked over to my dad's, I was a bit mad at him. I questioned him if he was calling my mother. He immediately answered me, "Yes," as he explained he wanted to know where my social security checks were going. "What checks?" I asked my dad with a very confused look on my face. "What's social security?" I questioned him again.

He explained due to him being sick, the state paid him and paid me social security checks every month. "Your mother gets them to take care of you," he informed me. I yelled at my dad, "I'm not living with my mother again." But my dad explained to me, "I want them going to Sandi's mother." He told me the money was so I had new school clothes and stuff I needed. But as the end of August approached, school was about to start and Sandi's mom was going through a tough time as her and her husband were divorcing. I told my dad about it and he expressed his concerns about wanting me to move in with my uncle. I told him I didn't want to be taken away from my friends. My aunt and uncle lived outside of Lowell which meant I would have to switch schools and miss all my friends. My dad and I talked a lot on the subject until I agreed that I would move back in with my mother since she didn't have a man living with her. "Maybe it will be different this time," I said to my dad. He was not happy I came up with that solution but he agreed with me. I called my mother and I told my friend Sandi who helped me carry my belongings into my mother's apartment located at 783 Lawrence Street in the South Lowell section of Lowell and right across the street from the Lawrence Street firehouse.

I confronted my mother about the checks my dad told me about and she took me school shopping at a mall. I didn't buy anything as we walked the mall. I wasn't interested in buying anything with my mother. I wasn't embarrassed being there with my mother, I just didn't want to be there with her. I didn't want to be anywhere with my mother. She didn't want to talk about the years prior and all I saw every time I looked at her was Dave, the monster who terrorized my childhood. That's what I saw every time I looked at my mother, my childhood on Fletcher and Pleasant Street. I convinced her to give me money so I could do my own school shopping downtown. She gave me eighty dollars and that was a lot of money for a teenager in 1983. I shopped at Zayre's, Cherry & Webb and Jordan Marsh for clothes. I went to Thom McCann's for a pair of Exersoles and a pair of canvas Nike sneakers. And soon it was the start of my freshman year in high school as I started school in the downtown area at Lowell High.

I took the city bus to school but I walked home so I could walk to my dads more often during the week. Eating supper at my dads and sleeping at my friend Sandi's house on the weekends made it real easy to avoid my mother; the woman I was once dead to. My baby sister was now seven years old, my older brothers were hardly home and I was having a hard time emotionally being back home with the same people who failed to protect me and who didn't seem to care what I had lived through. The more I had to go home, the more I hated my life. One day after school, my dad had a coughing fit, I watched him as he struggled to cough and breathe. I then grabbed his pack of cigarettes he had on top of the coffee table in front of him. I took the pack of smokes and went to sit at the far end of the coffee table so my dad couldn't reach me. I took a cigarette out of its box, used my dad's lighter and lit the cigarette.

Being a little cocky I said to him, "What are you going to do, ground me?" I questioned him in a real bratty fresh thirteen year old manner. My dad just chuckled as he hollered for my stepmother who was in their bedroom, "Hey honey." She came walking into the living room as my dad said to me, "She makes all the rules," while he continued to chuckle. My stepmother grabbed the pack of smokes off the coffee table and handed me a cigarette. Then she handed me another one and another one as she made me smoke each and every one until I was sick to my stomach.

My stepmom was a feisty little lady who was always sweet, kind and caring to me. My dad got a good laugh out of the way she made me keep smoking until it made me sick. Any call or visit I made to my dads was always a very welcoming one. I slept on dad's sofa that night as I was too sick to go home. I called my mother to inform her but she demanded I get home. I went home the next morning when I woke up.

Back at my mothers house, I was only home to shower and sleep during the week but I would still have to yell at my mother to stop yelling at me. Everyday I was always yelling at her, "Stop yelling at me." She would yell demanding to know where I was and who I was with. I would yell back at her, "You didn't care last year." As I would remind her of all the days and nights she didn't care where I was. I would bring up my childhood and my mother would quickly walk away. It didn't take me long to figure that out about my mother, how to make her walk away. I tried to talk to her about things Dave did to me and made me do but she would get upset with me for bringing it up. "Jesus Christ Cathy why do you keep bringing it up?" "He's in jail, you have to forget about it," my mother would snap, complain or yell at me. I tried to talk about Butler Avenue and why I had to live with the neighbors but she complained that I kept bringing up the past. I wanted to talk to my mother but all she ever did was yell at me.

I walked to my dads after school like I had been doing for a couple weeks already. It was the end of September and I noticed my dad was still sick so I questioned him, "Why are you still sick?" My dad just looked at me as my stepmother sat down right next me. They took turns explaining to me why my dad was still sick, the machine on the side of his chair, the tube in his nose and the cancer that was taking his life. At first I smiled hoping it was a joke, I kept looking back and forth at my dad in his chair and my stepmom sitting right next me. But it wasn't a joke. I could feel my heart, it fell right in the pit of my stomach as I listened to my dad and stepmom explain to me about my dad's cancer. He found out two years earlier that he had about two years left to live. I was so heartbroken as I listened to what they were saying to me. I cried, they both hugged me and we all cried together. My dad then went on about how my mother will pay some day for all the time he lost with me. "Even as a baby she kept you from me," my dad told me in a heartbroken manner. "Every time we got you, they made us give you back to her," he continued as he talked of my infant years to me. It was the first time I knew of anything from when I was a baby.

I sat on the couch for a few as I took it all in of what was just said to me. I kept shaking my head no. I'd look at my dad and shake my head. I did it a few times until I started thinking. Thinking of my life now, my life a year ago, my life two years ago, my life on Pleasant Street then I thought about my life on Fletcher Street and then I got pissed off. "Why did you have me?" I questioned my dad as I questioned him again before he could answer me. "Why did you and my mother have me?" I was now yelling at my dad. "Why did you have me?" I yelled again. "Why did you guys have me?" I yelled again "Huh dad?" "Why did you have me?" I screamed again, this time in my dad's face as I jumped up from the couch answering all my questions even before my dad had a chance to answer. "So I could be raped by my mother's boyfriend?" "So I could live with other people's families?" "So I could have no parents?" "Why did you have me dad?" I continued to yell causing me to cry as I could tell I was breaking my dad's heart with everything I was saying. I was so upset he was going to die on me and I just got him back in my life. "Just forget it," I yelled as I headed towards the door so I could leave.

"Ohhhh no you don't," my stepmother came running in between me and the door. Blocking me from leaving the apartment. "You're not leaving me with him after all you just said," she said with a warm smile as she gave me a hug and then said, "Get over there and go talk with your father." As she turned me around and directed me to where I was just sitting. My stepmother knew I was upset and she wasn't mean about how she approached me. She was concerned for my dad but she was also concerned for me. She placed a box of tissues on the coffee table and walked out of the room leaving my dad and I to talk. I sat on the couch and apologized to my dad. "Your baby sister's father?" my dad questioned me in reference to what I said in my tantrum about my mother's boyfriend. "Yes," I answered my dad. I told him about my mother always knowing that Dave was hurting me. I didn't call it rape when I talked to my dad, I told him I was forced to do sexual things.

I apologized and cried to my dad for not telling him in previous years about what was being done to me. My dad started being stern with me, "It was not your fault," "You were brainwashed," "You were just a kid," my dad continued as we cried to each other about how my life started out and how his life was about to end. I told my dad how scared I was on Pleasant Street, "That's why I ran to a friend's house." I said as I felt so humiliated the more I talked. "You were brainwashed to not speak of it," my dad repeated numerous times. He told me how he met my mother, about their short marriage, how he met my stepmother, about his first marriage, about my other siblings from his side and how he didn't know how many kids my mother actually had. "Can't believe nothing out of her mouth," he said in a disgusted voice. He told me my grandmother was actually his mother. He also told me how he was severely beaten in an alley when I was a baby and how many blame my mother for arranging it. My dad insisted I go live with my uncle and wanted me to agree so he could call my uncle with the news as he explained my aunt and uncle have always loved me.

I would have to move where my aunt and uncle lived which was to a city called Fall River. I told my dad I would go live with them. My dad wanted to do it that night but I told him I wanted to say bye to my friends. "Give me a week," I said to my dad as I explained that way I could tell my school, say bye to my friends and then move away. "I'm going to the hospital next week," my dad said to me as he explained they were doing more tests and assuring me he would be ok. He was concerned about me being back at my mothers house but I assured him there was no man living there and no way was I going to let anyone hurt me again. He said when he got back home from his stay at the hospital he was going to arrange for me to go live with my uncle. "Where she should have left you," he told me. "When you come home then?" I questioned him and he agreed. When he came back from his short hospital stay is when I would go live with my aunt and uncle in Fall River, Massachusetts.

It was another school night I ended up sleeping at my dads on the couch. It was too dark for me to walk home so I called my mother and told her I was sleeping there. The next morning we had breakfast, talked more and just enjoyed each other's company. My stepmom cooked dinner and I stayed the whole day before walking home to my mother's where she once again greeted me at the door yelling. "Where the heck have you been?" my mother snapped at me. I yelled back at her, "At my dad's." But she didn't care, she went on yelling, "As long as you live under my roof." A speech about me listening to her rules plus being yelled at for not going to school from my fathers house. "You know he's dying right?" I questioned my mother. "Big deal," she snapped at me. I didn't let a word she was saying get to me, never mind her rules.

I was having a real hard time being home with my family. All I wanted to do was talk to my mother about the things Dave did to me and forced me to do. But all my mother did was criticize and belittle me for, "Bringing it up again." I would see my brothers and wonder why they didn't help me after that last attack in the attic of Pleasant Street back in 1981. It was now October 1983 and my childhood seemed so far away in the past. I started to believe I would one day grow up and forget all the things forced onto me by my monster abuser. I just had to get to that day.

First week of October I stopped at my dad's for a visit and dinner. I was going to sleep over that weekend but my friend wanted me to go with her to a party. I last spoke with my dad on October 6, 1983 while I was at Sandi's house after school. Last thing he said to me was to have a fun weekend, I'll see you in a week and I love you. Just hearing those words from my father made me feel so rich inside. Any time I ever saw or talked to my dad he always told me, "I love you." I was sad about moving away from my friends and about my dad's cancer, so I went with Sandi to the party at her friends house. The party was in the backyard of 94 Grand St and I didn't know anyone except Sandi. It was in the highlands section of Lowell. It was a birthday party held outside with speakers blaring music. Sandi was in the same 10th grade class with a brother and sister who lived at the address. It was the brothers birthday party and his name was Jon.

There was a lot of food, everyone was nice and we left that night making plans for the next morning to go roller skating. I slept at Sandi's house and the next morning we went to the home in the highlands we were at the night before. The Porter family lived there; mom, dad, two sons and two daughters. As we piled in the house waiting to leave, I questioned where the bathroom was and Jon answered me, "Right here," he said as he opened a door and I went in it. Jon also walked in right behind me. It wasn't the bathroom, it was Jon and his brother's bedroom.

I quickly turned around to get out but he blocked the door. I looked at him confused as he quickly began acting silly making funny faces and crooked eyes. I attempted to grab the doorknob but he stopped me as he said, "Kiss me." I refused to kiss him but he got all goofy and funny about it so I went to kiss him on his cheek and he turned his face causing us to kiss on the lips. I then punched his arm and he opened the door. I walked out so embarrassed as I walked across the kitchen to where the bathroom actually was. I could never imagine the friendship Jon and I were about to begin.

Soon we all headed outside to get in his mothers car for the ride. Many kids piled on top of each other getting into Mrs. Porter's car for the drive to the High Hat roller skating rink. There were no seat belt laws then and as many kids that could fit in the car was how many were going. Between Jon's friends and his sisters friends, someone was sitting on someone's lap. As we were piling into the car, Jon who was getting in the front passenger side grabbed me and pulled me onto his lap. He was very friendly and funny towards me but I was definitely too messed up in the head to be flirting with a guy older than me. I was thirteen years old with a messed up family life and he was the cool fifteen year old with a family. Even at the skating rink he continued to bug me. He kept skating by me and circling me. He constantly kept asking me to skate with him. "Just hold my hand you're going to anyways," he continued to say to me as he skated by. I snapped at him, "You don't know me." With a smirk on his face he said, "You have no idea." I finally gave in and skated with him when he agreed to leave me alone if I did. We skated a song together and when the song was over he wanted me to kiss him again. I laughed at him as I told him no. He then said to me, "It's ok you're going to anyways." Then he skated away and left me alone the rest of the time we were there.

The week in school really dragged as I waited for my dad to call me either at Sandi's house or my mother's house. I ran into Jon a few times at school as he would go out of his way to say hi to me. Waving, jumping in front of me as I walked or hiding around stairways and jumping out at me. As the week went by I called my stepmother a couple of times and she told me how my dad was doing. One of the calls she informed me he needed to stay an extra couple days or week. As it got close to two weeks since I last spoke to my dad, I knew I would be hearing from him soon. Hospital's back then didn't allow kids to visit with or without an adult. So I wasn't allowed to see him. My stepmother also told me about my mother visiting him. She and I were not happy about that. I yelled at my mother later that day. I told her, "You have no right to visit my dad." But she just walked away from me.

Monday October 17, 1983 went by as any other day for me. But on October 18th I walked to Sandi's after school like I always did when I didn't walk to my dad's. It was a nice autumn day as a bunch of us teenagers were hanging inside of Sandi's house when we heard my name being called through the screen door. My older brother walked from our house to Sandi's house and yelled into the door, "Is Cathy here?" "What's up?" I questioned him as I wondered why he was at my friend's house "Your father died," he said to me. I looked at him, "What?" I questioned him as I knew I didn't hear him right the first time. "It's in today's paper," he said, "he died yesterday," he continued to say as I saw my whole life, body, heart and soul being ripped out of me. And like our mother, my brother then walked away. There was no hug, no empathy, just him walking away.

"No, no," I said over and over again. I was sure he was wrong so I called my stepmother. She immediately answered and I told her what was just said to me. Then she said, "Ohhhh I'm so sorry honey." I instantly broke down and cried at Sandi's house. My dad wasn't coming home because my dad died the day before. He died a little after four o'clock in the afternoon on October 17, 1983. I bawled like a baby at my friend's house. She didn't have the newspaper so I walked over to her neighbors. One of her neighbors had the newspaper and let me check out the obituary section. And it was true, my dad's obituary was in the paper. There was my name also listed as one of his kids. His wake was in two days and his funeral was later in the week. I thanked Sandi's neighbor for letting me borrow his newspaper and walked back to Sandi's where I cried even more.

'What do I do now,' I thought to myself. I felt so alone even though I had my friend Sandi with me. I couldn't stop crying. I went upstairs to where Sandi said I had a phone call and it was Jon. He called to give me his condolences about my dad. I thanked him for calling me at Sandi's and also thought it was weird he called me. Seeing the pity on Sandi's face killed me so I walked home. I knew everyone felt sorry for me, I was just sick of people feeling sorry for me.

I was once again thrown into a level of hurt I never knew I could feel. Though the pain was different, the hurt was the same. A hurt that is felt right down to the core of your soul. Just when I thought I had no more tears in me left to cry, I cried a million more. Where do they all come from? I believe the tears I cried in my short life were at least five times my weight, if not more. Sometimes life drops that thousand pound piano from a high rise building and right into your life. Stopping you in your tracks and all you can do is work with the keys until you can hear the music again or let it kill you. 'How much pain can one girl carry?' I'd question myself over and over again with each tear that fell.

I wasn't inside my mother's house for a minute when my mother questioned me, "Why are you crying?" I didn't answer her but she continued, "Your father?" she questioned as she continued more, "You didn't even know him." Now that pissed me off. "How would you know?" I yelled at my mother. I also turned around, walked out the back door and sat on the porch until late at night. My mother only came out to tell me she was about to lock the doors. I didn't go to school the next day and my mother yelled at me. I questioned her, "Are you going to my dad's wake?" My mother gave me a strange look and snapped at me, "What for?" As she made me feel stupid for asking her. "Well you visited him at the hospital," I yelled back at her before running out the back door so I could go meet my friend Sandi at her house when she got home from school.

I had never owned any nice clothes so Sandi let me borrow a dress and a pair of shoes. As the time approached for my father's wake, Sandi was heartbroken to know I was going to it by myself. She decided to walk with me so I didn't have to go alone. My father's wake was held at the O'Donnell Funeral home on the corner of Pawtucket and Fletcher Street. We walked from Agawam Street in south Lowell to the end of Fletcher Street in the acre section of Lowell. It was definitely a long walk. I guess I was excited to see my dad, not expecting him in the casket. I didn't really know who anyone was except my Godfather and uncle but they had adults all around them. Sandi and I decided to leave but it was now dark outside. So I used a phone in the funeral home to call my mother and I didn't ask her for a ride, I demanded one. When I first told her we needed a ride back, she snapped at me, "No," she said as she complained she wasn't going out. So I told her I would tell everyone at the funeral home that she wouldn't pick me up. A brief moment of silence then my mother said, "I'll be right there."

After dropping Sandi off at her home my mother drove down the street to where we lived. "I'll take you to the funeral tomorrow," my mother said to me as we walked into our home. I nodded my head to let her know I heard her, but frankly I didn't care if she did or not. The next morning I said not one word to her. Once we were at the funeral home I didn't see my mother again. I drove in a limousine with my stepmother and my dad's other kids; my two brothers who I met for the first time and the sister whose son our dad babysat when I slept over back in 1980. The funeral mass was at the same church I made my first communion.

All I could do was stare at my dad's casket as the funeral mass went on. I questioned myself over and over again, 'Why can't that be my mother in that casket?' We then drove to the cemetery where another prayer was said before everyone turned around to leave. I exchanged phone numbers with my sister and one of my older brothers offered to take me out to lunch and I agreed. We went out for pizza but I didn't eat much. I was very quiet. It's hard to talk about life without talking about the life you live. So it was easier to just be quiet. He took me to meet his mom (my dad's first wife.) She was a very nice lady. Then he drove me home, or so he thought he did. When it came time for me to be dropped off at home I had him drop me off on Agawam Street. I pretended to walk into the backyard and on the porch of another home. I waited for him to drive away before I took off to the house I lived at, my mother's house.

I started to skip school a lot. I would leave the house in the morning and walk the neighborhood. When my mother left for work, I went home and hung out for the day. When my older brother, baby sister or mother got home, then I would leave again. I'd go hang out at a friend's house or around the neighborhood as I met more friends along the way. Soon I was calling my dad's other daughter, my older sister. It wasn't long until I was walking to her house and then I began walking there almost everyday. That is until my mother showed up one day and caused a scene. Suddenly she didn't want me walking the streets of Lowell. As she declared, "You're only thirteen years old." Yelling outside my sister's house for all the neighbors to hear. I was so embarrassed and humiliated. What do I do? Do I tell my sister what kind of mother she really is? How do I tell without saying what happened to me? How do I explain it all? It was easier to get in my mother's car and go home with her. I didn't want anyone else to know I was raped, tortured and terrorized for six years of my childhood. But the more my mother and my brothers failed to acknowledge what they knew I lived through, the more I hated going home.

I got in trouble for not being in school when I got picked up by a truant officer. It was enough of a scare for me to go back to school. They took under consideration how I just lost my dad so I got a pass on detention. At school I would hang around after school just to be around whoever was around. Wasn't long before I was skipping school again. Only this time I was forging my own absent letters, calling my own dismissals or showing up for homeroom and taking off before first period started. I was making a lot of friends and constantly sleeping out. Even on school nights I was sleeping over friends houses. I was more prone to go to school when I slept out than when I slept at home. I was also getting detention and suspended for forging my mothers name on absent letters. I got my working permit on my fourteenth birthday and started a job at Dunkin Donuts on Church Street in the Zayre's Plaza.

I was sleeping at a girl Terri's house almost daily. Shortly after my birthday, her parents questioned me why I never wanted to be home or why my mother didn't seem to care that I was never home. They noticed I was embarrassed and they made everyone leave the room. Terri's parents were very nice to me as they explained how I was a good kid and they just wanted to know why I was never home. All I said to them was, "My mother is not a good mother to me." That was all I had to say as Terri's mom gave me a hug and told me, "You can stay as long as you want," "You are always welcomed in our home," she continued. Terri and I were very excited as I called my mother and questioned her, "I have clothes still there can you drop them off here?" My mother questioned me, "Why?" I answered her, "I'm living here now." My mother said ok before hanging up the phone. Later that night she drove up the street, beeped her car horn and dropped off what clothes I had at her house by hanging a plastic bag out her car window. And like back in 1981, my mother just drove away.

I was now living at the home of Mr. and Mrs. Jalbert. They had a bunch of kids and my friend Terri was their youngest. I had the same rules at

Terri's house as I had at my mother's cousins, my friend Sandi's, the Landry family, the Sullivan family and back at Sandi's, which was to clean up after myself, go to school and just be a kid.

On Christmas morning I decided to walk down to my mother's so I could see my sister. My mother invited me to stay for dinner but I declined. I couldn't shake the fact that I was a stranger in my own home. It felt like I had a hole in the pit of my stomach. It was either my childhood which scattered over all the floors of Pleasant Street or the lack of everything from my family or maybe both. Either way it was a hole in the pit of my stomach stretching miles long.

Terri had a bunch of siblings we would always babysit for and sometimes sleeping over and spending the weekends at their homes. After working at Dunkin Donuts for a few weeks, I told the boss I had to quit due to having a sucky mother. He let me go and offered me my job back whenever I wanted it. He was impressed by how I approached him about my decision to stop working. It was too hard to work and go babysitting with Terri and babysitting was more fun. When we weren't babysitting we were hanging out at the new pizza place not far down the street on Lawrence Street. We would get a slice of pizza, put money in the jukebox and play music for hours. It wasn't long until we were a regular face there as the owner hired us to fold pizza boxes, sweep floors and wipe down counters. We would get free pizza, fries, soda and jukebox money.

Being a teenager in 1984 Lowell, Massachusetts was really adventurous for a girl who was making a lot of friends. A million worlds away from the shame, hurt and the pain that came from living in my mother's home. Although I already experienced smoking marijuana a few times, living with a girl who's older siblings grew up in the 60s and 70s, I can say by age fourteen I was officially a pot smoker.

> *(In the 1980s marijuana was considered to be a narcotic drug. My birth mother would spend the next thirty years telling whoever would listen about the 'drug addict daughter' she don't bother with.)*

As the nice weather of springtime came, so did the temptation to skip school again. Terri and I skipped school one day, then another and another. Soon we were skipping a lot of school and hanging at the pizza shop during school hours. By March 1984, I was picked up on a CHINS (Child in need of services) warrant and taken downtown to juvenile court. I told whoever approached me how I did not want to live with my mother and telling them I wanted to go live with my father's brother Ray Mellen. I was told it would be looked into and then I was sent to Department of youth services (DYS) in Worcester, Massachusetts. I did school work while I was there and started to write poetry to pass the time. No matter who I asked about my uncle I was told they, "Would look into it." A caseworker asked my mother to get my clothes from Terri's home and drop them off to me. It was the only time my mother went to the DYS group home.

In May 1984, I was taken back to court where I was returned to my mother. I was given no choice but to go live with her because she was my mother. I was also given a probation officer. The probation officer got me a job at Price's Bakery on Chelmsford St. I worked with two elderly ladies. I also caught up with all my school work and I passed my freshman year at Lowell High School.

The job at the bakery was only for a few weeks and in July the city of Lowell had a summer park's program. I worked the rest of the summer for the parks program. Getting up every weekday morning, running from my mother's house on the corner of Lawrence and South Whipple Street. I ran down Moore Street, cut through the railroad tracks and onto Shaughnessy Park on Gorham Street for 7:00am. So I could catch the van ride and work for the day. You miss the van, you miss work for the day. We went to all areas throughout Lowell to cut grass, clean up trash on public walkways, roadways and parks. Making a small paycheck every week was a big paycheck to a fourteen year old.

I used my money to buy myself a ten speed bike. I asked my mother to drive me to Child World at the Chelmsford Mall in Chelmsford, Mass. She did and I got myself a candy apple red bicycle. Any time I was alone with my mother I would attempt to talk to her about my childhood. She never gave me a chance, always cutting me off, yelling and disgusted with me for, "Bringing it up again," my mother always yelled. I had barriers up with my brothers for not protecting me on Pleasant Street. Not for all the years of me being held in that bedroom on Pleasant Street. But for the last attack I suffered in that attic on Pleasant Street. They should have called the police. My baby sister only saw the anger I had in me for her mother and two older brothers.

I spent most of the summer of 1984 sleeping out, hanging with Terri, swimming, hanging over Sandi's who had moved to Pollard Street, hanging at the pizza place or riding my bike throughout the streets of Lowell and making many friends along the way.

I ran into Jon one day when I was out bike riding. I was riding all day and all around the city. It was later in the day when I came riding down Westford Street and Jon was at the park on the corner of Westford and Grand Street. I stopped and we talked for a while. He couldn't understand why I was bike riding by myself. He was baffled how a fourteen year old could be so far away from her home and I laughed like it was a normal thing to have so much freedom. He told me how his family wouldn't allow that and how he has a curfew and chores. "Yes, I get those when I live with other people's families," I said to him as I tried to make a joke out of my sucky unloving life. He questioned me about my family but I dodged his questions. I talked a little about my dad but it was still very heartbreaking for me so we quickly talked about 1984 summertime in Lowell. The night scene of 1984 downtown Lowell was the place to be. Bumper to bumper cars circling around Central, Middle, Merrimack and Market Streets for hours. Terri and I would ride our bikes down there, riding in and out of the bumper to bumper cars. Making more friends along the way as the majority were teenagers.

Before I knew it, summer was over, I was out of a summer job and my sophomore year of high school was about to begin. I got myself some corduroy Levi's in all colors at the Gap after my mother gave me money from my dad's social security check. She told me, "Because your father died you get a measly eighty dollars a month." Then she went on about how grateful I should be because she gave me money. I went downtown and shopped at Record Lane for the next new rock concert shirts. I got new Exersoles at Thom McCann and some school supplies at Woolworths. My mother had a friend at her work who needed a weekend babysitter. So I agreed to meet her. Gosh was my mother such a fake when she was around other people. I got hired to babysit their nine year old daughter, on weekends only. When I did babysit my mother had to drive me to the woman's house.

I was sleeping at Terri's for the Columbus day weekend when we took a walk to the neighborhood store Quelly's and I saw one of my older brother's there. We said hi to each other then I questioned him where everyone was. He said our oldest brother was with friends, our mother was home and our baby sister was with her father. "No he's in jail," I immediately said to him. But he didn't know what I was talking about. "She sees her father all the time," he continued to say like I was an idiot for saying what I said. I knew instantly my mother had lied to me. I ran from one end of South Whipple Street where I was to the other end of South Whipple Street.. I know it's impossible but it felt like I ran that in two steps, one, two and I was there. That's how quickly I ran.

> *Cruelty is the only word I can describe for how my mother treated me. I spent my childhood a victim of my mother's cruelty. I was always wanting what all my friends had with their mother's. I always knew the love wasn't there with my mother but I still held hope for the relationship even as I continued to see it be smashed into pieces over and over again*

I ran so fast down South Whipple Street by the time I made it into my mother's apartment I almost ran right into her. "Is he in jail?" I blurted out and questioned her as I got right into her face. She looked confused by my question as she answered me with a question. "Why did you see him?" she questioned with a smirk on her face. I told her what my brother told me just moments earlier at Quelly's. My mother then shook her head yes and said, "I only said he was in jail to make you feel better." "You told me on Butler Avenue he was in jail," I screamed at her. She put her glass of Pepsi down and said to me, "Cathy I only told you that because you looked so sad." As she went on explaining how pitiful I looked on Butler Avenue and for me to just forget about it all. "Forget about it?" I yelled at my mother. "What about what he did to me?" I continued to scream at her. "So forget what he did to me?" I was still screaming as I felt my heart being smashed onto the floor with every word that came out of my mouth. As our argument continued I yelled that Dave was going to hurt my baby sister.

I wanted to get her away from her father but my mother just yelled about my sister being his blood as she told me years prior. She went on explaining about Dave having another family now and it was only me that he did stuff to. "He turned his life around," she continued. Her voice carried over mine as we both continued in our huge argument. "Oh my God mom that girl from the highlands," I screamed as I started to breathe heavy at the thought going through my mind. I shook my head no, then I yelled, "Mom we have to go to the police." I pleaded to my mother as she insisted, "You were the only one he abused." She just stood there looking at me with that same smirk on her face she always had. I shook my head and was a bit taken back at what she just said to me. "No I wasn't mom and you know it," I sternly told her. "If he hurt that girl or anyone else after me I will tell the police all you knew," I continued to yell at my mother as we continued to argue while tears poured down my face with every cruel word my mother said. I guess she realized I wasn't backing down so she used her next best approach, pure cruelty.

As we yelled at each other, my mother finally gave up and got me where it hurt the most as she said to me, "You're just jealous because everyone has their father now but you." My mother went on talking about how my oldest brother had found out his father was alive and moved in with him. I didn't even know he had moved out of the house but I was never really home either and that's probably why I didn't know. "I'm jealous," I screamed out loud until I stopped arguing, I stopped yelling, I just stopped dealing with the wicked lady before me. I looked at the same cruel lady I knew on Fletcher Street, the same cruel lady I knew on Pleasant Street, the same cruel lady from Butler Avenue and she was the same cruel lady standing before me. My mother was still talking to me as I walked out the same back door I had walked into just minutes earlier. I wanted my dad and I walked as I cried.

I walked to the park down the street from where I lived. Then I went over to the river bank just across the street. I walked until I found an opening where I could sneak down to the river. I found a spot and I sat down. I watched as the water splashed against the rocks. I sat in peace as I listened to the river's rushing water. When out of the blue, "Oh shit," I yelled out as I remembered I ditched my friend Terri at the store after running into my older brother. I got up, headed to her house and told her about the cool spot I found at the river. I slept the rest of the weekend at Terri's house and when the weekend was over I returned home to where whatever relationship I did have with my mother would never be the same again.

I was so mad at my mother. It went through my head a million times a day, 'What did I ever do to her?' As much as I was steadfastly determined to get justice, I just needed that line of support. I was fourteen years old in 1984 and already lived one fucked up life and I just wanted my mothers support. I needed someone in my corner. I knew I had friends and their families but to talk of the actual abuse I endured to them. There was no way I wanted any of my friends to know what happened to me. So I wanted my mother to be my support, the one who knew about all the years Dave raped, terrorized and abused me.

AT SCHOOL I would look at the kids and think they could never understand what I've been through. I knew I was different and I found myself fitting in with friends who were like me; without parents. That older teenager Jon was calling me at my mother's on a daily basis. We would just talk about life, downtown, school and the future.

It wasn't long before my mother's friend needed me to babysit and my mother drove me there. My anger for my mother shined brightly since I found out Dave never went to jail and it made my mother nervous. "Cathy you can't keep being mad," she said to me as she drove me to her friend's house. I didn't say anything to her and she continued talking about how the lady was a good friend of hers and she didn't want me embarrassing her. I looked at my mother confused as I questioned her, "How am I going to embarrass you?" "They don't need to know about Dave," she snapped at me about her monster ex-boyfriend who never did any jail time for raping her daughter. She warned me that I better not ruin her reputation with her friend. The little girl I babysat would sometimes ask to spend her money from her piggy bank on her bureau. But I was already told by her mom how she tries it on all the babysitters. So I would always say no. This night I questioned the little girl and she was all excited as we took seventy dollars from her piggy bank. We walked to Lil Peach variety store on Roger's Street where we spent it all on candy and a Walkman radio.

When her parents got home and saw all the snacks, soda and the Walkman, they were not happy and I was fired from babysitting. The girl's parents drove me to Lil Peach, had me return the Walkman and had my mother pick me up at the store. I embarrassed my mother and she was so upset. She tried whacking me a couple times as she drove home but I grabbed her arm and yelled, "Stop hitting me." The rest of the short ride home went quiet and that's how I started getting my mother right where it hurts. My mother was so mad at me for what I did at my babysitting job. "I am so embarrassed by you," she snapped at me. I was extremely fresh to my mother as all I did was laugh out loud asking her, "How does it feel?" While giving her a sad smartass look over her ruined reputation. She informed me I was grounded but within moments of getting home I grabbed my bike from the back hallway where I always stored it and took off bike riding around the city. I continued meeting new friends whether it was at school, bike riding or just walking around the streets of Lowell with friends. Away from home I was who I was; a funny outgoing, adventurous, always smiling happy teenager. At home I was what was instilled into me, a shamed, humiliated, embarrassed, unloved, unworthy, unwanted, lonely teenager as the cruelty from my own mother continued.

A few days after being fired from babysitting, I came home from school and immediately noticed my bike wasn't in the back hallway. "Where's my bike?" I questioned my mother, brother and myself. "Where's my bike?" I yelled again so everyone in the apartment heard me. But like the abuse I endured for over six years of my childhood, no one seemed to know what happened to my ten speed bike. I went out to sit on the back porch before returning inside the apartment where I went right to my mother.

"You had my bike stolen," I accused her. And of course her response was with a question, "What would I want with your bike?" "I have a car," she continued. "You're evil like that," I said to her as I let her know that I knew she was behind my bike going missing. I continued going to school and hanging out with my friends. Jon was still going out of his way to say hi to me. Only now we were sneaking up on each other, giving each other wet willie's (wet your finger and poke an ear) or dope slaps upside the head, sudden quick not so hard smacks. As the many friends I was making at school, I hated going home. And going to school meant I had to go home. I loved living my life but I hated when I had to go home. I avoided being there as much I could. If no one was around the neighborhood then I would walk downtown where I was always guaranteed to run into someone I knew.

I soon got my job at Dunkin Donuts back. I worked whenever I could. When I wasn't working I was hanging around the place, helping to clean out back, carry supplies in, stock shelves or watch how the donuts were made. Which I always thought was so cool. Of course my mother would continue to yell at me every time I went home. I realized the more I worked the more I didn't have to be home and the more I had a reason not to be home.

By my fifteenth birthday December 15, 1984, I was working as many shifts I could including the overnight shift 11pm to 6am. Lowell Police constantly patrolled Zayre's parking lot where Dunkin Donuts was located and the police also received free coffee, donuts and muffins whenever requested. Back then Dunkin Donuts only sold coffee, donuts and muffins. My mother had a birthday cake for my birthday. I wasn't even expecting it and she definitely caught me off guard. I came out of the bedroom I slept in with my baby sister and there she was with a cake and lit candles on top of it. "Are you kidding me?" I immediately questioned as I was so flabbergasted at her attempt to rectify my last three birthday's without her. I started yelling at her, "No one cares about me in this house." As we looked around and only saw two people in the kitchen; my mother and I. Over a guilt trip my older brother came out of his bedroom and ate a piece of cake. I also expressed my feelings to him as he claimed I was wrong "That's not true," he told me after I also told him, "No one in this family cares about me." I was so mad at my mother and brothers for expecting me to just deal with what I lived through alone.

By January 1985, I was only going home to shower, wash my clothes and if my mother was home then I had to listen to her complain about me never being home. Every time I went home I felt more worthless and unwanted as no one seemed to care what I lived through before, during and after Pleasant Street. I used my tips from work to buy myself toothpaste, toothbrush and whatever else I needed so I didn't have to go home. The thing about having a job at Dunkin Donuts and a lot of friends meant I also had a lot of visitors at work. I would give free donuts and hot chocolate to them. My friend Mark from Butler Avenue was always stopping in with friends, his girlfriend or brother. Friends from South Lowell, Highlands, Belvedere and Acre sections of Lowell were also stopping by.

One night I was at work when one of my friends I've known for about two years came in to see me. He was with a couple of other friends I also knew and he had a question for me. I said, "Sure Eddie what's up?" He then questioned me if I wanted to help him throw a party. I was happy to help out as I answered him with a question, "Sure what do I have to do?" His answer to me was, "Lock the doors." I thought about it for a few seconds before I said, "Oh my God yes." We made a few phone calls from the landline phone at Dunkin Donuts and within an hour I had about ten friends inside Dunkin Donuts drinking mad dog 20/20 and eating donuts.

When a customer came to the locked door we would wave at them and laugh. We just talked, joked and laughed all night long until we left about half an hour before the next employee was due in. I locked the register, left the door unlocked with the key in it and left Dunkin Donuts.

A couple of us walked through downtown over the Bridge Street bridge and onto Bridge Street until we reached Burger King. We ate some breakfast then we all headed back towards downtown where we separated as everyone headed home. And there I was walking home, back to the home I've been running away from for years now. I wasn't home long when my boss called me and I knew I was fired. He was bummed he had to fire me and praised me for having the balls to do what I did. He thought it was super cool but because of company policy, he had to fire me. We cleaned up after ourselves, didn't leave the place a mess and he told me he appreciated it as I could hear him get a chuckle out of knowing I threw a party inside Dunkin Donuts.

Losing my job also meant I had to be home more. I didn't have my bike to ride around the city and my life just seemed to be stuck. I would continue to confront my mother any chance I got about going to the police. But all I had to do was mention Dave's name, my past or the police and my mother would start yelling and walking away. I would sometimes watch my mother for hours until I worked the courage to approach her. Only to be shot down and belittled within seconds of opening my mouth. I had a lot of anger inside of me for always having to keep quiet about my childhood that was ripped from me. I was never mad at my baby sister because I knew she was too young to know what happened to me. All she saw was her older sister who had so much anger for her family. I was struggling between being the huge happy person I was when I was with friends and being the small unworthy kid when I was with my family.

My friends' families liked me, I respected the elderly and I was considerate of others. But when it came to my family I was nothing but a troublemaking brat and I decided to let them believe it. One day I tiptoed into my brothers bedroom while he was sleeping and stole a ten dollar bill from his newspaper route money. I waited the whole day for him to notice but he never did. The next morning I tiptoed back into his room and put the ten dollar bill back. He caught me and I booked it out of his room until he caught me in the kitchen. He wanted to know what I stole but I laughed and told him I put it back. He counted it to make sure his money was all there as I continued laughing while saying, "Call the cops on me," and continued, "Oh you don't call the cops on family."

And like my mother, when confronted with my childhood, he walked away. I am sure it reminded him of that day on Pleasant Street a few years earlier in 1981, when I begged each one of my brothers to call the police on my abuser, but was told, "We don't call the cops on family."

With all the friends I had, not going home got easier and easier as springtime came. I started to distance myself from friends in the neighborhood as I drifted towards friends who had no idea of the cruel mother I had at home. What friends I did bring back to my house for a quick stop would leave the house asking me, "Why is your mother so mean to you?" They were right, she was always mean, cruel and pure nasty towards me. Only a few of my friends saw my mother out in public and assumed she was a nice lady. I learned how easy it was to get her to walk out of the room. All I had to do was question her if Dave was in jail and she would walk away. I tried mostly going home when she wouldn't be there but I wasn't always good with my timing. In 1985, I was still just a constant reminder to my mother of the man she lost because I ran to a friend's house that Saturday morning in 1981.

I was again skipping many classes at school. One day when I showed up at school, one of the security guards came to get me. Mr. O'Neil was my headmaster and he was not happy with me skipping classes. I was taken to the juvenile courthouse in a police car for being a juvenile delinquent. I was also questioned numerous times about why I skipped school so much and each time I answered, "Because I do not want to live with my mother." This time I was sent to a group home just outside of the Boston area. In just under a month I was released under good behavior and told by the staff that I did not belong there. My mother had to pick me up from the group home and we said no words to each other on the drive home. We got home to an empty apartment and I questioned my mother, "Where is everyone?" She told me my older brother was out with his friends and my baby sister, "Is with her father," my mother said to me as she stood there with a smirk on her face waiting for my response.

I was fifteen years old and I already looked into the eyes of fear. I already looked into the eyes of terror. I already lived through so much pain, hurt, unloved, unworthy, unwanted cruel abuse. But nothing could prepare what was left of my fifteen year old soul for the pure cruelty it was about to endure. My mother just stood there with a smirk on her face waiting for me to respond to her informing me of my baby sister being with her father. The man who raped, tortured, traumatized and brutally abused me for six years of my childhood. I didn't respond to my mother as I couldn't make sense to why she would smirk at me the way she did. I walked by her and sat at the kitchen table to collect my thoughts. 'Why would she say that?' I questioned myself as I shook my head in disbelief, insult or just shocked that a mother could be so cruel. 'What did I ever do to her?' I questioned myself as I sat in the kitchen.

My mother was in the living room and I was sitting at the kitchen table for what seemed like hours. I hated the pain I carried. I hated the hurt I carried. I hated my life. I hated the memories of what that monster did to me. I hated how they protected him and I hated how they didn't protect me. So much went through my head as I questioned myself again and again. I kept looking at my mother's kitchen sink and the dishes in the dish rack drying. She had some steak knives with other silverware drying in the rack. I kept looking at a steak knife in the dish basket. I thought about grabbing one and slicing my wrist, throat or maybe right in my heart, but I knew I wasn't suicidal nor did I know which artery would actually kill me. Besides, my mothers knives were very dull. Before I could think of any crazy thoughts I quickly got up and went to the bathroom. I looked around the bathroom and it seemed just like the bathroom of another family's home I once lived in. I saw the toothbrushes and as usual I didn't have a toothbrush in the holder above the sink. I looked at the cabinets inside the bathroom and I didn't know what was in them. Like on Pleasant

Street, like on Butler Avenue and here on Lawrence Street, I was a stranger in my own home.

I told myself over and over again as I looked in the bathroom mirror 'You got this, don't back down, you got this, don't back down.' I washed my face from the pale shocked look I still carried from my mother's smirk on her face as she told me where my baby sister was. I shook myself, I jogged my legs in place as I prepared to head out the bathroom door and tell my mother I was going to the police and pressing charges against Dave. 'Ok you got this Cathy,' I told myself as I counted one, two, three. I opened the bathroom door headed out into the kitchen, passed the table, the sink and washing machine as the thought of being yelled at by my mother sent all the courage I had, right back down to the scared girl who didn't matter to anyone.

I stood by the washing machine trying to work up the courage to walk in the living room and approach my mother about taking me to the police station. But I didn't get the courage back so I sat down at the kitchen table. There were those knives again and I looked at them for a while. 'Do I stab my neck, my wrist, my heart?' I questioned myself then I'd quickly tell myself, 'I don't want to die.' And I didn't want to die, I wanted to matter. I kept telling myself not to cry, to stay strong and get the courage back. My mother then walked into the kitchen and I startled her. She thought I left a while ago as she made a comment about how quiet I was in the kitchen. I just watched my mother as she refilled her glass with ice and Pepsi from her small glass bottle she kept in the refrigerator. I watched every ice cube that fell, I watched as the Pepsi was poured into her glass but I didn't hear a word my mother was saying as she was bitching about me being so quiet. When she was done she walked by me as she headed back into the living room and it reminded me of the time she walked by me on Agawam Street in 1982. That made me mad and my courage quickly came back. I followed my mother into the living room and when I got to the doorway between the kitchen and living room I questioned my mother, "Can we please go to the police station now?"

Of course my mother answered with a question as she questioned me,

"What for now?" The second Dave's name came off my lips my mother got screaming mad at me. Instantly yelling at me, "You got to forget about it," "you're always bringing it up," my mother continued as she spoke to me in a disgusted manner. She didn't want to hear anything about Dave. So I questioned her about the photos and film, "Don't you want those naked photos of your daughter out of that cellar?" But I got another question from her, "What good would it do?" she questioned me. So I questioned her, "What if someone finds them?"

My mother explained to me, "He buried it all into the sidewalk." As she continued to inform me new people were living there now. "You can't go disrupting other people's lives," she continued with excuses as to why I shouldn't go to the police. "It was all buried well before he put the rocks back," "They would have to go through the sidewalk to get to it," "An animal got to it," "The rain washed it away," my mother continued with her excuses.

I didn't care about anything she was saying to me as I insisted she come to the police station with me. "Oh my God mom, I'm your daughter, come with me," I yelled. "I want those photos out of that cellar," I continued yelling at my mother causing her to stop yelling her ridiculous excuses at me and question me, "Why to show your friends?" she snapped as I stood there shocked with tears pouring down my face. I just looked at her, "How can you be so cruel?" I questioned her as I continued to let her know I was going with or without her. I walked away from her and into the bathroom where I washed my face from crying so I could make the walk downtown to the police station. She was standing in the kitchen when I walked out of the bathroom. So I attempted to ask her again, "Mom will you please come with me?" I desperately pleaded with my mother. But once again she answered with a question, "Who will believe you?" I yelled at her, "You will be there." But my mother shook her head no telling me she wouldn't go. Telling me I was just a kid and no one would believe me. When I yelled at her how she knew it was all true, my mother decided to get more nasty towards me, if that was even possible.

"Come on huh, all them years, you had to let him," my mother said to me causing me to scream in her face, "I was a fucking kid." But my mother continued yelling over me as she blamed me and insisted it was me who let Dave hurt me. It was me who didn't fight enough. It was me who could have stopped it. "It's your fault he molested you," "you let it go on," my mother continued with her cruel and unloving words. I didn't care what she was saying, I headed towards the back door when I heard, "Let me get my keys," my mother said just as I was walking out the door. I turned around and questioned her, "You'll come with me?" She said she would and went to retrieve her pocketbook and keys, so I waited. I was relieved when my mother told me she would go with me, I didn't want to do it alone. As cruel as my mother was, I was always told to respect your mother and I wanted her support. She knew about the attacks, the rapes, the film, the photos, the abuse and about the attack I suffered in the attic of Pleasant Street in 1981. So yes I wanted support from my family. I waited in the kitchen for my mother, but she returned empty handed.

"What are you going to tell your friends?" she questioned me as she walked back into the kitchen with nothing in her hands. No keys, no pocketbook, nothing but a question. "This is about me not my friends," I answered her while noticing her hands were empty. "Where are your keys?" I questioned her as she ignored me. Instead of answering my question she informed me, "They're going to think you wanted it." I couldn't believe what my mother was saying to me. I snapped at her, "Oh shut up." I walked away from her and headed out the back door. My mother and I got into a scuffle as she grabbed my arm in an attempt to stop me from leaving. I kept trying to remove her hand but she'd quickly grab me by her other hand. I started to cry again as I kept telling her to leave me alone and let me go to the police. "I'm going with you," my mother said to me. "I just want you to listen to what I have to say," she continued while preventing me from leaving. "You're going to come to the police with me?" I questioned her. She answered she would so we stepped out of the back hallway and went back into the kitchen where I listened to what my mother wanted to say.

"All those photos will be all over the newspapers," my mother started her talk while she named my friends I was hanging with who didn't know,

"All the things he did to you," she said with a smile on her face. "Why are you saying this shit mom?" I questioned her as I questioned again, "Can we go to the police now?" "I just want you to understand the consequences," my mother said to me. "What would your friend Francine say?" she questioned me and I answered her, "She would hate you." But my mother wasn't done as she named more of my friends, "What would Steph think?" "What would Helen and Nicole say?" my mother continued. "What would your friend Jon think?" she continued to question me with her cruelty. I was answering her, "She would hate you," "They would hate you," by the time I was about to say, "He would hate you," my mother informed me, "Jon won't bother to call you again."

My mother's demeanor changed as she became caring towards me. "I'm only telling you this for your own good," "Cathy they will think you wanted it," she continued with her cruel ways of belittling me. I just started screaming at her, "Shut up, I didn't let him." While the tears poured down my face. "They'll all know you posed for all those pictures," my mother continued saying as she blocked me from leaving. "All your friends will look down on you," "All those photos and film will be all over the news," "In all the newspapers, even the Boston Globe," my mother continued as she still wasn't finished, "You'll be nothing but trash to everyone," "What would they all think if they knew you let it go on for so long?" my mother continued to question me as I screamed at her, "I didn't let Dave rape me." But she kept on, "Strangers will look down at you," "You will just be trash to everyone, all used up," she continued speaking. I stood there giving up on trying to leave and waited for my mother to stop talking. When she finally finished, I looked her right in her eyes and I said, "Thank you for being someone I never want to be like."

I quickly ran around the side of my mother and booked it out the back door bawling my eyes out, but finally on my way to the police station. By the time I got to the bottom of the back porch stairs everything I stood strong for, my mother had managed to degrade. what was left of my fifteen-year-old soul was shattered. Every ounce of courage I carried was smashed, shattered, and lost on the kitchen floor of my mother's Lawrence Street apartment. I fell to my knees on the bottom step where I bawled and bawled and bawled my eyes out.

It was nothing short of pure cruelty of how my mother belittled and degraded me. All I ever wanted was to matter to her. I told myself my mother was wrong. I told myself she was a cruel person. I told myself not to listen to anything she said. I told myself to just go to the police station. I told myself just get there, but I always had to deal with everything alone.

I was hyperventilating from crying as I sat at the bottom steps. Every time I'd wipe my tears and face I'd just start crying again. I couldn't deal with all she said. I was so shocked, taken back and insulted by her cold cruel demeanor. My brother came home as he went by me to get up the stairs and not saying a word to me. I didn't want my mother to know I was still around so I decided to take off. I got up and attempted to run, but that decision was quickly fizzled as I was in no mood to run or move, I just wanted to be alone. So I headed to the backyard, a little wooded area with a couple of trees and a few big boulders resting in almost a circle. I sat down behind one of the boulder rocks and I cried. I cried and cried.

How can a mother be so cruel? I went to her for six years of my childhood and now she threw it in my face as she blamed me for why I was raped, terrorized and abused my whole childhood. I ran to my friends house on Pleasant Street cause I had to deal with six years of horrific abuse alone, I didn't want to go to the police station alone.

I had my friends, I had many friends for a fifteen year old with a sucky family life. But I didn't want them to know about my childhood. There was no way I was going to look at any of my friend's knowing they knew what I lived through. Emotional abuse can put a beating on a body as I learned that day. I was not moving from where I was. I cried a lot, played with leaves (ones I didn't use as tissues) and said a lot of prayers up to the sky as nightfall came and the sky lit up with stars.

My mother's attempts of looking for me consisted of her walking onto the porch, looking over the railings and yelling my name. She did it two times as I stayed sitting on the ground hiding behind a tree and a boulder. It was different, the pain I was feeling. When Dave was abusing me I felt a pain unimaginable as I hurt from the attacks I suffered. But this time it was like my chest was ripped open. Like a roaring fire was scorching my heart and sending the flames all through my body.

All those horrible things Dave did to me and adding my family's cruelty towards me on Butler Avenue and Lawrence Street. Did they know what it felt like to be a twelve year old standing on the sidewalk with your family in a closed door straight ahead in a home you haven't lived in for a while? In a home where you were unwanted? Gosh I cried so much that night. I did fall asleep off and on as I sat there leaning against the big rock. I would wake up from the noise of a breeze making a tree branch move. I awoke early in the morning and needed the bathroom. So I went behind another boulder and watered the ground. I watched as my brother and my baby sister left for school. I said to myself, 'No school for me today.' A short time later my mother left for work. I waited until she was gone and came out from the rock I was hiding behind.

I went up the wooden stairs, lifted up one of the windows off the porch and went in through my sister's bedroom. I took a shower, made myself something to eat and I just sat in the living room with the television on but not hearing anything being said. Something happened to me the night before as I cried behind the boulder rock in the backyard. Maybe I cried too much? Maybe I had too much anger in me? Maybe not enough? Maybe my pride crumbled or maybe I just gave up and didn't care? For the next few days I went to school and I went straight home to my mother's after school. I would watch my mother and brother wondering how they can just go on with their lives. 'Didn't they care what I lived through?' I'd question myself a hundred times a day.

A few days later I went home to my mother's after school and the guy Vinny from Butler Avenue was sitting on the couch in the living room. He was happy to see me and gave me a hug. He reeked of booze and he was back with my mother. I knew something happened to me that day my mother degraded me so badly. I was in a zombie like state for days. Going to school, keeping to myself and going home. Until the day Vinny was there and though I didn't know what it was that happened to me, I knew what I had to do. The memories of Butler Avenue kept going through my mind as I sat in the living room with my baby sister and Vinny. I got up from the chair I was sitting on and went into the kitchen to collect my thoughts. I sat at the kitchen table and there were those cheap steak knives over by my mother's kitchen sink again. I was not suicidal and I did not want to die, I wanted to live. It's what I always wanted, just to live. I didn't want to be degraded anymore. I realized what it was that changed in me that night I was up in the wooded area all night long. I knew if I stayed living with this family any longer, I knew that I would someday kill myself.

'Nope,' I said to myself as I got up, went into the bedroom my sister was forced to share with me whenever I was living there and I put my clothes into a duffle bag. I told my baby sister I was sorry and headed out the door. I didn't want to be nothing and nobody anymore, I just wanted to live. It was easy for my family to move on, not dwell, get over it, not remember, forgive or forget because it didn't happen to them. The thing is it happened to me and they didn't care. So I did what I had to do in 1981, I ran away. Could you blame me? I didn't care where I was going but I knew I was running away. If I had to look at my mother's face again I would have stabbed myself in my neck and prayed I hit the right artery.

All teenagers had back then were either bikes and our legs for walking. With my bike disappearing off the back hallway, I had to use my legs and walk. I walked straight to a friend's house that day and what would be the start to a really awesome summer. I would leave my bag of clothes at a friends house and we would walk to wherever was the place to be. We would walk downtown, the High-hat roller skating rink and even to Rt3 cinema in Chelmsford Mass, which was one heck of a long walk. There was a method to our madness when we walked to the Chelmsford cinema. We would pay for a movie, sneak in our own snacks and hide in the cigarette smoke clouded bathroom stall after the movie, until it was safe to sneak into the next movie for free. It was easy to hang out and eat or sleep at a friend's house because there was always someone around. I was never alone when I was with my friends. I would go to Lowell High to pass the time as I waited for my friends to get out of school. I would show up at a couple of my classes, walking in and out of Lowell High as if I was a former student visiting. Jon was still going out of his way to say hello to me and finally convincing me to hang out on his street one day. That day became a few more days. He tried getting me to talk about my family life but I wouldn't. I loved how he talked about his family and thought it was cool he had a nice caring family. We were just friends, but he always acted so interested in me for some reason.

As high school ended it gave way for a fun start to the summer of 1985. My friends would tell their parents, grandparents or guardian that they would be sleeping at my house and we would hang out all night at another friend's house or walk around the city while making some really fun memories. We passed our days by walking, taking the city bus to the Billerica mall or finding someone to buy us some three dollar Mad Dog 20/20. If there was a house party going on then we walked there. We would walk to Lowell cemetery on Lawrence Street to hang out by the steps of Witch Bonney, a well known monument in the cemetery. We would hitchhike on the Lowell Connector to get a ride to Hampton beach in New Hampshire. We never got in a vehicle with more than two people in it and always had at least three of us hitchhiking at a time. We passed up a lot of rides but we also always got a ride. Although we never had to hitchhike home because we always ran into someone from Lowell at the beach.

The sadness, the pain, the hurt and the family I once had was all behind me now.

I was always welcomed whenever a friend took me home. Sometimes I stayed in their bedroom and the parents never knew I was sleeping there. I didn't miss my home life and the more I stayed busy, the more it got easy to push it all out of my head whenever a bad memory came to me. I was already known as the kid whose mother didn't want her by some of my friends and I was already known as the kid who had so much freedom by my other friends.

Walking down a Lowell street one day with a friend, a Lowell police cruiser pulled up beside us. The officers got out of their car and called my friend by her name. Next thing, we are both in the back seat of the police cruiser heading to the police station. I was told the friend I was walking with was reported as a runaway and that's why I was picked up with her. "Wait she's a runaway but I'm not?" I questioned the officers as I laughed. Then I explained to the officers, "I ran away over two months ago." As usual I was not reported as a runaway. One of the officers called my mother on the phone. When she answered he first questioned her if she knew where I was. Then he told her he had an award for me, then he told her I was sitting right in front of him as he scolded her and told her to get over to the juvenile courthouse. He was very nice to me as he explained I was only fifteen years old and he couldn't just let me walk out of the police station. He drove me over personally to the courthouse where I once again questioned about living with my dad's brother, my Uncle Ray and refusing to live with my mother. I was sent back to the DYS facility in Worcester where for the next three months I would be moved to foster homes in Worcester, Framingham and Grafton Massachusetts.

The 1985 juvenile court system labeled any child who didn't want to live with their parent(s) as a 'Juvenile Delinquent,' and that's what I was.

I was scolded, "My mother died, be glad yours is alive." I was judged, "Have respect for your mother." I was looked down upon, "She's your mother." I was an outcast, "You're the one with a problem." I was labeled a juvenile delinquent. I was so mad to have my life interrupted by a court system that wanted me home with my mother and my mother not wanting me to return.

Shortly after I arrived at the DYS facility I was sent to live at a foster home. My bag of clothes was still at my friends house in Lowell so once at the facility I was given a bunch of hand me down clothes. Within a month I was told I had a court date in Lowell and a van would be picking me up for the long ride back home to Lowell. I was taken once again to the juvenile courthouse where I again asked about living with my uncle and refusing to live with my mother. For every court appearance I was either picked up by a van or by a court appointed social worker. I had to take all my belongings with me for every court appearance in case I didn't return to the same foster home. A small bag of clothes, toothbrush, hairbrush and notebooks. At the courthouse I was taken to a cell where I waited for my case to be called.

I felt so low, I couldn't believe I was in a courthouse jail cell. I met a case worker and a probation officer who I told about wanting to live with my dad's brother and my refusal to live with my mother. But I was sent back to another foster home in the Worcester area where I would again live in a strangers home until my next court appearance. I didn't always have the same case worker at the courthouse and no one ever questioned me why I didn't want to live with my mother. At one of my court appearances I was told the uncle I kept asking about had been killed in a highway car crash along with his wife. Still refusing to go live with my mother I was sent back into the foster care system. I kept requesting they find out if it was actually true about my aunt and uncle. I barely knew them but I knew it was who my dad wanted me with. Did they really die in a car crash? For some reason I knew it was a lie my mother was telling.

There was only one foster home I ran away from. I was scared to sleep there the first night and when I questioned to use the bathroom, I booked it out the front door. I ran to a CVS store where the manager called the police and they called the DYS facility where I went for the night until going to another foster home. All the other foster homes were really nice to me, as hard as it was to be a stranger in their home, most welcomed strangers like me into their homes.

I would stay for a couple of weeks at one place until my next court appearance. The home in Grafton Mass I loved the best. They owned a Chinese restaurant and included me in their daily routine. They even offered to adopt me but the whole theory of a family scared me. I told them I would think about it, even though they were nice people, I wanted to be home with my friends. At another court appearance I was told my aunt and uncle did in fact die in a bad highway car crash. I then went in front of the judge who informed me I was a juvenile delinquent and scolded me, "Your mother is all you have." As the judge gave me sympathy about my dad's death and was stern with me for not wanting to live with my mother. He then told me to, "Work out your problems with your mother." I was released from DYS custody and into my mother's custody. It had been a few months since I saw my friends and I really wanted to see them. So I agreed with the judge. My mother waited for me in the large hallway inside the courthouse. When we walked out of the courthouse doors and headed down the cement stairs, things changed very quickly.

We weren't even at the bottom of the outside courthouse stairs when my life had a turning point again. My mother was walking ahead of me when she turned around and faced me. She told me that she was going to be moving in with Pete soon. Pete was my older brothers father. "He don't like you and it would be better if you didn't move with us," my mother said to me. "He don't know me," I snapped at her. "He knows the trouble you cause," she responded to me. As I responded in a disappointed manner, "He only knows what you told him." I thought about running back into the courthouse and telling the judge what my mother just said to me. But I knew I would be sent back to foster care so I looked at my mother and for once we both agreed on something; I'd rather not live with them either.

I started to walk away but my mother grabbed my arm and insisted I walk her to her car. "So they don't think anything," she said as she pointed to the courthouse. I yanked my arm away from my mother as I told her, "I don't care what they think." I walked away from the courthouse and away from my mother. I walked straight down the street to where in just seconds I was with my friends.

To a few I was just a kid who hated her baby sister's father.
To some I was just a kid who gave her mother trouble.
And to the rest, they were my friends.
I was finally free to be me.
It wasn't about going home to my 'family' anymore,
It was about creating my own.

A Teenage Promise and a Road Unknown

After yanking my arm away from my mother then walking away from her and the courthouse, I smiled the biggest smile I ever had. I wasn't afraid and I didn't care where I was going, I just knew I was getting as far away from my mother and the juvenile court system as I could.

I know you're not an adult when you're fifteen years old but I walked that short distance to the main strip of downtown like I was this big proud adult. 'I have to get a job and a place to live,' I thought to myself as I walked. 'I got this,' I reassured myself as I knew anything was better than living with a family I never mattered too. As I got to the main strip of downtown called Central Street I looked at the time on the tall old Victorian looking lamp post clock. My friends were still in school, as the new school year already started. I waited for cars to go by in both directions so I could cross the street when a motorcycle pulled up alongside me. I jumped backwards so I wasn't so close, but when he took off his motorcycle helmet I noticed it was my friend Mark from Butler Avenue. Mark always kept in touch with me after I lived at his aunt's house while my family lived next door. He drove up Agawam Street a few times, he stopped whenever he saw me walking and would visit me when I worked at Dunkin Donuts with his girlfriend and his brother. "Where you been?" he questioned me as he held his arms out for a hug. "Foster homes," I answered him as I hugged him back. "Why, who called on you?" he questioned as he already knew I had only one parent alive and it wasn't her who called on me. I told him I was walking with someone who was reported as a runaway. "Collateral damage again huh," he said as we both shook our heads in agreement.

Mark told me to go meet everyone under the clock. Under the clock was at the high school on the old building side, a huge green Victorian style clock that overhangs outside one of the entrances. It was the meeting spot for many high school students and teachers busting students trying to skip detention. I walked there not knowing what to expect but excited to see some of my friends again. Then I was going to see if I could sleep over someone's house. By the time I made it to the school and under the clock I already ran into a few friends. Nothing but loud screams and big hugs. "Where have you been?" the question with every friend I ran into. Loud screams and big hugs. It was so freaking cool and from the high school we all walked. We walked to the Acre section of Lowell and we walked to the Belvidere section. There was no stopping us if we had to get somewhere, we either got a ride or took a bus but mostly we walked. I quickly went right back into the same situation I had before I was sent to foster homes.

I would stay at a friend's house until it was late at night. Sometimes they told their parents I was sleeping over and sometimes they didn't. I just stayed quiet in their bedrooms. I'd sleep there, get up with them in the morning and leave when they left for school. My bag of clothes from before I got sent away was still where I left it at my friends house. I spent my days walking around the city with someone who skipped school for the day or I would walk to my mother's on Lawrence Street to see if she moved yet. I would remind her that I was still around and question her about my dad's social security checks. My mother wasn't as nasty towards me when I showed up unexpectedly because she knew I wasn't staying. That was all my mother ever wanted, was for me not to be living with her. She informed me after my dad passed away they stopped sending social security checks because he was now dead. "They can't pay for every dead person that lived," my mother snapped at me as she reminded me of her cruel motherly ways.

I was homeless but I slept safe at night. I had no family but I had friends who included me as one. I had no hope's, no dreams and no idea where I was going in life but I knew I was right where I belonged. I also knew I could throw a fit and order my mother to give me a roof over my head, food on my table and clothes for wearing. But why would I? Being away from my mother is when I felt my safest, my worth and my self being. So I continued doing what I knew best, letting my friends sneak me into their homes for the night or multiple nights at a time.

Sometimes I ate dinner at a friends house with their family and sometimes a friend would sneak me food after the parents went to bed. And I was never judged. I was never put down for having no parents. I was never put down for not owning a super nice wardrobe of clothes. I was never put down for not knowing when I'd eat again. I was never put down for being homeless. Hanging with my friends just meant we were making some real fun times and fun memories together. If I found myself feeling sorry for myself, being mad at my life or sad my life was the way it was, I'd quickly shake it off and remind myself that my abuser Dave Umpleby never touched me again and that made all my heartaches worth it.

In November my friends and I were told about a party in the highlands section of Lowell. We walked there and a couple of kids ran away from their homes just to show up at the party. So many kids from all around the Lowell area were there. Some kids set up their own band and we all listened to them jamming out. When the music wasn't playing, we were talking. A good twenty or so teenagers just sitting around getting to know each other.

Whenever I felt a question was coming my way about family I would get up and leave the room. I'd go to the bathroom, help clean up in the kitchen or chat with whoever was in the other room. My friend Mark told me if I behaved it would be ok for me to sleep at the home because the parents were gone for a few days. He already asked his friend, the one who lived in the home and who was throwing the party. It was a brother and sister who lived there and their parents were on a trip. The brother and sister were super cool. I did stay a few days there as I made a lot of friends and a lot of fun memories.

Anyone who went to the 1985 November party at the Casey home will also remember the night the School Street bridge went up in flames. Police knocked on the Casey family door and we all thought we were busted for the party but it was an evacuation emergency. The fire was extremely close to the colonial gas company so an emergency evacuation was placed and the Casey home was in that area. We all got into cars or trucks and cruised throughout the empty streets of downtown Lowell like we owned them and it wouldn't be long until we did. Afterwards we all went back to the party house and crashed. Sleeping on sofas, floors, chairs or staying up all night talking. I was allowed to shower there and I was treated like a person, like a human being and like I mattered.

I was sent for a walk to the corner store with another friend who was also staying there. As we walked to the store a police cruiser pulled up alongside us. "Uuurgh are you a runaway?" I asked her and before she could answer an officer said her name. She was a runaway and her parents reported her. "Where you heading?" the officer questioned me and I told him I was going to the store for some milk. The officer let me go on my way, minus the girl I was walking with. I continued walking to the store and returned to the party one less person. That's when the questions about my family life started. "Isn't anyone missing you?" "Where are your parents?" "Did you runaway?" Then when I answered, "No one is missing me," "My dad died and my mother hates me," and, "I have no one to report me as a runaway." I was overwhelmed by how many people couldn't understand why I was able to stay almost a whole week and no family was out looking for me. I stayed pretty much up until the day the parents were due home. I grabbed my small bag of clothes and left the house in the highlands wondering, 'Where am I going to go now?' I decided to walk to my dad's home and visit my stepmother for a few. I hadn't seen her since my dad's funeral. I don't know why but that's where I headed and like any other time, when she opened the door, her arms went wide open and she pulled me inside with her hugs. Only this time my dad wasn't there. We both cried and talked. I was so mad as she told me about the trouble my mother caused her with my dad's social security checks.

My mother tried claiming his death benefits. "You're getting your checks, right?" she questioned me. I could only imagine the look on my face as I answered her, "Ummmm no." She let me know she did indeed win my dad's death benefits and not my mother which made me so happy. She also let me know my mother was indeed collecting social security checks in my name from my dad's death benefits, which didn't make me happy to hear. It was getting into afternoon time and I had to leave so I could walk to a friend's house and have a place to sleep, plus it was breaking my heart being there because my dad wasn't there. He was at a cemetery instead and I missed him so much. I know he wasn't in my life long and he apologized for that.

My dad was always real to me, he called me and he said he loved me every time we talked. I had some really good conversations with him and I will always be grateful for that. But I didn't have the heart to tell my stepmother I wasn't living at home because I didn't want to go back to living in foster homes. So I left with a promise I would be back to visit. A visit that would take fourteen years to accomplish as I continued living this life given to me.

I was quickly back to sleeping at the homes of my friends. Nicole's dads in the acre, her mom's in the highlands, Francine's on Congress Street, Sam's on the same street or the sisters Lisa and Christina in Portuguese corner. I didn't mind the way I was living and none of my friends judged me or had looks of pity. The friendships I made were with teenagers who had no judgments on people in general. Unless you were a miserable person, everyone got along with everyone.

In 1983 - 1984 there was a lot of separation of people; the jocks, rebels, punks and preps. But by 1985 a lot of teens thought it didn't matter what, who or where you were from. It was who you were as a person that mattered.

I did walk to my mother's so I could confront her about what my stepmother told me of my dad's social security checks. My mother told me how they stopped when I was in foster care but just started back up again. She handed me eighty dollars and rushed me out the door because my older brother's father was on his way there to discuss my mother moving into his home. I headed out the door and walked into him coming inside the back hall. We said hi to each other and I took off to do what I always did, go hang with my friends. I wouldn't see that guy or my mother again until the weekend of my sixteenth birthday. I walked to his house in the acre just to remind my mother that I was still around. I went there with the sole purpose to be a smart ass to my mother. She told me my brother's father wasn't expecting me to live there so I showed up asking where my bedroom was. I also questioned about my dad's social security checks, but my mother claimed they had stopped. I only stayed long enough to piss my mother off.

I was still running into Jon a lot. Walking all over the city I'd run into him in the acre, downtown or passing by his street in the highlands. By now our friendship consisted of a lot of goofiness and laughs. I continued to sleep out, mostly staying on Congress Street at my friend Francine's home. I would always sneak in after her grandparents went to bed or hide in the back hall and sneak in when they weren't looking. Her grandmother caught on quickly and never minded when I was there. We made a lot of fun memories. Dancing to the movie Grease on a small television with aluminum foil antennas, making new hair styles with our hair, folding fitted sheets or walking to Woolworths for some new house coats for her grandmother. I spent Christmas 1985 hanging over Francine's house with her sisters.

Mark was still checking up on me every so often and by the end of 1985, Mark told me he had someone he wanted me to meet; a girl who needed an early morning babysitter. She was throwing a New years eve party and we all headed over to the highlands section on Lowell so I could meet her. Her name was Cissy and she lived on the corner of School and Somerset Streets in a three room apartment she shared with her daughter. I didn't immediately move in but it wasn't long before I was calling Cissy's apartment my home. Cissy and I hit it off immediately. Even though she was only two years older than me, she not only became a friend to me but also like a mother figure. I babysat her daughter while she worked as a painter during the day. Because her daughter went to sleep at her grandmother's some days, I didn't always have to babysit.

Mark was also getting me other babysitting jobs so I could make some extra money. Living at Cissy's in early 1986 was so much fun for this sixteen year old. Walking the streets at one, two or three in the morning while it was snowing was always a lot of fun. Walking up and down Chelmsford Street, we would switch metal signs outside of stores and businesses. Dragging the signs across the street or parking lot and leaving it in front of another business or store. We would climb up on the huge billboard sign on Chelmsford Street and sit on the footing area. Police showed up one night shining their flashlights on us and ordering us down. We all jumped off, made a run for it and ran all the way back to Cissy's house. There were always a bunch of teenagers at Cissy's including Mark, Mike, John, Frankie, Jamie, Andre, Stonis, Evelyn, Francine, Nicole, Shelly and many more. They would show up to check on us, hang out with us, watch VHS movies, play truth or dare or just talk for hours and hours. Laundry at Cissy's was always an adventure. There was always about four or five girls carrying big green trash bags of dirty laundry up the street to the laundromat. We thought twenty dollars to do over twenty loads of laundry was a lot of money.

Just weeks after calling Cissy's house my home, Jon wanted to start dating. He knew my life was too complicated to have a boyfriend but he wasn't buying that excuse. He was persistent and insisted we give it a try. My friendship with Jon had become a more trusting one as he always showed concern and an interest in me. I wanted to be a normal teenager and so I agreed to dating. Jon would pick me up at Cissy's and we would either go catch a movie at the Rt3 cinema, cruise around downtown, hang out at the boulevard or go to one of his practices for baseball or hockey. He was always trying to get me to talk about my years living with my mother, but I would always change the subject. He would get stubborn with me for not wanting to talk, but at the same time he was also understanding.

He told jokes, made me laugh and we were always being goofy with each other. I was my happiest when I didn't get questioned about my childhood. Jon however, constantly insisted I talked about it. I would be too embarrassed, ashamed or too many tears falling and Jon always praised, encouraged and cried with me. Jon knew the darkest secrets of my life and he didn't judge me. I appreciated his empathy and friendship even when he shared a bizarre secret, which he swore me to secrecy. Jon would always say some real freaky stuff but he always turned it into a joke until we laughed it off. We talked about the past, present, future and I always had a good time in his company. The year 1986 would become one of the best years of my young life. Filled with adventure, experiences, death and friendships to last a lifetime.

We didn't have cell phones back then and there was no house phone at Cissy's. So my communication with Jon was based on plans we would make from meeting him at his house, him picking me up at Cissy's or meeting downtown. As springtime came around, downtown was the place to be. Cars driving bumper to bumper down Central Street taking a left on either the cobblestone road called Middle Street or the next left onto Merrimack Street. Then taking a left onto Shattuck Street and a quick right onto Market Street where at the end you take a right onto Central Street. Some cars would circle the strip numerous times throughout the night. What would normally be a ten or fifteen minute ride would take up to two or more hours on a busy night. Mark and his friends would park their motorcycles along Central Street. Hanging out, talking, watching the cars circle around, making friends and some really great memories. Zayre's parking lot was the meeting place for when people wanted to take a break from driving or just to socialize. I was never without a friend or friends. There were many hang out spots downtown. We would hang outside of JJ's Pub, Espresso Pizza and Record Lane or hang out on the cement steps of a business, on the bridge or a public bench more further down Central Street. Cars pulled over to talk, make friends or go for rides to parties only to be dropped back off downtown. My friends and I were making friends in Chelmsford, Billerica, Tewkesbury and Dracut, Massachusetts along with friends in Hudson, Pelham and Nashua, New Hampshire. They would randomly show up at Cissy's house and take us for a game of basketball at two in the morning at one of the public parks throughout the city. A whole bunch of us, a good twenty or more playing basketball games in the wee hours of the morning. There were always cars and teenagers hanging out at Cissy's. Where everyone was getting to know everyone and having so much fun along the way.

My childhood was far behind me, like a trillion years behind me. Everyday there was always something going on at Cissy's. A card game of war or a game of truth or dare was played many times. I would always say dare because I never wanted to be a sore loser if I didn't want to answer a question. One time I was dared to drink vanilla extract, it was gross but the laughs were worth it. Staying up throughout the night talking, laughing and just having fun was very common in my life now. Sometimes it would take exhaustion to make us finally sleep.

One morning I was snoring so loud when some of the guys showed up to take whoever was at Cissy's out for breakfast. When I didn't wake up they wrapped me in a sleeping bag and carried me to the truck. They drove down to Joe's Diner on Chelmsford Street, carried me out of the truck and placed me on the public bench as they crossed the street to eat breakfast at the diner. I did wake up a bit confused, but then I saw the truck and my friends looking through the windows of the diner laughing. I let myself wake up before I walked over. I joined my friends, had some coffee and a whole lot of laughs.

Some of my friends had older siblings who were in my oldest brother's circle of friends, which confused many because they didn't know I had siblings. Hanging out downtown was real easy to find anyone you were looking for, including me. No one came looking for me but I did run into my oldest brother often when he drove around downtown. He never cared about me being on my own as a sixteen year old. Jon hated how I didn't have a curfew. He would drop me off at Cissy's after hanging out and I'd walk downtown with friends who showed up at Cissy's. I did it many times after Jon dropped me off. I wasn't being sneaky against Jon, he knew I did it and I did it because I could. I was sixteen years old and I had no rules or guardian. Jon and I talked about how it sucked that I couldn't be a girl you take home to meet your parents because the first question they'd ask, "Where do you live?" The second question would be, "What school do you go to?" "Who are your parents?" The questions would continue and Jon understood that and it made me want to understand him even more.

As May 1986 came around Jon and Mark had their high school graduation to get ready for. I was starting a new part time job at Dallas Texas Smokehouse on Chelmsford Street where another one of Mark's aunt was the manager who hired me. Warmer weather also had Mark picking everyone up at Cissy's and taking us all up to Hampton Beach where we would hang out for the day. As he did on Memorial day weekend where the whole gang from Cissy's house spent the weekend hanging out in the parking lot of Hampton Beach. We had fun, made memories and had no idea how much our lives were about to change in the blink of an eye.

Blood does not make you related, loyalty does and a heartache is only the blessed feeling of love.

There are not enough words to say how much fun my life as a sixteen year old in 1986 Lowell, Massachusetts really was. Babysitting jobs, hanging out downtown, walking around the highlands, acre and Belvidere sections of Lowell. Rt3 Cinema with Jon, cruising around with him, his crazy talks and winning my trust more everyday. Meeting so many friends and being part of a family, a circle of friends who accepted me without judgement. I was questioned by a few, "Why don't you live with your mother?" I'd answer, "My mother isn't a good mother to me." And that was it, no one questioned me to explain more. I never had to explain myself.

All my friends looked out for me, they had my back, they included me, they treated me as a person and they knew me. Mark was constantly stopping in at Cissy's apartment dropping off plates of food, left overs from his house, giving us rides when we needed them, always offering his help, his laughs and his friendship. He always kept in touch with me ever since I met him in 1982 at his aunt's house. He took me on as a baby sister. He used to tell me he was, "Your brother from another mother." And I always told him I was, "Your sister from another mister." More than half of my friends from the 1980s I met because of Mark. I was living at Cissy's because of Mark. Working at Dallas Texas Smokehouse and babysitting jobs was also because of Mark. As I was on May 28th when I woke up at Cissy's and walked up the street to Shaw Street where I started babysitting for someone Mark knew. It was a part time babysitting job for a woman named Darlene with three young kids. Mark called me there in the morning to inform me he would be picking me up after work and bringing me to the mall. I was promoted to waitress at my job and I needed black pants for work that coming weekend. Mark was meeting friends at the mall so he figured he'd take me at the same time.

Weirdest thing about babysitting when you're a teenager is the six hours of babysitting feels like thirty hours of soap operas, forty hours of Fraggle Rock, Smurfs and Curious George running around with the twins from the movie The Shining asking a thousand hours of the same one word question, "Why?" All done in six hours.

Mark showed up a little earlier than I thought and Darlene wasn't home yet. He was on his motorcycle, but I couldn't leave. He assured me that he would take me before Friday when I wasn't babysitting so I could get the pants I needed for work. He took his helmet off and gave me his famous big squeeze bear hug.

That was the last time I saw Mark.

Darlene was later than normal and came storming into her Shaw Street apartment about thirty minutes after Mark drove away. She was crying and screaming, "He's dead, he's dead, Mark's dead." I tried assuring her she was wrong, "He just left here about twenty-five minutes ago," I told her but she insisted she was right and that she was telling me the truth. I didn't believe her so I just grabbed my stuff and headed back down to Cissy's house. On my way there I ran into some friends who drove by, they stopped their car in the middle of the road and were saying the same thing Darlene was saying. I didn't believe them either, so I continued walking until I got to Cissy's apartment where everyone was. All our friends, the whole gang from Cissy's was at Cissy's. All crying, hugging and supporting each other. That was when I found out it was true, my friend, my brother from another mother was killed instantly in a motorcycle accident on his way to the Pheasant Lane Mall while driving along the boulevard. Just minutes after giving me his famous bear hug.

I was empty, numb, lost, blank with nothing to say. But the gang at Cissy's never left us alone. They got us to Mark's wake and his funeral. We were all together while we reminisced about how much fun Mark was. Making a toast in his honor to the sky and seeing a lightning bolt flash, left us all with the feeling of how unfair it was that Mark was taken from us. He was gone, like a flower plucked from the ground. His place on this earth left a huge void at Cissy's. Shortly after Mark's funeral, his mother showed up at Cissy's house asking for Cissy and I. She wanted us to know Mark included us as his sister's and we let her know he was always our brother. I was numb but without a doubt Mark was more of an older brother to me than anyone I had. I do hope if Mark's mother ever reads my story, I hope she knows how much his friendship was never forgotten, was appreciated and is always very much missed. Things quieted down at Cissy's after Mark's death. A bunch of us including me got in trouble for spray painting businesses downtown with messages of RIP Mark. Instead of pressing charges, the business owners made us clean up the spray paint and sweep outside their businesses, Espresso pizza being one of them. I didn't go back to work for Mark's family at Dallas Texas Smokehouse, I guess it was just too hard for me.

My life was so confusing, but the trust between Jon and I was something I knew to be true. We agreed the way our relationship was, it was working, so we kept us as we were. It wasn't a normal boyfriend/girlfriend relationship but nothing in my life was normal.

Hanging outside at Zayre's parking lot one afternoon got me my job back at Dunkin Donuts on Church Street, a third time. (They say the third time's a charm) My old manager saw me hanging outside, he called me in and offered me my job back. I was not expecting to ever work there again. He thought I was pretty cool for throwing the party and didn't hold it against me. I worked part time nights so I was available to babysit during the day for Cissy. Some nights Jon picked me up and some nights I walked home. The prostitutes on Appleton Street would walk me all the way to Westford Street as they stayed their distance walking on the opposite side of the street and yelling their names to me. They were being my bodyguards, just watching out for me. It never failed whenever I walked home from work, I always got a prostitute escort up Appleton Street, across the rotary and onto Westford Street.

Jon and I talked more about what he confided to me in secrecy and I promised to talk more of my childhood. I would half ass my way around talking about things related to my childhood and he would make it seem so easy to talk and cry about the difficult parts of my life. "It's not your fault," Jon always told me. When I would get embarrassed or ashamed to talk, Jon would interrupt me and continue to say what was too hard for me to speak of. Then he'd hug me and cry with me.

No matter how many times we talked over the summer of 1986, Jon reminded me how I always fought and how it was never my fault. A part of me knew he was very much right. I always fought, I always told my mother and for that I was a sixteen year old with no family. Deep down it did hurt but deep down I also knew I had to keep moving forward and so I did.

Throughout the summer, downtown became an even more popular and hopping place to be. Bumper to bumper cars and a guarantee to run into someone I knew. The 1986 streets of downtown were nothing like it is now in today's world of 2021. There were no used heroin needles lying around the streets and at any time day or night I always felt my safest when I was in the downtown area.

All my friend's at Cissy's and downtown did not know about my life living with my mother, but they knew I had a mother who I was better off without. My life was about Cissy's, hanging with Jon, working at Dunkin Donuts and hanging around downtown sometimes until three in the morning. The more we were downtown, the more friends we made. The more friends we made, the more friends were invited back to hang out at Cissy's. The more people at a small three room apartment, the more you're at risk of property damage. With property damage came an eviction and a lot of trouble we were in by Cissy's mom. We definitely got in a few good parties, memories and fun times by the time we had to move out of the apartment. I stayed with Cissy at her friends house for a couple weeks and I would stay over at Francine's house on Congress Street. Sometimes she would throw down her grandfather's car keys and I'd sleep in the back seat of his car. I'd either go into Francine's to clean up or we'd walk to the YMCA and I'd get a hot shower there.

One day Jon told me he wanted us to see each other less. "I don't want to break up or say goodbye, just take a break," he told me as I just assumed he was breaking up with me. But he insisted he wasn't. When he dropped me off that night I said, "So this is goodbye." He got mad at me insisting we were not breaking up. I was totally confused about what Jon wanted but my life was too busy to let myself get depressed about it. Cissy got another apartment by the end of the summer and I moved in with her again.

I wasn't babysitting anymore, and I still had my part time job at Dunkin Donuts. That is until a spontaneous question came my way, "Want to take a ride to Florida?" My friend Sam from Congress Street and her friend Chris questioned if I wanted to take a ride with them, how could I resist? I was supposed to work that day so I called out. I didn't call out sick. I called out by telling my boss, "I'm leaving for Florida." What an adventure it was. Sometimes a boring, sometimes an exciting long ride. We drove down to Florida, stayed for a few hours as Chris was dropping off the car we drove down in and was driving another one back. As we were driving back home and got near the state line of Florida, we saw an elderly man broken down on the side of the road.

We pulled over to help him but he was just anxious to get home and his car was completely dead. He lived in Maryland and we were heading that way. So we offered him a ride. He took his plates off his car, left the car on the side of the road and we headed towards Maryland with an extra passenger in the car. He was nervous being in the car with two teenagers and a twenty year old. We stopped at the first rest stop so he could call his wife, let her know where he was and who he was with. The rest of the fifteen plus hour ride was one of fun, laughs and cool story telling from the old timer. He called me a funny bugger and he was super nice. When we got him home safely his wife was waiting for us with a full breakfast buffet. She insisted we go inside and eat. When we walked in we were all like, "Wow." There was so much food. We ate, washed up in the bathroom, thanked her for her kindness and headed home to Massachusetts.

Once I was back in Lowell I went home to Cissy's. I showered, got dressed and headed downtown. First person I ran into was Jon and he is pissed off at me. When I questioned why he was mad, he told me because I went to Florida without telling him. "I thought you wouldn't care," I said to him as he looked at me with sadness. I truly didn't think anyone could care for me in a girlfriend kind of way. He hugged me so tight as he told me, "Because I'm your boyfriend and I care," "Look we'll talk later," he continued as we were surrounded by friends hanging out downtown. I was so confused, because I was positive we had broken up.

Taking off to Florida like I did let me know that three times was not always a charm. I kind of figured I was fired from Dunkin Donuts and a little mad at myself for getting fired. But it was a fun experience taking the trip to Florida so I wasn't too hard on myself. I just knew I had to find another job quickly. I was only back from Florida for a few days when I found myself in the back of a police cruiser again. Same reason again also. My friend Sam who I went to Florida with was reported by her parents as a runaway and once again I wasn't. "I'm not doing this again," I told the officers. I was only sixteen, so I begged and pleaded with the officers. I told them I was better off away from foster care and my mother. Even my friend who was the runaway pleaded for me. The officer agreed and allowed me to be picked up by Cissy who was eighteen years old.

I was on the right road. The moving on, not dwelling and getting over it road. In a city so large and family so few, friendship was all I really ever knew. Over the next few months my life continued to stay busy. I took babysitting jobs, helped Cissy with keeping the apartment clean and took a job at the Dunkin Donuts on Middlesex Street. I walked to work and started off as being a trainee. After a few days I was put on the register at the drive-thru window. I spoke into the headset taking orders, pressing them into the register and passing the order to the customer out the drive-thru window. I was only at work for about an hour when I went to hand a coffee to the person out the window, but I noticed immediately who it was. It was my baby sister's father, my abuser Dave Umpleby. I squeezed the coffee cup, loosening the cover and whipping the hot black coffee into his face as I yelled, "You raped me, you raped me."

I was skinny and tall, so I squeezed myself right out that drive-thru window as I chased after him. As soon as he got out of the parking lot and onto Middlesex Street he was gone. A woman who was in the drive-thru helped me to my feet as I just fell to the ground when I knew I couldn't catch him. I didn't know what I'd do if I did catch him. It caught me off guard seeing him. Instead of walking back into Dunkin Donuts, I walked home to Cissy's. She was cool about it too. We walked back to Dunkins a few days later and got my few hours of pay. I didn't have to explain what happened the day I squeezed through the drive-thru window. I'm pretty sure everyone at Dunkin Donuts that morning heard and saw me. I was too embarrassed, so I didn't go back to work there.

Jon was picking me up at Cissy's, downtown and sometimes having his friend Scott pick me up. I would go to his games or practices for baseball or hockey at Shedd Park, Alumni Field, behind the Bartlett School or Janis Skating Rink. We would hang outside of Jon's house, downtown, at the boulevard or Rt3 Cinema. Friends were always around at Cissy's even more than before, but no large crowds or parties. Just a whole lot of fun. If we wanted to get loud then we headed downtown where we walked the streets like we owned them. As teenagers back then, we definitely owned downtown.

I soon got a job at the Pheasant Lane Mall as a cashier at a store called International Foods. I would either take the city bus or Cissy's friend Louie would drive me and pick me up. I only worked a few days a week and was hired for the Christmas holiday season. My seventeenth birthday December 15, 1986 went by as quickly as the years since I first stopped living with my family in 1981. A few days before Christmas I was at work and there was my mother doing some last minute Christmas shopping. I approached her asking about my baby sister. I questioned if I could see her on Christmas day and my mother said I could as she quickly walked away from me. The mall was too crowded and I had to get back to work anyway. On Christmas morning I walked to the house my family lived at in the acre section of Lowell. I was very uncomfortable and only stayed a few minutes before walking back to Cissy's apartment.

As the days got colder I wasn't seeing Jon as much, but only because we were always busy. Before I knew it, the year 1987 was upon us. By the end of January and due to circumstances beyond my control, I had to move to the other side of the city in the Centerville section of Lowell on a street called Cumberland Road. I was already listing both my parents as being deceased when it came to doctor visits at the free teen clinic. Any form I had to fill out where its information is questioned, I was listing Jon as my emergency contact.

I moved over to the Centerville section of Lowell, into the home of a friend I knew from high school, Cissy's and downtown. Her mother told me about tax refund checks and about doing a change of address form. I knew nothing much about either of those, so I paid to have my taxes done and took the change of address form to my new home for some help on filling it out.

I knew my mothers address in the acre and that's what my friends mother told me to put down as a previous address. So I did and what a web it did weave. I didn't have a job when I first moved to Centerville but I did have to pay room and board. So I got up early in the morning and walked downtown to a place called Work A Day on Central Street. I had to be there by six in the morning to catch the van that took me to a factory or warehouse type of work. At the end of the day, the van drove myself and others back to the office on Central Street where I was paid between $60-$80 cash for a day's work.

It was weird but nice being in a home so warm with a family touch. Jon of course knew where to find me. After settling in for a few weeks at my new home, I decided to take a walk downtown to see Jon but he was outside already waiting for me. It had been at least two months since I last saw him. My relationship with Jon was becoming more trusting, real, freaky and caring. We continued dating but also dating others so we could get the experience of dating, not getting sick of each other and just doing life as a teenager in the 1980s. A part of normalcy I had in my life.

As I awaited my tax return check in the mail I instead received a letter from the city of Boston informing me to report to my nearest social security administration office. I took a day off from work and I walked to the cobblestone Palmer Street in downtown with my friend and my letter in hand. I picked a number tab and sat down waiting for my number to be called. After what seemed like hours my number was called. I handed my letter to the clerk behind the counter. She took my letter and disappeared towards the back of the building. Within minutes a man came to the front desk, called my name and asked me to follow him as he opened a door for me to walk through. I told him my friend was my sister so he let her come with me as we followed him. There were cubicles throughout the one floor building. We walked towards the back where he had me sit in one of the cubicles. He informed me how I filled out a change of address form and filed for a tax return. "Is this correct Miss Mellen?" he questioned me. "Yes," I answered him as I shook my head happily. "Do you know what social security fraud is Miss Mellen?" the man questioned me a bit angrily. "No," I answered the guy not so happily. He looked at me strangely but then explained how collecting social security checks while working was against the law.

I kind of chuckled at the guy. "I'm working cause I don't get social security checks," I told him. Then he questioned me, "When did you move from your mother's School Street address?" "Move," I sarcastically giggled to the man. "I never lived there," I continued to answer his question. I explained my living conditions since 1981, where I was living now and my distant relationship with my mother. The man was not happy at what I was saying to him. I got a bit nervous over his reaction, but he assured me that it was not me who he was mad at. Then he said my dad's name as he questioned me, "You're his daughter correct?" When I answered him I was his daughter, he got up and told me to sit where I was. "I'll be right back," he said to me. He wasn't right back. My friend and I waited what seemed like hours for the guy to return.

He returned with a stack of rectangular shape copy paper in his arms. It had light green and off white stripes, like from a Xerox copy machine. He sat down, asked me to sign my name a few different ways on a piece of paper and so I did. Then he showed me a copy of a cashed social security check. I looked at the cashed check he was showing me. It was written out to my mother, in care of me on behalf of my father. Then I looked at the date February 1987 and I was a bit confused. I looked at the copy with the date of February 1987 and my signature over and over again. It had my signature but I didn't sign it. "This was last month," I said to the man as I thought to myself, 'my mother cashed this last month.' The man informed me how my mother had been collecting social security checks for me on behalf of my father every single month since 1982. I was speechless as confusion went through my head while the man kept showing me more and more copies. "Is this your signature?" "Is this your signature?" he questioned with every new copy he showed me.

There were so many copies of cashed checks and all had my signature on them, but not one did I sign. I started to cry and he stopped. He informed me how much trouble my mother was in for stealing my dad's social security checks since 1982. While other people took care of me, while Cissy and I struggled for months at a time. How dare my mother do that. She told me they had stopped and I am so glad she got caught. The man had me sign some paperwork and assured me that I would not have to face my mother in court. "We at social security will take care of her ourselves," he said to me reassuring me that I was not in any trouble at all.

I left the social security office questioning myself, 'How could she?' I told my friend, "That money could have helped Cissy when I lived with her." I was so hurt, mad and confused as I wondered how after all my mother did to me throughout my life, she continued to spit in my face with every social security check she cashed every month for over five years. The checks were meant to support me not her. I walked back to the home I was living in, now awaiting two checks in the mail and wondering, 'How could my mother do that?' That was $417.00 a month for five years. Like my friend Sandi's mom once told me when I lived with them in 1981, "Shame on her." Now it was 1987 and those words were still so very much true.

Jon thought it was funny I had something while living on Cumberland Road I did not have in a long time, a curfew. His persistence convinced me to enroll in night school classes at Lowell High. I wasn't able to get my diploma with my graduating class of 1987 but I was able to get my GED. I had class three nights a week which Jon would always pick me up from. The only thing about going to class was the reminder of what school was to me. A place I always went to when I lived with my mother. I can definitely say I hated school. I continued to work at my Work a Day job during the week and had weekends off to hang out with friends. I was still catching a movie at Rt3 cinema or hanging out downtown but only on weekends now. I was still walking all around the city to get to places my friends and I wanted to go.

I finally had the rules and curfew of being a teenager, but I also had the overwhelming responsibility of keeping a roof over my head. I knew I had to pay my weekly room and board or I wouldn't have a room to sleep in. First thing I did with my money every week was make sure I paid my room and board of sixty dollars. Even though Jon and I agreed on dating other people, we were also still seeing a lot of each other. I started to date a guy from Christian hill but he didn't like the idea of the friendship I had with Jon so it didn't last.

After I told Jon what happened at the social security office and my mother stealing my dad's social security checks, he was even more disgusted in the woman I kept calling my mother. "She's your birth mother," he told me one day. It was also the first time he told me my mother would have to line out her lies. I didn't understand him at first but he explained how one day she would have to line out all the lies she has told. It wasn't long before my mother was spotted driving her white escort around the street I was living on, looking for me. She was seen on numerous occasions driving around the block and circling Cumberland Road. My friend's mother told me about seeing her. "Why would she be looking for me?" I questioned my friend's mother and she answered me, "Your dad's social security checks," "She wants them back," she continued. I pretended it didn't bother me but it did. Anywhere I walked I kept looking over my shoulder, looking behind me, watching every white colored car that drove by me. I was mad, I was hurt and I couldn't understand why it took money for my mother to finally want to look for me.

On April 10th after seeing a movie with Jon at the Rt3 cinema, Jon drove to an empty field under the Lord Overpass Rotary on Middlesex Street and parked his car. He wanted to go for a walk and sit under the stars. It was something we did usually at the boulevard but it was interesting being around the train tracks and seeing all the graffiti spray painted. We sat on some huge logs that rested on the ground by the railroad tracks and we did what we did so well. We talked and we talked. Jon wanted us to make a promise to each other that no matter what happens in life, we would wait for each other. Whether it was life or death, he would wait for me should he die before me and I, the same for him. I didn't have to think about it. "I promise," I quickly said to him without hesitation.

He was always concerned over the troubled life I lived and he always wanted me to experience more of what life had to offer. Even though I didn't see Jon everyday, he was always so caring and poetic with me. It was his way to let me know he was always thinking of me. Jon was persistent, stubborn and funny, which made it easy for me to comply with his promise to wait for each other.

We made so many promises to each other that night as we squeezed our pinky fingers together tight and rolled our promises into one. We joked a lot, laughed a lot and had a really fun time. Jon and I were never about the secrets we shared, he was always a friend, a hug, and an ear away. Before our night ended we did a poem together. Something we had done many times before. Jon would say one line and I would say the next line, then I'd go home to where I was living and write it down. I'd write poems about life, friendship, breakups, goodbyes, death, heaven, angels and more. The night came to an abrupt end when Jon reminded me I had a curfew. He dropped me off at my Cumberland Road home where April 10th 1987 became the night I would remember for the rest of my life, it was the night I swore my heart and soul to Jon Massey Porter. When Jon picked me up the weekend after we made all our promises, we both admitted what we did was a bit weird, freaky and yet it was also a lot of fun. Some days I didn't know what to make of Jon, but only because sometimes, he really did leave me speechless.

One day my mother caught me as I was leaving the Cumberland Road apartment. She stopped her car in the middle of the road and jumped out calling my name. Jon was picking me up and that's why I was running out the door because he pulled up and beeped. I headed towards Jon's car as my mother was stopped behind his yellow car. She hollered to me, "I just want to talk to you." I looked at Jon who was now standing outside of his car. He walked over to my mother, stood about a foot away from her and just stared her down. I got into Jon's car as I watched my mother just look at Jon before hopping back in her car and driving away. She didn't say one word to Jon.

By the first week of May I figured out why my mother was driving around looking for me. It wasn't because I was her daughter nor was it because she was my mother. It was because of my dad's social security checks. It had to do with mail I received from the social security office, a check in the amount of $417.00 and a few days later I received another check from social security, this time for six thousand dollars. That was a lot of money for a seventeen year old teenager in 1987 and I did what any teenager would do, I went on a shopping spree. I shopped downtown, I took buses to the Chelmsford, Billerica and Pheasant Lane Malls. I took time off from my job and Jon took me to Central Savings bank so I could open a bank account. Jon was so proud and happy for me, but he knew I wasn't as happy as I should be. "Talk," he said to me as he pulled his car over after driving away from the bank. For some reason, I don't know why but as we left the bank that day, it was the first time I realized that I was seventeen years old. My childhood was gone and I never had a chance to be a kid without being terrorized. It was the first time I realized I never had a childhood. Jon just hugged me as I cried and cried.

In June I received another check from social security and I would continue to receive those checks every month until my eighteenth birthday. It felt so good to wear clothes that belonged to me, to wear shoes, jackets, sweaters and a bathing suit that belonged to me. For the first time in years I wasn't wearing hand me down clothes. I had a place to live and I had people in my life who wanted me in theirs. I had everything that I didn't have when I lived with my family. I had safety, I had security, I had love, I had trust and I had faith knowing despite what my 'family' thought of me, I was doing right for myself. Something I still remind myself constantly.

By the time July came the people I was living with had decided to pack up and move to Oklahoma. I was offered the chance to go with them but I declined as I was scared of the thought of living in another state. I ended up moving in with my friend and her boyfriend but it quickly became an uncomfortable situation for me. And by the end of July I was on my way to Florida with my friend Francine and her young son. It was spontaneous although I did plan a phone call to Jon to let him know where I was going. Then Francine, her young son and I walked to the train station where we took buses to Springfield Mass, New York and continued onto Florida. We stayed with Francine's family in St Petersburg and in Clearwater. Spending almost two months down in Florida enjoying the sun, the palm trees and the experience. I tried finding work while I was there but I had no luck in finding a job. As the weeks went by so did our money and before we knew it, we were broke. Francine and I were both back in Lowell by early September. We were both tanned and both full of experience. I stayed at Francine's for a few days after getting back home, calling Jon as soon as I could.

As October came around most of my friends who were my age were busy getting their licenses, driving cars, applying for college or joining the Military. I was just looking for a room to rent. I finally found one in the Christian hill neighborhood of Lowell on Fremont Street. I rented an attic room from a woman and her husband. They seemed like really nice people. I was allowed to have friends over, I was always invited to watch a movie with them and they always saved me a plate if I wasn't home for dinner. I got a job as a waitress in a small Brazilian restaurant right downtown on Central Street. I also enrolled in self defense classes at Belvidere Martial Arts. Often taking random walks to visit my dad at the cemetery and as random as I was, so wasn't Jon who always showed up there to give me a ride home. I used to pinch him all the time to make sure he was a real person. I'd just shake my head and thank my lucky stars for having someone like him in my life.

After living on Fremont Street for about a month, it seemed everything was normal and there was no reason why I should have thought any differently. But there I was, just home from work when I put my key into the front door keyhole and it didn't fit. I tried again but the key wouldn't fit in the keyhole. So I knocked but no one answered. I knocked again and after knocking for a long time, I started throwing whatever I could find on the ground at the windows. Rocks and sticks until finally the husband opened the front door.

I was about to walk inside when he stopped me from doing so. I looked at him confused. That's when he told me his wife had issues and didn't want me renting from them anymore. He informed me because his wife was my size and needed new clothes, he was also allowing her to keep my clothes. Then he slammed the door shut. I was so dumbfounded over what happened, then I was mad over what happened. I started to throw bigger rocks at their windows. I was screaming their names out on the street causing neighbors to look outside at what all the commotion was about. I asked one of the neighbors to call the police and they did. Shortly after a police officer showed up at the property of 102 Fremont Street and he knocked on the door until the husband answered it. The officer ordered the husband to return my belongings to me. A few minutes later the front door opened again and the husband threw a green trash bag of clothes on the porch as he slammed the front door shut. I looked through the bag and immediately noticed not all my clothes were in the bag. The officer informed me how the husband and wife were known to the police. The husband was a known drug user and his wife had a lot of issues. The officer also told me I could file a small claims lawsuit against them for the remainder of my belongings, but I declined to do so. I watched the police officer drive away as I realized I was once again homeless.

I was so mad at the couple I rented the attic from. They kept my jean jacket, red Reebok sneakers and a bunch of my clothes. All I could do was gather my green trash bag of clothes and walk to the only place I knew as a home that was always there whenever I needed it to be; downtown Lowell Massachusetts. I walked into Woolworths department store where I found a duffle bag, paid for it, went outside and switched my clothes into my new bag. I'm not sure if I blinked my eyes and life changed or I walked through a door and life rearranged. Either way there was always friendship and music around, for that I am forever grateful for. I used a pay phone to call Jon as I was so embarrassed, humiliated and ashamed that I was once again homeless. Jon picked me up and I used my money from my dad's social security checks to pay for a room at the Motel Caswell in Tewksbury, Mass, just outside of Lowell. I was too young to rent a room so Jon booked it for me, paying a day at a time.

Jon would pick me up before he had work in the morning and dropped me off in Lowell for the day. At the end of the day, I'd catch up with him. If I wasn't sleeping at a friends then he would drive me back to the motel where sometimes he ended up booking a week at a time so I didn't have to always go into Lowell and Jon didn't always have to worry about picking me up. Jon took me to the store for snacks, reading materials and puzzles so I stayed busy. It was a long period in my life. The motel was gross no matter how much I cleaned it up. I was alone a lot and I cried a lot. I started to get scared, scared of my future because I did not want to be where I was. As the colder months came, so didn't the month of December, my eighteenth birthday and my last social security check.

 I spent Christmas eve and morning with a friend I knew from downtown Lowell. She lived in Billerica and had all kinds of animals on her family's property. It was a beautiful home, her mom was so nice and even gave me a Christmas stocking with health and beauty products in it. There were younger siblings in the home and it was so cool watching their excitement on Christmas morning. At one point I was overwhelmed with sadness as I realized I had spent every Christmas since 1981 with a different family. I tried holding back the tears but I was overwhelmed and I started to cry. The mother of the home handed me her cordless phone and told me to call my family, so I called Jon. Shortly after my phone call to Jon I got dropped off at Shedd Park where Jon was already waiting for me as we planned on the phone. We sat in his car for a while just talking about so much. I was emotionally torturing myself over things that were out of my control. I didn't have a normal family life, a normal school life, my virginity was ripped from me, my childhood was lost and it was my sixth Christmas without my family. I was an emotional wreck.

 Jon always had a way of saying the right things. My virginity he compared to a rolling pin and questioned me, "If I hit you off the head with a rolling pin would you consider yourself a cook?" He then handed me a clipping of a Dear Abby article that I still have to this day. Jon reminded me how Mark was my brother with or without being blood related. Letting me know Mark loved me like a little sister. I knew that long before Mark died, but I was thankful to Jon for reminding me of the sibling love I had with Mark. Jon always reminded me that as tough as my life was, I was now free to live the life I was given. That it was me who had control of my life now. After chatting for what seemed like hours, Jon dropped me off at another friends house on Smith Street where I was invited for Christmas dinner by a family I did babysitting for. Jon's hug, kiss and our, "see you soon," was the most normal part of my unstable life that I had become very accustomed to. Before I knew it, the year 1988 was here.

One day I walked to the department of youth services on Lawrence Street to see what I could do to still receive my dad's checks after workers at social security sent me there. Because I was homeless, I automatically qualified for a Job Corp program that started up. The only catch was I had to move to New York City. I would live in a dorm like place, go to class and other benefits in career oriented programs. I would be allowed to leave every other weekend to travel back to Lowell if I wanted to. They gave me a few days to think it over and that's what I did. Of course the more I talked about it, the more exciting it sounded. An adventure, I kept telling myself. Jon was all excited also, he insisted he would pick me up every other weekend and he was excited about visiting me in New York City. My friend's all thought it was a good idea and so I called to notify them I would accept the offer for Job Corp. I was leaving the next morning so I hung out all night in the downtown area. Just hanging out with Jon and friends. Some friends went home, some friends had no curfew and some friends just stayed for the fun. And it was always a lot of fun. Zayre's parking lot was where everyone would meet to hang out after the police kicked us off of our hang out spots on Central Street.

By 1988 the Lowell police were putting a stop to all the kids hanging around the downtown area and trying to ease the amount of cars cruising around the center. When morning came I had to walk to Lawrence Street and meet my caseworker who was driving me to New York City. I thought a lot as I walked from one end of Lawrence Street to the other, 'I just turned eighteen, New York was a big city, I would be alone in another state where I had no family or friends.' The more I walked, the more I thought. The more I thought, the more my anxiety raced. 'I have plenty of friends in Lowell who consider me as their family and I still have money in my bank account,' I told myself as my anxiety of being alone got the best of me. I quickly turned around and walked to a friends house. I felt like I was at a crossroad in my life as I made a quick decision to take a right turn and walk to a friend's house, instead of walking straight up Lawrence Street towards the department of youth services. I was also relieved as my anxiety calmed down knowing I wasn't going to a large city where I knew no one. Ditching the Job Corp opportunity meant I had to find myself a job before my bank account drained. I got to sleep at my friend's house where we cleaned up before heading downtown before the night crew showed up.

Even though the Lowell police were putting a stop to us teenagers hanging out downtown, we were all still meeting down there and heading over to Zayre's parking lot where we would hang out, make plans and take off in cars to hang out at someone's house. A few friends were disappointed I blew off the Job Corp experience. A few others offered me to live with their families and many friends just stayed and to hang out with me, as in the blink of an eye my emotions would take over my life as I suffered one too many blows after the other.

It started that night, the night I should have been in New York city. Jon wasn't expecting to see me and I wasn't expecting to see him drive by me with a girl in his car. I know we dated other people and we talked about people we had dates with or dated. We talked, laughed and explained our dating ways, but I never actually saw him with another girl. I was hanging on Central Street as he drove up and he quickly gunned his gas around the corner. As I watched him drive up Middlesex Street, I just froze. I hyperventilated as I was shocked or maybe I was crushed? I was so hurt as I saw my band aid covered heart smashed all over downtown Lowell.

My friend saw the girl in his car also and she quickly took me away from the downtown area. We walked to an older friends house and he went to the liquor store for us. We got things to make fuzzy navel drinks, some nips and some marijuana. We got drunk, we got stoned and then we headed back downtown. That was my mistake, never go downtown drunk with a broken heart. It was the middle of winter and I was the warmest I had been in days. It was a lot of fun walking downtown until we cut through Zayre's parking lot and there was Jon. His face dropped when he saw me and my two middle fingers were already up as I screamed at him. He tried walking towards me but I yelled louder so he backed away. I could tell by the way he was looking at me that he was disappointed in me, which pissed me off even more about the girl I saw him with.

I started accusing him of being a freak, a fake and a jerk. I was so mad at him, so hurt by him and so confused by him. I told him to stay away from me and stay away from my life. For the next few days, I did not care about my life. I closed my bank account, spent most of it on alcohol and the rest on pizza, cigarettes, SuzyQ cupcake snacks and soda. I walked around the downtown area all day and night. I walked to Dunkin Donuts in Zayre's plaza when I had to use the bathroom, brush my teeth or splash my face with water. I would hang out in a phone booth, bus stop booth or a hallway in an apartment complex if it got too cold or windy for me. I was carrying nips of alcohol in my coat pocket. As cold as the winters are in Massachusetts, I was pretty warm when I had alcohol in me. After many days of living that way, I started to wonder what I was going to do with my life. I had a complete meltdown when everything just came crashing down on me. I cried and I cried, I tried everything not to cry which caused me to cry more. There was no stopping me as the tears poured down my face. A friend took me back to her apartment where we talked for hours over a cup of hot tea. I got some sleep, a shower and a promising start to a new day.

For a period of a few short weeks I would be knocked into the lowest time of my adult life. It had been a few days since I had my drunken emotional breakdown and a few days since I last saw Jon. I wanted to see him but first thing first, I needed to get myself a job. Where else to find one but none other than downtown. I headed down there in hopes that my old job at Work a Day was hiring. As soon as I got to the area of Zayre's, I ran into a friend who was also out job hunting. We decided to walk together looking for help wanted signs outside of businesses as we walked by them. When we crossed Church Street and continued onto Central Street, I was suddenly cut off by a man who came walking fast outside of JJ's Pub. I stopped quickly so I didn't walk right into the man. He didn't see me, but I saw him. That uncle I kept requesting to live with after my dad died, that uncle I was repeatedly told had died, that uncle the Lowell juvenile courthouse verified had died way back in 1985. Yes, that uncle was the man who just cut me off and stopped me in my tracks. "What are you doing?" my friend said back to me as she was still walking but quickly turned around and was by my side.

"That's, that's, that's my dead uncle walking," I said in a confusing manner, yet determined to catch up to him for verification and so I did. "Uncle Ray?" I questioned as I ran up to the man. He looked right at me and smiled as he grabbed me saying, "Catherine." He kissed me all over my cheeks and hugged me as he was so delighted to see me. I was beside myself, dumbfounded, empty, yet so happy that he and my aunt were alive. He kept trying to give me money. I was giving it back to him as he kept giving it to me, insisting he just won on the lottery. I didn't care about that, I was asking him questions and telling him what I was told. But then I noticed he had a bit of a buzz going. It was around noon time and he reeked of alcohol.

He was funny and we only talked a few minutes when a cab pulled up. The driver got out and helped my uncle into the cab. I told the driver who I was as my uncle threw more money at me before the cab drove away and just like that, my dad's brother was alive all along. The juvenile court system back in 1984 and 1985 didn't look into my request to live with who my dad wanted me to. They just took my mother's word that they had died. My uncle gave me a total of a hundred dollars that day, so my friend and I went out to eat at Captain Pizza on Merrimack Street. I was bummed how the encounter with my uncle went so fast as it settled in what had just happened to me with seeing my uncle alive and well.

I started to think about my dad's social security checks and it made me realize just how much my mother has taken from me. First my childhood as she handed me to her boyfriend on a silver platter for six years, my father who she kept me from as much as she could, my father's social security checks that could have helped every person who took me in and my stability by denying me the right to live with my aunt and uncle. The more I thought about my mother, the more I lost my appetite to finish my pizza. I was about to bawl my eyes out in front of my friends, have a complete meltdown or get mad. So I decided to get mad. I questioned myself again, 'How could she?' I wondered why she kept me from my uncle and aunt for all those years. I couldn't stop shaking my head, I was beside myself, a loss for words yet having so many questions of why's. Why was my mother so cruel to me? Why didn't she ever stop him? Why didn't she protect me? Why did she allow me to be abused? Why did she keep me from my father? Why did she tell me my father was dead when he was alive? Why did she tell me my uncle and aunt were dead when they were alive? Why did the court system believe my mother who had numerous children she didn't care for long before me? Why? Why? Why? I said over and over again until my friend questioned me, "What can you do about it?" I'm not sure if it was a question or statement but I answered her, "I want to go ask my mother why." That's what my friend and I did, we left the pizza place and headed to my mother's house in the acre section where she had been living for a couple years already. I had a bit of resentment, jealousy and sadness that I was never included with my family. I just wanted to know why, why did my mother always have hate for me?

It was a quick walk from downtown to where she lived on School Street. I walked to the back porch and knocked on the door. I walked to the front door and I knocked. I continued to knock on the front door, the back door and then I knocked on windows. I then picked up a rock and used it to knock on the window. I picked up rock after rock throwing them. I thought about my uncle who I thought was dead because of my mother. I thought about all the memories I missed out on with my dad. I thought about all the checks that could have helped when I lived at Cissy's. I thought about my older brothers and baby sister. I thought about my mother shunning me away because I was being raped, terrorized and abused by a man they all defended. I thought more about my dad's family and I had so much anger in me from my childhood.

I threw rock after rock for every thought I had. I was breaking windows and I broke one enough for me to climb inside, and so I did. I climbed in and just started throwing things, smashing and tossing it all onto the kitchen floor. I took things out of cabinets, counters and wall shelves. I then went into the refrigerator and started throwing stuff from inside onto the floor. I was making a mess of the place. I was mad because I walked there for an answer and I had to leave without one. I heard a scream and a yell for me to get out. I looked up and saw it was my baby sister. I didn't understand why she didn't answer the door, but I immediately stopped trashing my mother's house and I left. I walked half way down School Street when a police cruiser pulled up along the sidewalk with the cruiser lights on. My friend and I stopped walking as we waited for the officer to get out of his cruiser. "I bet my mother called them," I told my friend.

That was exactly why they were stopping my friend and I. "Did my mother call?" I questioned the police officer as he looked at me confused. "Your mother?" he questioned me as he continued, "The call was for an intruder." I did inform the officer I was the intruder and I trashed my mother's house because she deserved it. I was placed under arrest right there and taken down to the police station in the back seat of a cruiser. After some paperwork, I was then transferred to the same courthouse I was in just years earlier. They took me to the same cells down in the basement. That's where I sat for a few hours until my name got called. I admitted to myself it was dumb what I did. That woman was a rotten mother, how much could I take? I was a newly eighteen year old and I still had a lot to learn.

I went in front of the judge who gave me a bail of fifty dollars and a lecture about making better choices. I was then taken back down to the cell until I got myself bailed out. I was questioned a couple of times about calling someone for my bail, but I declined each time I was questioned. For once I wanted to go to a foster home so I could get a good night's sleep. I was emotionally drained and I was so tired of my unstable life. During my time in the cell a guard kept checking on me and talking to me. He pleaded with me to call someone because it was getting late. I told him I needed a good night's sleep and wouldn't mind going to a foster home this time. His face dropped as he explained to me I was now eighteen years old and I wouldn't be going to a foster home if my bail wasn't paid within the hour, I would be going to Framingham State Prison.

My face dropped as I questioned the guard, "What?" I didn't know who to call. I didn't want to bother my friends and I definitely wasn't calling Jon. I didn't want to do it, but I gave in and I called my mother. When she answered I quickly questioned her, "I'm eighteen now so I'll go to prison, please pay my bail and I'll pay you back?" "Nope," she answered me and hung up her end of the phone before I was even done talking. I told the guard not to worry about me and I thanked him for being so kind to me.

I just co-existed I guess. I sat in the courthouse cell for a while and when the prison van showed up, I was put in ankle cuffs, waist chains and handcuffs as I was escorted into the back of the van where each prisoner was separated by gates made of metal. I was on my way to Framingham State Prison. It was a long, cold uncomfortable ride to the women's prison facility in Framingham, Massachusetts. I looked through the metal grates and out the tiny window on the prison van back doors. Saying the words, 'what the fuck,' to myself a million times. I wasn't the only female prisoner being transported but I definitely was the youngest. I looked out the window and all I saw was how quickly my childhood and teen years were gone. I was mad, I felt like a loser with no family. Once we arrived at the prison facility we were all ordered out of the van in a single file line. I then experienced the normal protocol that is required for prisoners going to jail. The humiliation of a strip search. The standing in the nude, bending over as we are told to let out a cough and taking an open shower. The one on one meeting with an officer of the prison who documents every scar, tattoo and any other information required. I was then taken down a hall, through some steel doors and into a cell with three other women. I was told the left side top bunk was my bed. So I jumped up onto the bed, rolled over to face the wall, scared shit at the thought I was in prison and fell asleep.

I woke up the next morning to the prisons wake up calls through the intercom speakers. When I sat up from the bed, all three women in the cell with me introduced themselves. They were serving time but were in the section of the prison where I was because they all had court dates and they got transported from that section when needed. They also informed me it was breakfast time and for me to stick with them as we were about to be taken to the full population of the women's prison, the cafeteria. When the cell doors opened we were taken on a long walk down stairs, through halls and metal doors all while walking in a single file. I guess I didn't expect it to be what they were explaining it to be. When we walked through the door into the cafeteria of the prison, it was like a whole city all in its own. Everyone was wearing the same blue pants and shirt I was given upon my arrival to the prison. There were male and female guards but all the prisoners were women. The food was as bad as they warned me it would be, totally gross! It was a cold rainy day which prevented us from going outside after breakfast. According to my cell mates it was a good thing. We walked back to our cells and because we had a toilet in the cell, there were no bathroom stops along the way. I went back to the cell, jumped on the top bunk and rolled over. I cried into the pillow until I fell asleep again.

Then it was lunch time, which went the same as breakfast. I sat with the women in my cell and the food was still gross. We were sent back to our cells where I jumped to the top bunk again. I cried again, slept again and was just minding my own business. A few hours into the afternoon one of the women hollered to me, "Hey little girl in the top bunk, don't you have to pee?" she questioned in a calm but funny manner. I immediately sat up and answered her that I did in fact have to go pee.

I had to go really bad but I was embarrassed to go with three other women in the small cell with me. She then questioned me, "Are you embarrassed?" When I told her I was, all three woman stood up and formed a wall for me. All had their backs towards me as I finally went pee. The funny lady then says, "Damn girl, how did you carry all that in you?" It felt like I peed forever. Afterwards I stayed in conversations with the three ladies and one of them was also from Lowell. About an hour before what would have been the prisons dinner time, there was a knock on the cell door. The small window opened, a guard hollered, "Mellen you're being bailed." I was a bit confused but wasn't going to question it. A few minutes later the guard opened the door to the cell and escorted me down the hall, down some stairs, down another hall and through a door. I was suddenly at a small window, signing my name, getting my belongings and walking out of prison. Not knowing who bailed me out, I walked outside of the prison doors and there was a car filled with about ten of my friends from the downtown area. They paid my bail and we got as far away from Framingham as we could. I stayed at a friends house one day, another friends house the next day. I was carrying everything I owned in a duffle bag, in my pocketbook and I was tired of living that way.

I was hanging out downtown one afternoon with a couple of friends when I saw myself at a crossroad in my life again. My friend who moved to Oklahoma had already moved back to Massachusetts and back to the Centerville section of Lowell. I knew I could continue to live my life on the streets hanging with my downtown gang or I could walk to my friend's new home in Centerville and ask if I could room and board with them again. It was a decision that popped in my head and I knew it was a good decision.

I didn't know where I was headed in life but I knew I had to take care of myself and that's exactly what I did. I quickly told my friends I had to take a walk across the Bridge Street bridge for a few and that I'd be back within an hour. I walked across the bridge, across the intersection and continued straight up Bridge Street. I walked there for the sole purpose of finding stability in my life and I did. As much as I wanted to stay downtown and hang with my friends, I knew walking to Centerville was in the best interest of myself. I gave myself a pat on the shoulder for doing the right thing. Even if I couldn't stay there at least I tried. By the end of February 1988 not only was I living with that family again, I was also working full time at a box making factory in Dracut, Mass called Beauty Box. Working full time, babysitting and living in a stable home again made hanging out downtown a very scarce thing to do. When I did get a chance to go downtown no one was really around anymore. It wasn't long before Jon started to show up at the West Fourth Street apartment I lived at. I'd get out of work and he would be parked out front. I apologized for being an ass towards him the month before and I punched him for seeing him with the girl I saw him with. He was funny about how he accepted my apology.

He gave me a lecture about alcohol not solving anyone's problems let alone my problems. I told him about my dead uncle actually being alive and he gave me a big squeeze of a hug. Jon always told me he considered me a very head smart person. Although despite all I've lived through, he said I didn't have a clue about the one thing I needed. When I questioned him what that was he answered me, "Love." Jon insisted we continue to date others as it was part of the experience in life. He wanted me to have the chance to experience the life given to me. Jon had a way of seeing the positive in any kind of situation and always had a way of making you feel good about yourself, no matter the sucky family life you had. He would remind me numerous times how my mother was not my mother. "She is just your birth mother," he told me many times. For the next few months, life continued and so didn't work, babysitting and living with a stable roof over my head.

I realized one day what a lousy older sister I was to my baby sister. I knew she was getting older and it made me want to see her. I looked up my mothers phone number in the telephone book. I called her and the second she knew it was me, she hung up her end of the phone. I called her back and she hung up again. I called again, she hung up again. It went back and forth until a little time went by before I called her back. All I could think of was the loud scream I wanted to scream, but couldn't. I waited a half hour to call her again and when she answered her phone I immediately said into the phone, "You need to listen to what I have to say." My mother's voice on the other end of the phone snapped at me, "What do you want?" I told her I wanted to see my sister and she snapped at me again, "Nope." I then threatened my mother that I would show up at my sisters school and tell her everything about her rotten mother and father. My mother doubted me for a few as we argued back and forth before she gave in and made arrangements for me to pick up my baby sister for a few hours. I was excited and nervous, I felt like I owed my baby sister an explanation. But how do I tell her? Where do I start? Who do I start with? Her mother, her father? What would it do to her? Would she hate me? Would she call me a liar?

I picked my baby sister up a few days later and we spent the day together. The friend I was living with took the long walk with me to the acre. We then walked downtown for pizza, I took my sister to Kent Jewelers to have her ears pierced and we walked back to the Centerville apartment I was living at. It was really good to spend the day with my baby sister but it also made me realize I was not good for her either. I hated her mother and I hated her father. It killed me emotionally because as much as I loved my baby sister, I hated both her parents.

I started to realize that I was also a baby sister. I had siblings from my dad's side. I had an array of siblings from my mother's side. The hairdresser sister I hadn't seen since 1980 and the siblings I lived with on Pleasant Street who never cared where I was all these years. I was eighteen years old and an only child with about seven siblings out there somewhere. (Or so I thought.)

It hurt but I didn't blame my dad's kids because they were raised by their mother. The hairdresser sister was raised by her dad. My baby sister was too young and I believed my two older brothers would have helped me. Then I would find myself wondering, why didn't they help me? Like a closed fisted hand slammed into my chest and ripped my heart out just so it can twist it around and place it back in, one punch at a time. That one question hurt me to the core and also became the easiest to bury.

Ironic how things you do everyday as a teen slowly drifts away as you find yourself standing in adulthood, scratching your head wondering, 'How did I get here?' I continued to work, babysit, save money and by the end of the summer 1988, I was offered the opportunity to pay a third of rent/utilities/food for an apartment with a friend I knew from downtown. I checked out the apartment and within two weeks I was moved into 401 Lakeview Avenue. I had no curfew, my own bedroom with a door, my own closet and something to be part mine. I also had something I never really had to call my own, my own house key.

Having a roommate was cool. Many fun memories were made living with my roommate and his girlfriend. I paid a third of the monthly bill's and always over spent when I did the groceries. I learned how meatloaf does not take four hours to cook, boiling water does evaporate and a lot of other cooking mishaps. Jokes were being played on me until I realized my roommate had an identical twin and they got some good ones on me. Having me run up and down the stairs fetching something as a favor or sending me to the store and I'd return to him insisting he didn't ask me to go. All in all it was a lot of fun and laughs. I was still working at Beauty Box, mostly walking to and from work. I didn't like working in the factory setting so I started looking for jobs elsewhere. I was filling out applications and checking the newspaper ads for places hiring in a quest to find another job. It wasn't long before I found one at Lowell General Hospital. One of my big reasons for accepting the job was the benefits. I worked in the cafeteria and was responsible for bringing supplements to patients throughout the hospital. I would walk downtown and catch a city bus to the hospital for 6:30am. There was a bus stop outside the hospital, I just had to climb a lot of stairs to get up the hill where the hospital was.

Getting out of work everyday at a normal time also gave me too much time on my hands and I quickly found ways to keep myself busy. I would babysit, clean apartments, take part time jobs that included being a gas station attendant at Merit Gas Station in downtown and a telemarketer for the Lowell sun newspaper which did not last long as I didn't return after a bathroom break one day. I started to buy myself things I would need for my own apartment, which I'd get myself one day. Every week after I cashed one of my paychecks or money from cleaning and babysitting jobs, I'd go shopping at Woolworths and Zayre's.

I would buy pots, pans, a sugar bowl, matching butter dish, plates, cups, knickknacks and more. Then I would walk to the bus stop with bags in each arm reminding myself not to shop as much next time. Although it is easy to fill up a store carriage, carrying heavy bags to the bus stop was very exhausting. I also spoiled myself with new clothes and shoes. For Thanksgiving and with the help of my roommates, I made my first Thanksgiving dinner and it came out delicious. Just like that, I was moving on, getting over it and I wasn't dwelling. I wasn't bringing up my childhood as it was a whole world behind me, or at least I thought.

December 15, 1988 I turned nineteen years old. I already spent the past eight birthdays accepting the fact that deep down I didn't matter to my family. I treated the day as if it was no different than any other day. I was required to work Christmas day at the hospital and I still made the walk to my dads cemetery. Jon was still popping into my life whenever he would. Picking me up at the cemetery, outside my work, driving up alongside me as I was out walking, waiting at a bus stop or wherever I was going. He'd drive up and holler, "Where ya been?" It was one of many regular sayings we had. We would make plans to hang out, we called each other as I finally had a landline phone in the apartment I lived at and I continued living life as I was doing. Working, making good memories and before I knew it, the year 1989 was here. Walking around the Bridge Street area one day with a couple of friends, I heard a man's voice say my name and when I looked at the direction the voice came from, I noticed it was my oldest brother. He was living in an apartment off of Bridge Street and I was walking by his home. He invited my friends and I inside. We stayed for a bit talking about life in general and not the life I once lived. We exchanged phone numbers and promised to keep in touch with each other. As weird as it sounds, despite everything I have been through in my life I was super excited to have a real blood related brother in my life. Even though I've seen this brother numerous times throughout the years from him driving by me downtown, it was cool to reconnect with him and finally have a piece of family member in my life. It also made me wonder about my hairdresser sister who I hadn't seen since 1980.

    I started to do my research to find out where she was. I called a lot of hair salons throughout Lowell and surrounding towns to find out where she was working. I would request a hairdresser by my sister's name and for every phone call with a helpless response I got, I felt hopeless. I continued to call hair salons and when I finally got one where the voice on the other end informed me that a hairdresser by the name Pauline worked there, I hung up the phone. I guess I was used to having no luck on calling hair salons throughout the city. When one finally said yes, I panicked and hung up the phone. Over the next few weeks I'd call the salon and ask for directions or I'd call and ask their prices. Until I finally called and set up an appointment to get my haircut by my hairdresser sister. I only gave my first name and scheduled the appointment for after work a few days later.

Talking with Jon on the phone I agreed to meet him at Toni's Restaurant on Aiken St which was right down the street from my apartment on Lakeview Avenue. We ate some food, got an ice cream and headed down to the boulevard. We talked and as we were getting older our talks became more about finding explanations, reasons and whys to our lives. Jon was always encouraging, yet stubborn, persistent and funny as he was this day also. For years Jon was always asking me what I wanted out of life and I would never answer him. I always thought my answer was stupid. Most girls wanted diamonds and I just wanted to be part of a family. On this particular day Jon was acting all secretly as he kept his back towards me. He would look back at me and the more I tried to stand in front of him, he would quickly turn himself so his back stayed turned towards me. He did this for a few minutes until he finally turned around with blood dripping from his hand. As quickly as I grabbed his hand and questioned him, "What the heck happened?" Jon just as quickly grabbed my hand and with a sharp object he sliced my finger. After screaming ouch and trying to get away from him. He quickly rubbed my bloody cut against his bloody cut as he said, "There, we're family now." I looked at Jon so confused. "Why did you do that?" I questioned him. He just laughed as he told me, "Now at the end of everyday you have family."

Jon wanted us to not be intimate with each other for a few years. He again insisted he didn't want to break up or say goodbye. I knew we had secrets about each other, I knew I had his trust, I knew I had his love and a part of his caring heart. I also knew he was right as he explained we had the whole future to look forward to. Telling me how life has so much to offer us and we still had so many questions we wanted answers to. Everything Jon was saying seemed to make perfect sense. I never knew how to be a daughter, a sister or an everyday girlfriend but only because I never had the proper experience to be one. But I knew how to be a friend because I was one to Jon and he was one to me.

When the day came for my haircut appointment, I took the city bus to the other side of the city in the highlands. I went inside the hair salon off of Stevens Street and I showed up for my haircut appointment. I recognized my hairdresser sister right away but I knew she couldn't possibly recognize me as I was only a kid when she saw me last. I sat in her chair and she proceeded to play with, wet and cut my hair as she also made conversation with me. I gave a lot of short answers and a lot of small talk. More than half way through the haircut she whacked me with the brush on my head. Lightly but enough to let me know she knew who I was all along. We talked more and she had nothing nice to say about the woman who gave birth to us. I loved the haircut she gave me but when I left the salon she worked at, it killed me emotionally for days as I blamed myself for things my mother allowed to happen to me. I knew I couldn't keep in contact with my oldest sister because I was to her what she was to me, a reminder of our birth mother.

The guy from Christian hill who I dated the year before was coming around the apartment I lived at and soon we were dating again. He didn't believe two people who dated for years can be still friends, so he had a hard time understanding my friendship with Jon. He was a lot of fun to be around and always cracking jokes. We had a lot in common and with his help I got myself my first apartment. It was an apartment his sister lived in and she was moving out. I met with the landlord, paid the down deposit and moved in, a day after the apartment went empty. I was so excited, I got cable at twenty dollars a month, a phone and a phone book. I started calling everyone as I was excited over my new place and Jon of course was super excited for me. He was even happier when I told him I was dating the guy Ken from Christian hill again and he was moving in. I felt safer at night with someone there and it was my apartment, if it didn't work out then Ken would move out. Besides the promise I made with Jon meant no marrying anyone else and it was an easy promise to comply.

I started the summer at the age of nineteen years old in my first apartment. Now I just had to get to the day when I would forget all the horrible horrific images I see in my head, hear in my ears and smell in my memories. Seeing friends with their family members made me long for the one thing I ran from, family. Moving into 176 Barker Avenue was definitely an experience for me in so many aspects of my life. Ken's friends and family came to see the apartment. His dad offered to pick me up in the morning so I didn't have to take a cab or walk downtown to catch the bus for work everyday. The only catch was I got dropped off a little too early in the morning. But I didn't mind it as I saved three dollars a day on cab and bus fare. I stopped in a diner every morning for a coffee and muffin which cost under one dollar. Getting picked up every morning quickly became a routine as did stopping in for coffee at the diner Kennedy Bacon & Eggs which was located right downtown on the corner of Bridge and Merrimack Streets.

Jon was super proud, happy and excited for me. He was happy I was living with someone, even someone I was dating. Since Jon did the blood thing with our fingers we agreed not to break up or say goodbye but also not date each other for a bit. He insisted he was now every male relative I'd ever need and he was also a friend first. Jon respected Ken's boundaries and only visited me when he wasn't home. Most of the time we sat outside on the stone wall, chatted for a bit, gave big hugs and always said, "See you soon." A part of me still longed for the roots of a blood related family and soon my oldest brother would visit with his girlfriend. I got my other older brother's address and started writing him letters as he served in the United States Army. I lived my life as if my childhood didn't happen. I was living to get to that day when I would forget it all. A few weeks after moving into my apartment, I was at the coffee shop when I noticed the owner was stressed out, so I questioned him what was wrong. He replied in a question, "Do you know how to cook?" As he also told me his cook called out again. I told him I wasn't a cook, then he questioned me, "Do you know how to follow directions?" I told him that was something I did do well. He offered me a ridiculous amount of money plus tips if I would help him out for the day. I called out sick at the hospital and started what would be my first day in a twenty-seven year cooking career.

My life quickly became all about home and work. I quit my side jobs and my full time job at the hospital. I quickly became a full time cook and baker at the coffee shop. I learned how to cook breakfast, lunches, soups, chowders, muffins and more. I loved every part of it. My relationship with Ken was always a fun one but also one that had a bump in it. Only because I stood by my decision to abide with my promises I made to Jon as I knew Jon was keeping his promises with me. Jon always praised me for doing well with my life despite all I have been through. The relationship I had with Jon may have been a confusing one but his friendship never was.

The next few months living with Ken went real smoothly. He worked long days and nights. I worked at the coffee shop, babysat Ken's daughter and went shopping at Stuart's department store on Bridge Street, which was a quick walk from my Barker Avenue apartment. By August, I was still keeping in contact with my oldest brother and though we never talked about my childhood years, there was so much more to talk about instead. Anytime I had a memory, a flashback or a reminder of my childhood, I would just push it out of my head because it was my childhood that I was trying to forget. I truly believed one day I would forget all about what I once lived through as a child. I was jealous, I was always jealous. My two older brothers and baby sister had a bond and they had better memories of their childhood. They had a mother and even though I was also a baby sister in between the youngest of the older brothers and our other baby sister, it was as if they skipped right over me and just assumed it was ok why I lived with other people's families as a kid and teen. It was as if it was ok how I didn't have a relationship with what was also my mother. It was as if it was ok for me to just forget and forgive what I lived through as a kid.

By late September, early October things started to change for me at home. Ken started to become possessive of me, picking me up after work from the diner and bringing me back to his work until he finished. He stopped me from babysitting his daughter while criticizing me for becoming friends with our neighbors, my friendship with Jon and reminding me of the lack of family I really did have. The constant fights and arguments made me realize that our living arrangements were not working out. It took a couple of weeks for me to work up the courage to end the relationship with Ken and ask him to move out. I knew he had family to move back home to and it was something we discussed before he moved in. I got up for work one day and I was going to tell Ken later that day. After work that day I had my six month physical at the women's clinic which was located right across the street from St. John's Hospital. (What is now known as Saints Memorial Hospital.) It was a normal physical where I undressed, wore a hospital gown, had a physical and blood drawn. When it was over, I waited for the nurse to come in with my six month prescription of birth control and the next appointment date. Instead the nurse came in and asked me to follow her to the doctor's office, so I did. That's when I was told I was pregnant. I just looked at the doctor in a blank stare. I thought I heard her wrong, maybe she was mistaken?

I left that doctor's appointment, walked home and realized the doctor was not wrong. She wasn't making a mistake and instead of ending my relationship with Ken, I was going to tell him he was about to become a father to my child. I never made it upstairs to my apartment as Jon was sitting on the stone wall outside waiting for me. I told him I was pregnant, I cried to him and as usual Jon said everything right. We talked about saying he was the father, but then I'd be like my birth mother by lying to my child. We talked about a lot of positive's in a world so filled with negatives. My neighbor came outside and joined us in the conversation. Jon left shortly afterwards and soon Ken came home. My neighbor now knew I was pregnant and I was still in a funk over the news. Ken got out of his car and our neighbor yelled, "Hi daddy." If looks could kill, I'd be dead. Ken was so mad at me for telling my neighbor before I told him. Thinking I was helping the situation I replied, "No Jon knew first." I explained he was outside when I got home, I explained how shocked I was over the news and I explained how confused I was, but he didn't care. He yelled, he smashed his hand into the wall and when he heard Jon knew first, he got real nasty towards me. His anger caused him to say some real mean things to me and I ran out the door, down the stairs and for one of the longest walks of my life.

I walked and cried. I cried about things done to me as a child, I cried about having no family in my life and I cried about Jon not being the father of my baby. I found myself standing on the Bridge Street bridge. I had an emotional breakdown as the reality of my family life hit me hard. I knew I could end all of my problems with just one flip, all I had to do was flip myself over the railing on the bridge. I would hit the rocks below, I wouldn't be in pain anymore and I wouldn't be an inconvenience or a reminder to anyone anymore. Then I thought of my dad, my friend Mark and how I hoped to see them again one day when I died. Then I thought about Jon and the baby inside me, a family to call my own. I had one question I couldn't answer that kept going through my head, 'What am I telling the baby about my family?' That's when I got pissed off and walked back home very upset with the way Ken treated me. I let him know that if it had been him I met in 1983 and not Jon, then I would have jumped over the railing of the bridge and it was because of Jon's friendship that I did not jump. I then told him, "Be thankful I have a friend like Jon."

Things continued to stay rocky with Ken and I, but only because I continued on being me. I was keeping my friendships with my neighbors, my friendship with Jon and if I found no reason to justify an argument, then I didn't. During the Thanksgiving holiday I went into work to find out the diner was being sold. The new owners were not taking the old employees with them and I was quickly out of a job along with a weekly paycheck. As my twentieth birthday went by, I was still getting use to being pregnant, jobless and without a paycheck. I spent Christmas visiting with Ken's family and spending the rest of the day at home. Soon the year 1990 was upon us and my first ultrasound where I was told I was having a boy. Jon insisted they were wrong.

I took small part time jobs throughout the early start of 1990. It was hard to find a job while being pregnant. I took jobs at Anton Cleaners, Stuart's department store, Dunkin Donuts on Bridge Street and some babysitting jobs. By early spring I was battling with the decision of what to tell my baby about my family. Do I tell my baby his/her grandmother was dead? Do I tell my baby his/her mother has no family? I didn't want to lie to my baby. I didn't want my baby to grow up and find out I had lied to them their whole life about my family and I didn't want my baby to think

I kept them from the family they had, like my mother kept me from my dad and his family. I battled with the decision of whether or not I should call my mother and offer her the chance to be in her grandchild's life. I got my mother's phone number from my oldest brother and I worked up the strength to call her. It took me weeks of picking up the phone and hanging up before I made the call. It took me weeks of staring at the phone number and not being able to pick up the phone. It took me weeks of crying over the memories that flashed through my mind every time I thought about making that phone call. And then I finally made the call.

Even though I had not seen my mother in a few years, when she answered the phone, I knew it was her by her voice. I immediately said who I was and told her, "I'm pregnant." I continued talking as I told my mother she had failed me as a mother but I was offering her the opportunity to be a grandmother to my baby, but only if she wanted to. She said she did and we made plans for the following weekend so she could come by my apartment and we could talk in person. After speaking with my mother on the phone I was speechless and motionless as I sat beside the telephone in my living room. Over the next week I walked a lot, cleaned a lot and kept myself busy. I honestly didn't think my mother would show up. Ken told me it was a mistake. He didn't know about my childhood but he knew I had issues with my family. He knew my mother was not a nice mother to me and he knew she didn't deserve me.

My mother was scheduled to come over to my apartment the following Saturday and by the time Saturday came, I realized I didn't want her inside my apartment. I questioned my neighbors if I could use their picnic table in the yard and they agreed it wasn't a problem at all. When it got close to the time she was to arrive, I went outside with Ken. We sat at the picnic table and waited for her to show up. Then a car pulled up and there she was sitting in the passenger seat of the car. I quickly sat up from the picnic table and walked over to the parked car outside of my building. I waited for a door to open and when it finally did, it was the driver who got out first. I met her when I lived that short period on Butler Avenue in 1982. Her name was Elaine and she immediately said hello to me as she gave me a hug. Then my mother got out of the car with a look of shock on her face. My first time speaking to my mother face to face in years and the first thing I said to her was a question, "Are you shocked to see I am still alive?" As I was saying it I felt every being of my soul just crushing away into dust. I could feel the rage in me as I had things I needed to say but I also knew by saying it, meant I was being a disrespectful unappreciated daughter. I didn't bother inviting them upstairs to my apartment and was glad I decided to do the talking outside. Just the look of my mother's face disgusted me.

I apologized to my mother's friend for coming off as being rude but I also informed her that what I was about to say, needed to be said. I looked right at my mother as I sat across from her at the picnic table. "You lost any right to say you are my mother," I told her. I continued to tell her what she put me through was despicable, disgusting and no excuse in the world could explain why she allowed the childhood she gave me. "I am trying to forget the life you allowed me to live," I continued to say to the woman who was my mother, but who I could only call by the name I knew her as, Lorraine, besides birth mother sounded too corny. After all I said to Lorraine, I sat there just looking at the woman sitting across from me as she said not a word. She was looking at me with a smile on her face, nodding her head as if she was agreeing with all I was saying to her. Yet she had no tears, no remorse and no apology.

Her friend was yelling at Ken to stop being rude. He kept calling Lorraine nasty names in pretended coughs and sneezes. I actually found it to be funny. It was a strange, puke stuck in my throat feeling as I sat across the table from Lorraine. Her friend was not insulted by the way I talked to Lorraine and even gave me a hug before they left. They didn't stay long and I told them I would inform them of any baby shower in the future. After they left, I let it all sink in and instead of being sad, jealous or upset for reaching out to my mother, I was instead proud of myself for having a heart. Something I knew she did not have, I mean how could she? She has other children. What about them? Did she just forget them like she wanted to forget me for so long? Have they reached out to her? Why did I reach out to her? Do I really want this lady in my life? So many mixed emotions went through me after I reached out to my mother. As much as I hated the childhood she gave me, she was still my baby's biological grandmother.

I hated the memories that flashed through my mind of my mother, yet I was curious as to how she could be a good mother to some of her children while tossing me and my hairdresser sister off to the side as if we never mattered. In a sense I was a bit jealous of my two older brothers and baby sister for having that foundation of a rooted family. They had a mother who was good to them and though we had the same mother, my mother was not a good mother to me. I knew by reaching out to my birth mother meant I was doing right by my baby, I just wasn't sure if I was doing right by me.

My stomach started to grow as did the morning sickness and the flutters of kicking I was feeling in my belly. The experience of being pregnant was a cool and fun experience knowing I was about to have someone who was going to love me everyday of their life. The thought of labor, I pretty much avoided and figured I'd get a front row seat in the experience of being in labor soon enough. Even though my doctor said I was having a baby boy, I was still undecided as I kept thinking of what Jon had said about them being wrong. Sometimes when it came to Jon all I could do was shake my head and smile knowing I had a friend like him in my life.

By late spring, Ken was doing a lot of side work for a man who owned property throughout Lowell. It wasn't long until we moved into one of his apartments, moving not far down the street to 119 Hildreth Street. We were now calling each other boyfriend/girlfriend and I pretty much made money just from babysitting, leaving Ken to pay all the bills. He was working late into the night and coming home arguing with me about my day. Asking who I was with and what I did. During my whole pregnancy he never came to one doctor's appointment with me. He criticized my friends and when I tried to talk to him about my childhood or why I was sad over a memory of it, he would quickly hush me up. "Shhh that's the past," he said as he continued, "Forget about it." That was one thing we both did agree on, I had to forget about my childhood.

Grown children respected their parents, you had to forgive and you had to forget. Family was all you had, bury the secrets and close the door on the past. It was the rules of society. I thought I was being selfish, I didn't want Lorraine in my life but I didn't want to be known as a selfish, disrespectful, ungrateful daughter.

Some days Ken would come home from work and find me deep in cleaning, waxing floors or rearranging. He would get a chuckle as he laughed saying, "What the heck are you doing?" I would respond that I was, "Just forgetting things." As I kept myself busy in an attempt to not think about my childhood. We decided to have his brother and wife be our baby's godparents so it stayed in the family. They wanted to throw me a baby shower and I gave her a list of phone numbers including Lorraine's. My due date was for the end of July and I had a healthy pregnancy. Some days I did a lot of walking around the city of Lowell. At the end of June I went to a cookout at my soon to be baby's godparents home. When we arrived I found out the cookout was actually a baby shower for me. Once we went through the backyard fence there were over sixty people there, if not more. Ken whispered to me, "Who are these people?" I looked around the fenced in yard and started to recognize some faces. There was Lorraine, her sisters I met when I was younger, their kids who were also my cousins. Along with friends and of course Ken's family. The yard was packed with people and it was an overwhelming experience. I knew what his question was referring to so I answered him, "They are my relatives." As he immediately said something to me that stuck with me for years, "Where have they been the past ten years?" It was a question I could not answer.

I received over a year's supply of everything in colors of blue, green and yellow. I thanked everyone individually, I also thanked Lorraine for reaching out to her relatives, then I invited her over to my place so she could see everything I received. By late July 1990 I had another ultrasound done to see the position of the baby. I was given a photo of my baby's ultrasound with a pointed arrow aiming right at the penis of my baby boy. I stopped babysitting and waited for the arrival of some real bad cramping.

I spent my days walking from Hildreth Street in the Centerville section of Lowell to my doctor's appointments on Varnum Avenue in the Pawtucketville section, then I would walk back home after the appointment and always walked a different route home. Jon was still checking in on me and even though I shoved the ultrasound photo of my son in his face, he still insisted I was having a girl and the doctors were wrong. On August 6th my doctor scheduled me to be induced on August 9th which is also my baby sister's birthday. The day before I was to be induced, I awoke to minor cramps going across my small beach ball of a belly. Ken went to work as I had a pager with me at all times so I could page him when I needed to. I didn't know what to be ready for and was nervous being home alone so I walked to a friend's house down the street. I stayed there for the whole day waiting for Ken to pick me up. By the time he picked me up we headed home and then a quick detour to the hospital where on August 8th I gave birth to a beautiful healthy baby girl.

Being pregnant was an interesting healthy experience but labor was a very painless experience for me as it all happened so fast. Just as quickly as everything was moving in my delivery room, a nurse notified us of our baby's grandmother being outside the room. We both assumed it was Ken's mother, but it wasn't. In came an oversized stuffed animal and behind it was Lorraine. Suddenly everything went quiet and all I heard was her voice, all I saw was her face. Then I told myself, 'Nope,' and everything was back; all the noise and movements of the nurses in the room. I politely told Lorraine I didn't want visitors and she informed me her niece works at admission that's why she knew I was admitted.

Once at home, I took a lot of walks with my daughter before the cold months came. Stopping in on friends along the way. When Jon visited me after my baby was born, I wouldn't let him see her, but he saw me walking one day and parked his car along side me as I walked. When I noticed it was him we played cat and mouse as I tried dodging him from seeing my daughter. I soon gave in and let him indulge in the fact he was right, I was having a baby girl all along. Ken was always working so I thought I was doing right by keeping myself busy. Being a mom was a whole new experience for me and one I loved being a part of. I was mesmerized over the relatives on Ken's side, he had great uncle's and a nana who all were close as a family should be.

As mid September approached I was already back in my old clothes. Every Thursday I went over nana's for a polish pork lunch with my daughter. Lorraine was visiting me any chance she could. She was always trying to hold my baby and always seemed happy to be in my life. What I didn't understand was, why she didn't want me in her life? I had a wall up and at times I had to remind Lorraine of it. She would act as if we were best friends for decades causing me to just stare her down. She would stop what she was doing and I'd remind her, "I still don't trust you," and I didn't, I didn't trust her at all.

One day Jon took me and my daughter to visit my dad at the cemetery. When he dropped me off at home, Ken was already home and ready to yell and argue with me. When I wouldn't argue back he took offense to it. We constantly argued over money, what I did with my day, who was I with and how I needed to get a job. Then we argued because I had a job. I could never win an argument when the argument was an unnecessary merry go round. He always assumed I was laughing at him but I wasn't. I was being who I am, something I couldn't do for the first eleven years of my life, I was being me; a funny, laughable and likeable person. Soon it was my twenty-first birthday where I stayed home all day with my daughter. My friends called to wish me a happy birthday and so didn't Lorraine which was a bit emotional for me to handle. So what does a girl do at Christmas time when she is trying to forget a childhood she lived? She goes Christmas shopping.

So many times I just wanted to take my mother by her head and scream in her face, "For all those years, why did you let him?" But I knew it would be me causing an argument by bringing it up again. I would have been reminded that I had to, "Forget about it." I went through the emotions of taking her calls one day and not taking them the next. Anytime she left my apartment after visiting me, I would get so depressed over my family life. I hated myself for reaching out to her. I hated myself for being respectful enough to do what society said I should do, 'learn to forgive your mother because you only get one.' Yet I had more mother's in my life who were just that, a mother.

I soon had Lorraine picking me up instead of coming in my apartment for a visit. We would go shopping instead. She would pick me and my daughter up for a few hours of shopping, lunch and with Christmas coming, I shopped a lot. Ken continued to work long days and late nights. When my daughter slept, my mind wandered and before I knew it, I'd be sobbing like a baby over things that happened to me in my childhood. Ken knew I was having a hard time with Lorraine in my life. He would offer advise about cutting her out of my life or not, but also telling me I needed to decide one way or the other. Deep down I knew he was right. He surprised me shortly before Christmas when he came home with a real Christmas tree. It was my first Christmas tree in many years. We then went out shopping for lights, garland and decorations for the tree.

Ken came home one day to see the living room packed with gifts coming out from under the tree and he questioned what it all was. When I answered him it was our daughter's gifts for Christmas, he laughed and questioned me, "All that is hers?" I told him they were and asked why he was questioning me. He laughed as he answered me with a question, "How is she going to open them?" I looked at my four month old daughter sleeping in her swing, then I looked around the living room and realized I needed to control my shopping. I also unwrapped all her gifts during the holiday week. We spent most of Christmas day at Ken's parents, stopped at Lorraine's who only had my baby sister at her house before we headed home.

I survived the holidays and the U-Haul truck of gifts my daughter received. I also realized I had a lot of anger for Lorraine and I promised myself I would learn to put my anger to the side for the sake of family. As the 1991 new year was upon us, so were the New England winters. We had a lot of snow on the ground making it hard to take my daughter out for walks in her stroller. Feeling bummed out we were stuck inside one day, I started organizing my daughter's room when I remembered the sled she received as a Christmas gift. It was a box baby sled with an attached rope to pull it. We were soon out everyday. I would bundle my daughter up, secure her in the sled and head out on the street getting where I wanted to go. I got so many thumbs up from passing motorists as I pulled the cute baby sled with the adorable baby in it. I also started to experience cooking more. I loved being a mother and just experiencing life one day at a time.

On the phone one day with my oldest brother a conversation came up where he talked of Pleasant Street. So I took the opportunity to question him about what he remembered about me and Pleasant Street. But he insisted he did not remember anything bad regarding me from back then. I accepted his reason but it also bothered me, 'How could he not remember?' When I couldn't find an answer to my question, I answered it myself, 'He was too young to remember.' It was easier to accept that than have an unanswered question.

Soon it was tax season and I made plans with Lorraine to pick me and my daughter up for a day of shopping. I waited outside with my daughter in her car seat. A lot of questions filled my mind as we waited for Lorraine. Did Lorraine know what flashed through my horrific memories everyday? Did she know the hurt I carried every day? Did she know the pain, the shame, or the emptiness I felt every day? Did she even care? When Lorraine pulled up in her car I immediately put my daughter in the back seat, seat belted her car seat in and I sat in the front passenger seat. "Do you know what kind of memories flash through my mind of my childhood?" I blurted out to Lorraine and even before she could answer me, I blurted out another question, "Why didn't you stop him?" Not giving her time to answer me, I continued, "Why, why, why?" I was so mad how I had to even ask a question like I was. I just kept asking, "Why," over and over again until I broke down crying. Lorraine, who still had her car parked outside my home, leaned over to her glove compartment and handed me some tissues before becoming her famous motherly self. Lorraine's response to my questions, my hurt, my pain and my tears was of course in the form of a question. "Do you want your daughter to grow up and know her mother was molested?" she questioned me as she looked towards her back seat pointing at my daughter. It made no sense to me that the horrible woman sitting in the driver's seat said that to me. I screamed in her face, "He raped me." Then I told her to shove her word molest up her ass and I quickly hopped out of her car, took my daughter from the back seat and cancelled my trip of shopping with that cruel woman. I was so mad and hurt that she had the balls to say the word molested to me. Molest is just a word adults use to make sexual assault on a child sound lesser in meaning. I wasn't just molested, I was raped, tortured, terrorized and viciously attacked sexually and physically.

I went back into my house so mad at myself for letting my childhood get to me. It just piled up on my shoulders and I couldn't hold it in. I cried as I played with my daughter, cried as I fed her, cried as I changed her and then I cried until I cried myself out. It was a long day at home with my daughter that day as I realized I didn't remember my life without a broken heart. That was the day I wondered, 'Oh my God are there others?' I thought to myself. It was the first time I really put thought into it, 'Were there others after me?' It made me remember the girl from Lowell who went missing and found murdered. As quickly as the thought came in my mind, I called Lorraine from my home phone. The second she picked up I questioned her, "That girl, did he kill that girl?" She acted like she didn't know what I was talking about. So I mentioned all that happened when I ran to my friends house back when I was ten years old in 1980. Lorraine agreed it was 1980 and informed me how, "Those girls went missing years later." As she continued to tell me Dave was married by then. I interrupted her, "Girls, what girls?" I questioned her. Of course I also got a question, "What are you talking about?" Lorraine questioned me. I reminded her, "The August when I ran to Sandi's house," I said to her. She told me they caught the guy who murdered that girl, but I didn't believe her and figured I'd do my own research.

By early spring 1991, I was walking downtown with my daughter who was now back in a stroller. We went to the public library where I would spend about half an hour each time going through old newspaper articles looking for missing or murdered girls from June 1980 to July 1981, because I knew my family and my abuser Dave stayed living on Pleasant Street a year after I ran from there. I don't know why but a part of me wouldn't give up until I looked through every newspaper clipping between June 1980-July 1981. After numerous trips to the Lowell library and looking through old articles of the Lowell Sun newspaper, I didn't find anything. I wasn't going to ask anyone or go to the police because I was twenty-one years old, a mom and doing what society and my family expected of me to do; move on, get over it, stop bringing it up, stop dwelling, forget, forgive and deal with it. So that's what I did. I left the library for the last time thinking what an idiot I was.

Back at home, no matter how many times I tried to talk about my friendship with Jon to Ken it caused him to start arguing with me. We had a good friendship with a lot in common, I just thought he understood he was with a girl who promised to marry someone else. I was just a poetic train wreck in the making not knowing how to be a girlfriend or a mom. Ken had a lot of freedom with me and I was always happy being with my daughter at home or in the company of friends. Jon would visit for a few, always questioning me about Lorraine and my oldest brother. He would ask me if Lorraine apologized yet for the childhood she gave me and I would answer him, "I'm trying to forget my childhood." Jon would ask if my oldest brother had talked to me about my childhood and I told Jon again, "I'm trying to forget my childhood." I would then talk about other things just to change the topic.

Jon was very sincere as he explained he just needed a couple of years to figure out his life. "It will give her a chance to know her real father," he said to me as he looked at my daughter. I told Jon I didn't have much of a choice and that it was him who chose this for us. "No it was the someone up there who chose this," Jon said as he looked up to the sky. Jon insisted we were on the right path and he assured me that we would be together as a couple again soon. He wanted me to mention my childhood to Lorraine and my oldest brother again. "I want to know what they have to say," he said to me. I told Jon, "Maybe they were clueless to what was happening to me." Jon responded, "No way," as he shook his head and explained how if one of his siblings disappeared even for a night, he would demand answers. He told me he would have kicked that bedroom door down on Pleasant Street and I knew he would have. Jon talked about his parents, siblings, friends, morals and what a family is.

My friendship with Ken's parents was becoming a closer one. I would often walk up to their Christian hill home with my daughter and hang out in their yard. Having a cup of coffee, playing cribbage or helping them around the house. They went to bingo weekly and were always trying to get me to go with them. Ken was out of work early one day so I decided to go with them as they left early around dinner time. I rode in their car, they helped me around buying bingo cards, giving me a dauber for when numbers were called and excited for me to meet their bingo partner Lorraine. "Wait, what, huh, your bingo friend?" I questioned them in a dumbfounded manner. Ken's parents didn't know much of my childhood, but they knew I didn't have a good childhood or a good mother. They knew I always lived with other people and they knew about my dad's social security checks being stolen by my birth mother. After my initial reaction to their friends name, we all laughed it off as there are many other Lorraine's out in the world. Besides the lady they described was not my birth mother at all. I didn't win at bingo but the old man did and their friend Lorraine never showed up. The next four or five weeks went by, every week they would tell me about their friend Lorraine at bingo, she was a funny lady who lived a lonely life.

On a spontaneous moment I decided to go to bingo with Ken's parents again. I didn't win and their friend Lorraine didn't show up either. I questioned myself, 'Could this be my birth mother?' A few days later Ken's mother who everyone called, "Ma" informed me why her friend didn't make it to bingo, because she was helping one of her kids out. I remember thinking to myself, 'Ya, no way that's Lorraine.'

Things pretty much stayed the same until Ken was out of work early one day and wanted to go visit his parents. We were going to hang out, eat dinner and play some cribbage. We walked into his parents house through the front room and into the kitchen where they were usually found sitting at the kitchen table. They were there, along with company, their friend and bingo partner Lorraine.

As Ken's mother was about to introduce us to her friend, I noticed who it was. I immediately rushed past Ken and right to the kitchen table as I blurted out, "That's Lorraine." Ken's mother responded it was as I interrupted her, "That is Lorraine." While pointing my finger at the lady sitting at the kitchen table who wouldn't even look at me. I said it a few more times and at first Ken's mother thought I was making a joke for finally meeting their friend. She figured it out by the look on my face that it was Lorraine, my birth mother. Ken drove us back home, we ordered a pizza and I just waited for the day when I would forget all the horrible, horrific things I've seen, felt and was once forced upon me. I had not spoken to Lorraine since she used the word molested towards me a few months earlier outside of my house.

I was so mad, hurt, confused and full of why's as I tried to understand how Lorraine became bingo buddies with Ken's parents. I tried to wrap my head around the fact that this was happening to me. I was so mad as I was trying to forget my childhood, yet it kept popping back into my life and I couldn't understand why? Ken's parents were very supportive and kind old folks as they explained how they knew Lorraine from bingo. Needless to say I never went to bingo with Ken's parents again but I also appreciated their communication with me on the matter. They did not approve of the mother their new bingo buddy was, but they did like the friend she was to them.

By late spring 1991 we were given the opportunity to move up to Christian hill in a first floor duplex right next door to Ken's parents. It was a beautiful apartment with a yard, porch, washer/dryer hookups, a great neighborhood and a school right across the street. We soon moved into the apartment. Not long afterwards Ken's parents offered to babysit if I wanted to go to work part time. I refused to allow anyone to babysit my daughter except for her grandparents on her father's side, so when they offered, I thought, 'Sure why not.' It wasn't long before I found a job. When we first moved into the first floor duplex there were no tenants in the second floor apartment. Being home one day, Ken and I heard the moving truck pull up to the two family duplex. We knew immediately new neighbors were moving into the upstairs apartment. As I went to look out the window to catch a glimpse of my new neighbors, Ken said, "You don't need to be friends with every neighbor." I informed him I knew that, but at the same time I recognized the voice I was hearing as I looked out the window. "No way," I said out loud as I headed to the front door. There she was, my new neighbor and old friend from Cissy's house, Shelly and her boyfriend Mike. I didn't have to get to know my neighbors because I already knew them.

My new job was as a cook in the cafeteria of Middlesex Community College downtown campus. Ken's father quickly went back to driving me in the morning as he would drop me off at the college on his way to work. Living next door to each other made meeting outside at his car a regular routine in the morning. I lived on a city bus route and working in the downtown area made catching a bus ride home from work real easy. I also knew my daughter was in good hands with her grandmother while I worked. Although working also added to the list of arguments Ken would start with me.

He wanted me to be a full time mom but also wanted me to work. He wanted me to work but also didn't want the responsibility of taking our daughter out in the morning to his mother's, even though she lived next door. He wanted me to have friends but not with all my old friends. He wanted a cooked dinner every night but was never home to eat. I went to work every morning leaving a diaper bag filled for my daughter and a note reminding Ken of the bag I packed and to not forget anything before leaving.

It wasn't long before I had to start planning my daughter's first birthday party. I sent birthday invites out including one to Lorraine, after all she was my daughter's grandmother. A bunch of people filled my house for my daughter's birthday party along with her fathers family, my friends from

Cissy's house, Ken's friends and my birth mother along with my oldest brother. Not long after the birthday party started, one of my friends from Cissy's house who I've known since I was fifteen years old questioned me, "How do you know him?" As he pointed to a guy at my daughter's birthday party. I answered him, "That's my oldest brother." My friend then walked over to my oldest brother, gave him a dope slap on his head and questioned him, "Where the heck were you?" My friend knew me from Cissy's house but he knew my oldest brother because they hung out together. Small world huh? They had been good friends for years and he never knew we were related. Soon I would face many trick questions I would face for the rest of my life. Questions to some that would seem so easy to answer. Co-workers, customers at work or the new friends you meet along the way in life who ask simple questions. How many siblings do you have? How old were you when you moved out of your parents home? What parent did you live with? Along with so many questions I would continue to face.

Shortly after my daughter's first birthday, my other older brother came home from serving our country. Lorraine drove him over to see me and meet my daughter for the first time. Though we wrote small letters to each other while he was overseas, I had not seen this brother in many years. When the car pulled up outside my house he came running into my apartment and just hugged me. He was so excited to see me. It made me feel so happy knowing how excited he was. Though I had mixed emotions about reconnecting with Lorraine, I was very happy to reconnect with the siblings I had when I was a kid.

The arguments continued with Ken as I was required to work early mornings, leaving him with the task of bringing our daughter next door to his mothers. He insisted he shouldn't have to bring our daughter every morning because he worked harder than me. I basically left him with no choice but to bring her every morning because I was already gone to work. Living on Christian hill also made it more common for Jon to stop by and visit. Sometimes he gave me a ride home from work when he saw me walking towards the bus or we would meet across the street from my home in the school yard, up the street at the reservoir, down at the Reed Street convenience store or he would rev his engine from his motorcycle outside my house to let me know he was there. Jon and I were still talking about our secrets and how we managed life on a daily basis.

He continued to bring up Pleasant Street to me, trying to get me to talk more about my childhood, insisting I needed to talk about it in order to understand it. Until one day he just looked at me with sadness as he questioned me, "You really don't remember?" He then went on explaining to me how I would have to remember in order for it to make sense to me and for me to not be disappointed when I find out I was fighting for a family I never really had. "They are the only family I have," I responded to Jon but he just hugged me as he said, "No I am the only family you have." I just looked at Jon knowing he was right, even though deep down I was wishing he wasn't. Jon tried to convince me to submit my poetry to be published or write a book about my childhood. I told Jon I would not want to become a famous writer or poet because I wouldn't want people to know what I lived through. I was embarrassed, humiliated, ashamed, hurt and I just wanted to forget my childhood. To get off the subject I'd quickly change the conversation back to Jon's life and he would just as quickly put his helmet on while saying, "See you soon," before taking off on his motorcycle. Sometimes I would shake my head at Jon but every time I would smile. How could I not? Jon was a great friend who would show up in his car with a car seat in it just so he could take me and my daughter to visit my dad at the cemetery or to take us out to eat for lunch. Though Ken didn't understand my friendship with Jon, it was only because he chose not to. All Ken knew was that I made a promise to Jon and it was a promise I had no intentions of breaking.

By the fall of 1991 Lorraine was coming over on Saturdays to visit with my daughter, myself and drink coffee. Bringing up the past wasn't working for me, so I promised myself I would move on, get over it and finally stop dwelling. I would talk about my daughter, the future and things on television. Until one Saturday Lorraine questioned me about driving over to her friends house so she could meet my daughter. It was her friend

Theresa, the one whose house I slept over when I was ten years old. The one who said I would never be abused again. The one who I haven't seen since. "Yes I want to go see her," I said to Lorraine, but it was only because I had a question to ask her, "Why didn't she ever check on me again?" I immediately packed a diaper bag, got my daughter and myself ready for the quick ride over to Lorraine's long time friend Theresa. She was now living in Dracut Mass, just down the road from where I lived and about a five minute drive.

It crossed my mind many times as I was getting older and even at twenty-one years of age, I still wondered about it, What do the people from my past remember? How many knew I was abused? Who blamed me for being abused? How many blamed me for our mother and baby sister's father splitting up? Was it my fault? I was finally about to get some outside information on an opinion, answer, closure, anything to help me make sense of my childhood, my feelings, my life and most of all, myself.

Answers can give closure like a spark can give a fire. Either there is an explosion of light as the questions become crystal clear or the flame sits smoldering on the back burner of life just waiting for the water to boil over and burn another unanswered question into your soul.

She looked like the same cute little lady I remembered, just a little older looking. It was ten years since I last saw her. She was all smiles as she opened her door, gave me a hug and kissed my face. Then she was taken away by cuteness with my daughter asleep in her cars seat. "She's beautiful," she yelled. We all got situated at her kitchen table, she made coffee for Lorraine and I. When she finally sat at the table to talk, I blurted out the question that was steaming in my head as it exploded out, "Why didn't you ever check up on me again when I was younger?" Theresa's happy smiling face instantly dropped into sadness as she answered me, "Oh no honey I did call, but you went to go live with your dad." "No I didn't," I immediately responded to her as I looked over at Lorraine who was now looking at the floor. I looked back at Theresa and I told her what happened to me that day I left her house ten years earlier. I told her Lorraine drove me back to

Dave and how he tied me up downstairs in the cellar. She was certain I went to live with my dad. Theresa told me she gave my mother graduation cards to give to my father who then gave them to me. My 8th and my 12th grade graduation cards, Theresa insisted I got them. "You were still living with your father when you graduated high school," Theresa said to me. I sat there shaking my head no, "Besides my dad passed away in 1983," I answered Theresa as we went back and forth about the life I lived.

When Theresa heard me say my dad passed away the whole kitchen went quiet. We both looked at Lorraine who was still looking at the floor below her. "No he didn't, your father is still alive," Theresa said as a last ditch effort for me to agree with her. She had a look of disbelief in her friend Lorraine as I took the copy of my dad's obituary out of my wallet. Theresa read the obituary as her eyes filled with tears, she hugged me as she cried how sorry she was. "I didn't know, I didn't know," she said a few times before we took all our attention and put it towards my daughter who was waking up in her car seat.

It was a very quiet ride back to my house from Theresa's that day. It was really nice seeing her again, as for my birth mother, the lady I was calling Lorraine, I had a whole lot of gasoline twirling up in my brain as I felt the steam being tugged out of my ears with every sound coming from the cruel woman who was driving me home. Lorraine knew I was very upset with her and I went home to where I once again learned to forget a childhood I once lived.

When the following Saturday came, Lorraine came by for coffee as if nothing had happened the week before. I was so mad at her, I went off on her and though it sounded like I was being mean to her, I was only speaking the truth about what happened to me. It was just my daughter and I at home, so I spoke very freely about my childhood to Lorraine. As I was looking for closure in my own life, I was also feeling bad when I was telling Lorraine all the horrible things she did and allowed to happen to me. I was feeling bad for making her feel like shit. Then I was the one apologizing, fucked up right? I know it didn't make sense but then I realized it was because I had a heart and I hated to see anyone hurt including Lorraine.

I did wonder how many more times I was abused after that day I left Theresa's in 1980. How many more times Lorraine could have saved me but failed to do so. I had so many reasons to explode but I would just breathe in and breathe out. I continued to breathe in and breathe out until I walked back into my living room where Lorraine was sitting on my couch. "I am sick of your lies," I told her as I insisted she look at me while I spoke to her. I told her I wanted the truth to every question I asked her. "Is your mother really dead?" I questioned her. Lorraine answered, "Yes." I questioned, "When did she die?" Lorraine answered, "Before you were born." "Do you have any other kids?" I questioned Lorraine. She answered, "No." But she explained my hairdresser sister Pauline went to live with her father, she had a son who died of sudden infant death, my two older brothers, baby sister and me. That was all she had for kids. "Are you telling me the truth?" I questioned her. Lorraine answered, "Yes."

As the colder months came Jon would stop by to check up on me. "Because that's what family does," he would say with a smile. Jon would question me about the promises we made and my childhood. He wanted me to find the closure I deserved and to remember the reason why I ran from my childhood home. I had so many years of abuse that all ended on that Saturday morning I ran to my friend Sandi's house. "There is so much I do remember isn't that enough?" I questioned Jon as he hugged me and told me another fun story about his family and what a family is supposed to be like. His stories always added a warm smile to my day.

I continued working at the downtown college as a cook. I actually worked for the catering company which worked the kitchen. Along with getting side catering jobs such as weddings, political parties and graduations, I was making pretty decent money as a cook and caterer. Of course working, keeping my friendship with Jon, my neighbors and some days just being happy caused an argument with Ken. He could hold a grudge and show his animosity towards me very openly. Dirty looks, not talking for days and before we knew it Christmas 1991 was upon us. Ken and I had no choice but to get along as we were both super excited for our daughter's second Christmas. We knew she was going to be so much fun and we spoiled her.

Of course she got the best 1991 Christmas gift ever, the popular Barney the Purple Dinosaur.

I was now twenty-two years old and I was learning to except the emptiness I felt every day. Like an arm ripping into my chest and pulling a piece of me out. I was learning it wasn't going away, sometimes causing me to panic as if it was suffocating me. Like I was standing over pieces of my childhood soul scattered across the cellar floor of Pleasant Street. It's feeling like dirt, no matter how many showers, baths or scrubbing bubbles you take, you always feel that shaming, humiliating, emptiness pile of dirt resting in the pit of your stomach. Some days I would wake up telling myself, 'You're normal, just forget the past, you got this.' If I needed extra reassurance then I'd remind myself, 'Besides there is always someone worse off.' All words of advice I continued to offer myself.

There was and there is always someone worse off. Those words would be my reminder for the next twenty-five years as I dismissed my own hurt, my own pain and my own unanswered questions because there was always someone worse off than me. As the new year 1992 was upon us, I was being a mom and keeping my home a warm and comfy home. I worked 6am to 2pm then I went home, cleaned, cooked and played with my daughter. I cooked dinner even though Ken wasn't home much, I still had to eat. I was becoming high demand at my job as I was offered all the over time with catering jobs outside of the college campus. I would do three or four hour gigs where I'd show up at the required location and start cooking. I'd also go home with some really good money for working the side job, not to mention I loved cooking. What I didn't love was with all the new people I was meeting. There were also those tricked questions I was always being asked.

Inside it broke me every time I was unexpectedly caught off guard with a question from a coworker, a customer at work or even a stranger at a store as they make conversation while ringing up your grocery order. I would hear the words, "Remember when you were a kid," and boom, it was all nails going down a chalkboard. What seemed to be a perfect day of happiness was shot down to crumbles as I just smiled at the person until I found the best possible answer that would keep me from falling apart.

Working more, meant needing Ken to watch our daughter while I did my extra side jobs. Along with him also working a lot, it caused us to argue more than we were already arguing. I realized he was treating me with the same anger and animosity as I was treating Lorraine with. We always argued and spent most of our friendship arguing. From how long it took me at the grocery store, how long it took me to get home from work, what I cooked for dinner, too long of a shower, too much time at his parents and so on. I always had to explain or defend my actions and he was so quick to criticize my poetry, my past, my life and me. He was a super cool father to our daughter and that made me happy. I guess we were becoming comfortable in the situation we created for ourselves and though he blamed Jon as the reason for most of our arguments, most of our arguing had nothing to do with Jon.

In early 1992 Jon showed up at my house for a visit and he was all excited. "I have exciting news," he said to me with a huge smile on his face. He was so happy and speechless as I kept saying, "Well, tell me." He told me, "I got picked for a professional hockey team." His words weren't even out of his mouth when I screamed in excitement. I was so happy for him because I knew this is what he wanted. Jon told me he would be leaving in a few weeks for training so he could be ready for the 1992-1993 hockey season. He also informed me how he didn't want me to call his house, look for him or ask about him because he wanted it to be a surprise. He wanted to surprise his family and as he explained, it made sense to me. I was full of questions, "When are you leaving?" "How long will you be gone?" "When's this happening?" I continued with my questions. Jon answered every one of my questions with answers which seemed to make sense.

Unfortunately Jon was there to give me a, "See you soon hug," he said to me. He had to get his stuff in order, but also told me he would be home for about a week after summer and before the hockey season started. "I'll stop by then," he said to me as he put his hand over my heart. "Besides you can always find me right here," he continued. We talked a lot that day, he commented how Ken was a jerk to me but a good father and he praised him for that. "I feel better you living with him than a family who assumed you should accept an apology you never received," Jon told me as he continued with his disgust towards a family I was trying to be a part of, all the while trying to forget a childhood I once lived with them. Jon also repeated something he has told me since we made promises to each other back in 1987, "If the world was going to end tomorrow, I'd marry you tonight." And he always explained the world was not ending anytime soon. He also let me know how this gave me time to remember what I needed to remember. "When you're an emotional train wreck, just start from the beginning ok?" Jon said to me as he gave me his super big see you soon hug.

As summer arrived, I was still battling with the decision of whether or not I wanted Lorraine in my life. Some days, no most days I wished she just went away and never came back. I'd occasionally talk with my oldest brother on the phone, my other older brother was back and forth serving for our country and my only conversations with my baby sister was through Lorraine. Anytime I had to refer to Lorraine as my mother, I'd get this pit in my stomach rise up into my throat and just rest there until the feeling of dirt wore off once again. My daughter's godmother would stop by and visit on her days off from her work. One day she questioned why I didn't have my license. I told her of my several attempts to get my permit in 1987 and 1988, but with the help of my daughter's godmother, by the end of June I not only got my permit, I also became a Massachusetts licensed driver. After the excitement of having my license was over, it soon didn't make a difference because I didn't have a car.

I learned it was easy to avoid Lorraine when she called, I simply didn't answer the phone when it would ring. But her unexpected visits to my house made it impossible to avoid her and she showed up unexpectedly many times. I wanted to not answer her knocks on the door. I wanted to close all the curtains and shades. I wanted to scream in her face to go away, but she was my daughter's family. She was my daughter's grandmother so I let her in my home. It never failed seeing Lorraine always put me in a down mood as I still had a lot of hurt, pain and questions I kept to myself because no one wanted to hear it.

Ken would start arguments with me insisting I was with Jon, telling me Jon was just at the house or I was out driving with him. I admit it, I let it go on for a few months until I finally told him Jon had not been in the state of Massachusetts for months. The arguments went back to everything else like before. Jon did stop by my house in late summer time but I missed him. Ken was home when he showed up and Jon had a few words with him which resulted in an argument between them.

I told Ken that Jon was just looking out for me and how he got picked for a hockey team. Ken being a hockey fan seemed impressed as he said, "Wow congrats to him." After a week went by I knew I missed seeing Jon and was pretty bummed but also so happy for him on the career adventure he was on. After work one day in October I kneeled over in sharp pain throughout my stomach as I thought I was peeing myself, when I went to the bathroom there was blood everywhere. Ken immediately drove me to Lowell General hospital where I was told I had suffered a miscarriage and again I was told I needed a stronger monthly pill prescription. I was given a doctors note and three days off of work as doctors scheduled me for a DNC. A procedure normal to women who experience miscarriage/short term pregnancies. So I went home and did what the doctor said, I rested and stayed home with my daughter.

Ken held animosity towards me for my friendship with so many people as I held animosity towards Lorraine for being so cruel. I started to question myself about whether or not it was me who was being cruel to Ken. Gosh I was so confused as a twenty-two year old. The morning of my procedure Ken dropped me off at the hospital and left his pager number for nurses to call him when I needed a ride home. A problem arose when the doctor who was performing the procedure canceled it quickly. I looked at him, about to ask why, when he informed me that I was still pregnant. "What, wait, huh?" I said dumbfounded and confused. I'm pretty sure that was Ken's response when I paged him about twenty minutes after dropping me off and not the four hours later like he expected. I think it was the quietest we were as he drove me home. There I was in October 1992 and pregnant with my second child.

I soon went back to work and just a few days later I received a phone call at work from my daughter's doctor. She informed me my daughter tested positive for extremely high levels of lead paint poisoning. I had my daughter checked just the week before because of the paleness of her skin. Blood results came back and I was informed I had twenty-four hours to leave my home and health officials were also heading to my house. I immediately left work and walked home. Along the way one of Jon's friends hollered my name as I walked up Christian hill. I waved back and hollered down to him, "Where's Jon?" But he didn't hear me and I needed to get home to deal with the health officials who were standing outside my house as I turned onto Beech Street. It was true, I had to leave everything behind and wash it all before taking it where I was going to. Ken reached out to our old landlord from Hildreth Street and he happened to have an empty apartment we could stay in as long as we needed too. He also helped us with all the information we needed about lead paint in the home and how it works, as well as the doctors informing us about special diets for my daughter.

The apartment we moved into on Lakeview Avenue was a three bedroom sardine box. Not good for a daughter to see her train wreck in the making pregnant mother and animosity grudge holding father argue over everything from spilled milk to a sneeze in the ear. As we waited to move back into our Christian hill home, we were instead told to clean what we wanted and stay living in our sardine box until further notice.

I don't know how I did it. I worked, got my daughter after work, unpacked my apartment on Lakeview Avenue and walked to Beech Street where I washed everything I owned with pine sol and water before packing it into bags and boxes. Ken would pick us up after he got out of work. I could not believe a three bedroom apartment could be so small. In two of the bedrooms, I was able to stand in the middle of the floor, spread my arms and touch opposite sides of the wall without stretching. In my bedroom, I had to sit on my bed just to open the drawers to my bureau. The kitchen was a small space and the living room was every reason not to own a coffee table. But it was the 1990s and I had a coffee table, making for a whole lot of stubbed toes and banged legs.

    I slowly started to hang some of my wall hangings up as I tried to make my new home a bit comfy, homey and cozy. With a change of address, electricity, gas and cable change overs, we made the sardine box into our home. Christmas scared me as I was overwhelmed with adding things into the apartment. We didn't have room as it was. A four foot Christmas tree was humongous in the tiny living room we had. We also had to store half the living room set down in the cellar for the holiday. I was pregnant, turning twenty three years old and spending Christmas in a tiny apartment. I continued working, walking and doing what I only knew how, living my life.

    Ken was rarely home. He either worked late, was on a couple dart teams, a bowling team, a coworker night out or a night out with friends. We argued over everything, as just bumping into each other in the tiny apartment caused a three week fight of silence and animosity. On days he was able to be home, he would cause an argument just so he could walk out the front door. It wasn't like he was able to storm into another room. Like my first pregnancy, he did not come to any of my doctor appointments for this pregnancy either. Only this time I had my daughter with me who came to every single appointment for her upcoming sibling she was about to have. As the 1993 year was upon us, my stomach grew as it did for my first pregnancy, small and slow. I also started to realize as much as I tried to forget my childhood; all it took was a single word, photo, face, sound or simple reaction to something that startled me and it would cause a memory, flashback or reminder of the childhood I kept trying to forget. It also caused for some very mixed emotional days as I tried to deal with the pain from my childhood all by myself. I was trying to forget the mixed emotions about Lorraine like I was trying to forget my childhood, but every time I saw Lorraine I only saw the birth mother who gave me the childhood I was trying to forget. The lies my mother told would take me on many unanswered roads throughout my twenties.

As the first few months went by, the arguments, animosity and silence was the home life we were growing accustomed too. Ken would occasionally question me about what hockey team Jon was playing for, insisting his name wasn't on a team's roster and teasing me for believing in Jon's friendship. I started my maternity leave on May 21st. Leaving me a few days with my daughter before her sibling was born and I decided not to know the sex of the baby as they didn't get it right the first time for me. Two days later my labor pains started around five in the morning. Long before the fishing tournament on the boulevard started, but it didn't stop Ken from still leaving to join his buddies on their planned fishing trip. By 7:00 in the morning I was home with my two year old daughter and fifteen minute apart labor pains. My old neighbor from Barker Avenue who I became good friends with over the years was now living in her own home just up the street on West Sixth Street. I called her and she came to hang out with me and my daughter for the day. By five o'clock that afternoon I was at the hospital in a room waiting on Ken who was being pulled out of the fishing tournament and the delivery doctor who got called away from his Sunday afternoon game of golf. It was fitting with the thirteen hours of hard labor I was going through which was nothing like my first baby. Complications arose during delivery at one point, but with the grace of God and a great medical staff at Lowell general hospital, on May 23rd I gave birth to a healthy beautiful baby girl.

I was soon home with both my daughters where I was able to be home for the whole summer while I collected twelve weeks of maternity leave. Living in a tiny apartment made everyday, a day worth going outside. Even in the rain I walked with an umbrella over my girls and raincoats for us all as we walked up the street to my friends who did daycare so my oldest daughter could play with the other kids. I finally got the nerve to tell Lorraine to stop showing up unexpectedly. It was too much living in a small apartment, arguing with Ken and dealing with seeing the woman who was so cruel to me when I needed her the most. I wasn't mad she didn't stop Dave from abusing me, I was mad she let him continue for all those years and it would be an argument I would argue with myself for the next twenty plus years. My other older brother was home again from serving our country. Often visiting me for coffee and a game of cards. Talking about my childhood to him wasn't something to bring up at the time as we were just getting to know each other again. Though I kept myself busy with my daughters throughout the whole summer, the arguments between Ken and I only worsened. We argued over what time a television show was on, we argued over a good day being a good day, we argued over space, even the space we didn't have.

September came and it was time for me to go back to work. Days before I was scheduled to go back my boss called me. I was offered an opportunity to be laid off and collect unemployment benefits and I took the offer eagerly so I could stay home with my daughters for another couple of months. Ken was happy also as he didn't have to take them out in the morning and he was happy with me being home with them. As the weeks in September went by I wondered where Jon had been. I figured he realized I didn't live up on the hill anymore. I called him a couple of times, but I got hung up on.

One day in late September I left my girls with my friend and I borrowed her car. I drove straight to 94 Grand Street. I thought the reason why I had not seen Jon yet was because I had moved. I parked the car outside of his house, I walked up the inside stairs and knocked on his door. Only to find out he nor his family lived there anymore. I was confused. Where was he? This had been the longest since knowing Jon that I had not seen him. I missed him so much and I couldn't wait to see him again. I knew I would so I got back in the car and drove back to my friends house where my life continued.

I made plans with some friends for a night out, including with Ken's sister. It had been at least two years since I last went out with friends and it caused an argument as I needed Ken to be home with the girls. He insisted I should be home with my daughters, I insisted I needed a night out with my friends and that's exactly what I did. A bunch of us ladies met for a night of drinking, dancing and bar hopping throughout local bars in Dracut, Massachusetts. I went home to where in just one week it would be the 10th anniversary of my dad's death.

It was a Sunday and Ken still wasn't on talking terms with me for going out with friends the week before. He was getting ready for his brother to pick him up when I asked him to pick me up the Lowell Sun newspaper so I could check for any memorials for my dad. He quickly snapped at me, "There's nothing in the paper." Then questioned me, "Why should you care?" While he continued, "He's been gone for how long now?" Ken stood there staring at me and waiting for me to answer him. I just shook my head and answered the front door as his brother was now knocking on it. Ken and his brother were total opposites, along with being my oldest daughter's godfather, he was also a very empathetic man. After coming into the apartment Ken's brother informed me his coworker was at his house earlier and recognized me in a photo he had on a shelf. I questioned who his coworker was and he answered he was a guy Jimmy who at one time lived on Grand Street and also knew my friend Jon. I thought it was cool he mentioned it to me and I told him to say hello to him at work the next day. He informed me he would then he said to me, "Sorry about your friend." I looked at him confused. "My friend?" I questioned him. "Ya he died, my condolences," he answered in a sympathetic manner. I looked at him and blurted out, "Oh my God he died, your coworker Jimmy?" As I continued, "Oh my God I am so sorry, that's so sad," I continued as I attempted to walk away when I heard him say, "No your friend Jon." I immediately looked at Ken who quickly said to me, "I didn't know how to tell you." "What, what, no, no, no fuckin way," I went on saying. Then I immediately snapped, "What did you just say to me?" I questioned Ken without waiting for an answer, I just as quickly walked out my door and up the street to see if my friend had the local newspaper. Not realizing it was similar to what I did just ten years earlier. I didn't let myself cry because I knew it wasn't true. It was like my insides went completely empty as I heard the words, "No your friend Jon." Then Ken saying, "I didn't know how to tell you." I said the word, "No," hundreds of times out loud and to myself as I walked out my door and up the street to my friend's house.

I knew she got the newspaper delivered as she was a coupon collector. So many thoughts came to my mind, 'No way, it's a miscommunication.' Then I'd tell myself, 'No way God would do that to me.' I continued to reassure myself the news of Jon's death was a mistake. I apologized to my friend for showing up without calling first but she didn't mind at all. She made me a coffee as I told her what I just heard and why I was there. She did have the newspaper for that day, October 17, 1993. She informed me there were no bad accidents in the paper or anything to draw concern as she handed me the newspaper for me to check it out for myself. I started on page one, then page two and so on. There was nothing about anything regarding Jon. I continued flipping the pages of the newspaper looking to see if anyone did a memorial for my dad in the obituary section of the newspaper. I looked through the obituaries and there was nothing. As I continued reading the obituary section, I quickly saw his picture but I was confused, shocked and frozen in time. Why was Jon's picture in the memorials?

I don't know how long I gazed at the article in the obituary section of the newspaper. I read the memorial under Jon's photo at least a thousand times. I looked at the clock on my friends kitchen wall and it was a little after three in the afternoon. Chills went through me, I was completely empty as I put together timelines in my life.

- 1983... It was my brother who came to my friends house to tell me my dad had passed.
- 1993... Ken's brother came to my house and told me Jon had passed.
- 1983... I walked to my friend's neighbors so I could read the Lowell Sun newspaper about my dad.
- 1993... I walked to my friend's house so I could see if there was anything about Jon in the Lowell Sun newspaper.
- 1983... I found out about my dad's death on the 18th one day after he passed away.
- 1993... I found out about Jon's death one year after he passed away.

It was his one year memorial I was reading.

I was finding out very similar to Jon's passing how I found out about my dad's passing. I hadn't run into anyone in the past year who could have told me about Jon. I wasn't able to go to Jon's wake or funeral because I didn't know. What I also didn't know was, why was this happening? I was in shock while I was at my friends house looking through her newspaper, but It was the walk back to my house where it started to hit me. I walked home to where Ken was with our daughters. His brother left without him as he couldn't leave because I left him home alone with the girls. My face was covered in tears and mucus from crying so hard. "How long have you known?" I screamed at Ken immediately after walking inside the apartment.

Before he could answer, I stormed into my bedroom and slammed the door shut. I cried and I cried for hours. I screamed, threw things and bawled my eyes out. Ken had known since the year before. He kept it from me for a whole year. He also knew to stay away from me, it was the most help he had been to me in years. He left me alone and he took care of our daughters while I cried for hours upon hours inside our bedroom. I was so hurt, I was so confused, I was lost, I was empty, mad, alone, in pain and just wanting it all to go away. Jon died on the one day he told me was the only day out of the year that I deserved to cry on, the day my dad died, October 17th.

How did this happen? Was I living in a bad dream? Was I living another nightmare in my life? Just when I didn't think I could cry anymore, there I was crying more tears than a lifetime should allow. Ken fed our girls their dinner, got them ready for bed and continued to leave me alone. I couldn't stop crying because if I did then I had to accept that Jon died and that he died a whole year earlier. It would be another eight years before I found out how it happened, when it happened and the lie Jon told me about the hockey team he never left the state of Massachusetts to join.

The next morning Ken came into the bedroom insisting I had to clean myself up. "The girls can't see you like this," he told me as he explained he needed to get to work. Which meant I had to clean myself up and be a mom to my daughters. I knew Ken was right. My face and eyes were all puffy from crying so much, so long and uncontrollably. I did what I had to do, I cleaned myself up and took care of my daughters. Holding them both a little extra in my arms as they gave me the strength I needed to go on. I got us all dressed and we headed up the street to visit with my friend for coffee. I was still lost, a piece of me was anyways. It was like I was in a fog between reality and what I knew I deserved; for Jon to be alive. My friend had cut Jon's memorial out of the newspaper for me and told me to use her car to visit him at the cemetery that was listed in the memorial.

I never went to that cemetery, but I soon found myself driving there. I parked the car once I drove through the entrance of the cemetery and I cried even more. So many things Jon said to me raced through my head. So many questions I asked myself. How can this be true? How could God do this to me? Why was this happening? As much as I didn't want to believe it, Jon was buried here and it killed me knowing that. I walked throughout the cemetery until I found a stone wall near the back of the cemetery where I sat and cried some more. My eyes were so full of tears that I didn't notice I was sitting diagonally across from Jon's monument. I walked back to the car, drove back to my friends house, got my daughters and went home to where I was never the same again. I was lost and I was hurting. I went from being a happy, strong independent woman to being an old unworthy, stay a secret, afraid to speak my mind, kind of girl that I would continue to be for the next seven years of my life.

As quickly as I was mourning the loss of Jon and trying to understand how I didn't know about it for a whole year, I was also hit with a new apartment to move into. Ken found a duplex in the Christian hill area. This time the duplex was on Myrtle Street, one street down from our former Beech Street duplex apartment. I was an emotional wreck over Jon's death which made moving into a new apartment exhausting, by Thanksgiving we were all moved in. I solely concentrated on raising my daughters.

It was hard adjusting to not looking for Jon driving by. It was hard not checking every motorcycle that revved its motor. It was hard getting used to knowing I would not see him again in this lifetime. But one thing I did know was, I shared an undeniable bond with Jon. It would be a bond that would take me on a lifetime of love, faith and understanding. As the year 1994 came upon us, I would muster enough courage to finally question my other older brother about what he remembered from Pleasant Street and the abuse I endured.

My voice stayed silent, my secrets kept and I was allowing my mother back into my life, but only this time it was because I wanted her there. I thought it was what I deserved. I deserved the hurt and I deserved the pain. I deserved to feel so unwanted, unworthy and unloved. I deserved to feel all of it because Jon wasn't here. It was my fault I always remembered my childhood, it was my fault why Jon was gone, it was my fault for being abused when I was younger and it was my fault for all the pain I have ever felt. It was all my fault. *Family will protect a man who inflicts horror on a child then tells that child to get over the one thing they will never forget. We grow up to stand our ground, speak our mind and move on. It's finally over, it's time to forgive and time to forget, right? It's all part of life, growing up as a statistic in a world full of abused children who were growing up. There were no handbooks for this. Sometimes my mouth would open and I could feel this hollowness of space going down my throat into the open pit of my stomach, resting like a hundred pound boulder.*

We watch families be just that; families. When wanting validation becomes unnecessary drama to others, it becomes easier to blame ourselves for wanting justice. Slowly belittling our own selves in the process. We learn to accept the mimics and ridicule as a normal way of life. Making the explaining easier to avoid. So many saw me as a happy independent girl and so many saw me as a quiet shy girl. Years of battling who I was continued due to my older brother's answer to my question, "Do you remember what happened to me on Pleasant Street?"

A Life Given To Me: Under God's Watch

I started going for walks and visiting a cemetery when I was a teenager. Every cemetery has an area dedicated for infants and as I got older, no matter who I visited at a cemetery, I never went to their gravesite. Not my dad's, not Jon's, not Mark's and not my friend Lana's. I would park my car and walk around the cemetery I was at. Before leaving, I always left roses at the graves of the infants. I knew my loved ones in heaven wouldn't mind if I did.

Life emotionally got hard, I was empty, my heart was bleeding, my stare was blank, my mind was a big fat question mark. I would look down a street and I had to keep reminding myself Jon was gone, but at the same time I wanted to see him come down the street. I kept myself busy unpacking as I made my new apartment a home, doing some Christmas shopping and staying busy with my girls.

Jon always wanted me to find closure from my childhood and by that he meant an apology, some acknowledgment, a bit of support and maybe a dash of protection. But unfortunately, I surrounded myself with people who assumed I should accept an apology I was never given. I surrounded myself with people who never acknowledged my horrific childhood. I surrounded myself around people who failed to support me when I was a kid and then again as an adult. I was surrounded by people who failed to protect me. That was my driving force behind getting the courage to question my other older brother about what he remembered of my childhood and the abuse I endured. Whether it was morning, day or night, there was always a time in my day when I would wonder why they hadn't acknowledged anything I went through. I couldn't understand why? It built up as I continued to keep it to myself everyday. Yet I wanted to scream it in the faces of my two older brothers and my birth mother. It was either ask the question or explode and sound like a raging lunatic, so I questioned.

My other older brother came home from the service again, he would stop by for coffee and some card games of rummy or scat. He always came with a friend or stayed busy with my girls, never giving me the opportunity to question him about my childhood. One day, I just finished making us a fresh cup of coffee, I was about to question him about my childhood when he suddenly remembered he had somewhere to be. It happened so fast, I sat down at my dining room table with my coffee and he got up saying bye to my daughter's while telling me he had to go. There was no way I was holding it in any longer, he was a foot away from the door and I blurted the question. "What do you remember of the abuse that happened to me?" But I was quickly told, "Forget about the past," "What matters is you are here," "Live for today," "She's your mother and you have to forgive her," my brother continued talking and not letting me get a word in at all. "You have to forget it happened, no one needs to know, besides you have your girls now," my older brother went on as he still didn't let me get a word in before he headed out the door.

I wasn't happy we didn't talk but I was happy at least one of my siblings acknowledged my childhood. His words stuck with me for a few weeks.

I would stop myself from thinking of my past, I would remind myself I am alive and I lived for the day. I looked towards the future, I forgave my birth mother, I forgot her cruelty and I had my daughters to concentrate on. I kept my pain, hurt and childhood to myself because no one needed to know. Yes, my older brother was right, or at least I told myself that hundreds of times a day. I started to blame myself for every time I thought about what happened to me when I was younger. I blamed myself for all the images that flashed through my brain everyday. I blamed myself for all the terror and evil I once lived through. I blamed myself for not accepting that I was just another statistic in a world full of abused children who have been molested. As much as I hated the word, I was now admitting I was also molested.

As I continued to live my life, I realized I had no one to talk or tell my side of my childhood to. I was always shunned away, told to forget about it or how it was my fault I kept bringing it up again. I was seeking approval from the same people who refused to remember me. It was ok to be accepted by them as long as I didn't bring up my childhood years. When I did, no one wanted to remember or talk about it. It was my fault I lived with other families. Or maybe it was their lack of caring why I was tossed to other families. Either way, they didn't care.

Despite all the obstacles, heartaches and blessings I was given in life, I lived my life. I knew it was what my dad, Jon and Mark would want for me. I had three angels in the sky, how lucky was I? I kept my promise to Jon as I promised myself I would live my life. What I didn't realize was that my life was living for me. I did not ask for the many memories, flashbacks and trick questions that I have faced on a daily basis, but it is my life, this is me, living the life given to me. As the years went on, I grew to be smitten, blessed and grateful for the bond I had with Jon. It's like I knew he was gone, yet I felt him with me all the time. I went back to work part time as a cook on the weekends. I worked overnight, got paid good money and I loved cooking in the back kitchen of a restaurant. Ken and I would throw birthday cookouts for our daughters. Always a good turnout with a huge family on Ken's side having a lot of great uncles and aunts. My baby sister, older brothers and Lorraine would also show up. Sometimes I tried to impress them in hopes to belong and other times I held resentment for feeling like an outcast. Not realizing my bouts with depression was being caused by the same family I was trying so hard to be a part of.

I struggled with every little thing that put a reminder, an image or a sound of the childhood I was still trying to forget. A simple conversation would still trigger a memory, an image or a nightmare. Answering questions that to many may seem easy to answer or topics which to some are easy to discuss, was not always easy for me to answer or easy to discuss; 'Remember your sweet sixteenth? Wait, you're whose sister? Don't disrespect your mother. How many siblings do you have? Remember when you were a kid?' I was learning it was easier to avoid those questions and topics than it was to tell the truth and see the look of pity on their faces. What seemed to make it all go away was being home with my daughters.

First time I heard Lorraine refer to me as her daughter, everything around me went silent as my insides wanted to come puking out of my throat. It bothered me, I wasn't her daughter and she definitely wasn't my mother. Gosh I hated it, but I sucked it up. I let the image or maybe it was the thought of having a family get the best of me. It was what everyone else had, so I wanted it too. I wanted my daughters to know their aunt, uncle's and grandmother on my side.

I stayed busy and I ignored any reference to my childhood. I continued to blame myself for every bad memory I had. Then one day out of nowhere, Lorraine's lies just started smacking her in her face without warning. It was a phone call I received from my oldest brother informing me our grandmother passed away and Lorraine was at her funeral. He always considered my dad's mother as his grandmother, so I informed him she died when we were kids. But he informed me it was, "Our mother's mother," he said. "Our grandmother on our mother's side?" I questioned him in confusion. "Wait, what, huh," I continued to say.

I questioned Lorraine when I was a teenager and I questioned her again when I was a young adult. I was told by Lorraine numerous times throughout the years that her own mother had died long before I was born.

So how could Lorraine be at her mother's funeral if she died decades ago? The answer is Lorraine lied, her mother was alive and well until the mid 1990s. Finding out about a grandmother who I was told died long before 1969 had recently died, really pissed me off, but also made me feel the disappointment in Lorraine.

My brother was also informed of an uncle I never met or knew about. He was Lorraine's brother and he lived out of state but was in Lowell for his mother's funeral. After hanging up the phone with my oldest brother, I immediately drove to his house. He owned the home and rented the first floor to Lorraine. I was so mad and I wanted answers from her. Why would Lorraine keep us from her own mother? I parked my car outside my brother's house and headed up his front stairs. I was just about to ring the bell when the front door swung open and a man yelled, "Susan," "You're not Susan," the man continued to say to me. "Who's Susan?" I questioned the man, who I found out was my uncle. As for Susan, well she was another daughter Lorraine had and didn't raise. Just like that, I had another older sister. I could feel the steam coming out of my ears. I went inside Lorraine's apartment where everyone was meeting. We all sat at her table as we tried to understand why she kept us from her mother, her brother and another daughter. I told her brother everything. I told him of all the lies she told, of all the people who raised me and of her boyfriend who she allowed to abuse me. I didn't say rape, terrorize or molested, I just used the word abuse. Lorraine's brother had empathy as he looked at Lorraine in disgust. But not one of my brother's nor Lorraine said a word. I was so mad as I screamed at them all for not backing me up. I stormed out of the apartment and drove back home where I once again learned to forget the childhood I was trying to forget.

Ken reminded me how I can't keep having them in and out of my life. He insisted I had to choose one or the other for the sake of our daughters and I was emotionally beating myself up over it. Our oldest daughter heard us having that conversation about my siblings and Lorraine. "I'm glad Ma is your mother and Memere is dad's mother," she blurted out to me as she came into the room. Suddenly I had some explaining to do.

Ma and Papa Foote were Ken's parents while Memere was Lorraine. I had such a great relationship with Ma and Papa that even their neighbors got confused on who was their child. I was always unsure of reconnecting with Lorraine from the beginning. As much as I tried to make it work having a relationship with her, there was always something there that made me jumpy, mad, insulted and unimportant are just to name a few.

A mother is known as someone who raises her children and Lorraine had nothing to do with the person I grew up to be. I have myself for being smart enough to run that Saturday morning when I was a kid. I have Sandi's mom, Jon, friends, my kids and all the good hearted people in this world. That's who had everything to do with the person I grew up to be.

I continued battling the emotions I dealt with everyday in regards to my childhood. A simple sentence from a television show, a simple question from a coworker, a conversation with a store clerk, a chat with a group of friends or a news brief of another abused child would cause me to be scared or startled. Even the smallest gesture would remind me of so much from my childhood. It was slowly eating me up from the insides out. I never doubted Jon or his friendship and some days, I missed him more than others. Did it suck like so much in my life, carrying another heartache on my sleeve? Yes it did. I yelled at my dad for dying on me, I yelled at Jon for leaving me, I yelled at myself for having to deal with it all alone as I literally had no self worth. I wasn't proud for surviving my childhood, I was angry with myself for always remembering it.

I began to drill it into my head that I was the only one Dave abused. 'There were no others, he lied about the girls he claimed to have killed, I was the only one,' I continued to remind myself constantly. I even called myself dumb for thinking it was as bad as I remembered it to be. I made one more trip to the city library to look through old newspaper clips in the local newspaper. I had to make sure one more time, were there any missing or murdered girls between the time I ran from Pleasant Street and the time Dave moved out? Which was July of the following year. Lorraine moved in the springtime but Dave stayed until July with my oldest brother. So I checked old newspapers again for June 1980 - July 1981 and there was nothing. For some reason I truly believed it was 1980 when I ran. After finding nothing again, I went back home and lived my life.

I tried making the relationship with Ken work. Raising our kids, having cookouts, birthdays and holidays. The perfect American family, right? I loved living life, but many times late at night, I would cry my eyes out. Falling to my knees, punching my bed as the pain came out in words of, "Whys?" Through sobs of tears, hurting so bad, all I could do was grasp the breaths of reality and return to the secret, strength and silence I was very aware of carrying. I would brush myself off and life continued.

By my mid-twenties, I was finding out how easily I was insulted by the selective memories from the same people who claimed to love me; my two older brothers. I was always teased about being the one who hated my baby sister's father. I was always the one they assumed wanted to live with other people's families. I was always the one who claimed to be abused. I was always the one who needed proof and I took it like a grain of salt. Even as the subject always got quickly changed when I went into defense mode.

At a cookout held at my oldest brother's home, I was sitting outside on a lawn chair when he made a conversation about Pleasant Street. When I overheard the conversation, I immediately said, "I don't remember that." My oldest brother stated, "You must have been living with Sandi then." He then went back to the conversation he was having. I sat there a minute or two. "You think I wanted to live with other people's families?" I blurted out to my oldest brother, but he just shooed me away. I waited for my heart to finish crumbling right through me, through the chair I was sitting on and onto the pavement below me. "This is bullshit," I said as I gathered my kids and we left. So many times a simple conversation came up and it was like I was in a vocabulary prison when it came to Lorraine and my older brothers. Soon it was them telling me about the abuse I suffered. "It wasn't that bad," one said to me or the conversation would change once I came into the room. Sometimes we went weeks or months not speaking to each other, usually using Christmas to put away all our differences or in my case, all the hurt. Christmas was becoming a routine as we all met at Lorraine's for breakfast and did gifts with the kids. The house would get a bit chaotic with young kids running around the small apartment. But I was with my baby sister, both my older brothers, their kids and Lorraine. I was learning if I focused on the family, it made dealing with my mixed emotions a bit more bearable.

One Christmas as I helped clean up from everyone eating breakfast, I smiled but like nails on a chalkboard and shivers down my spine, there came another conversation of Pleasant Street. My baby sister blurted out a question she wanted to know, "So what happened on Pleasant Street?" she questioned everyone in the room. I froze, stared at her and then said to my two older siblings and Lorraine, "Ya, why don't you tell her what happened on Pleasant Street?" But no one said a word, they changed the subject as they talked about other things. And on life went, where I was belittled, ridiculed and mocked by my own siblings on something so serious. All they had to do was listen, support and love me, but they never did.

I started to feel insulted, disrespected, offended, jealous and unfair when it came my siblings. Why could they talk about their childhood? Why did they grow up together? Did they know there was a sibling between my baby sister and them? If they didn't, well it was me. Why did Lorraine choose them to love? I felt like such an outcast in my own family.

One day after work, a waitress questioned what my mothers nickname for me was when I was a kid. I quickly responded, "Assholes kid." I continued doing my clean up before punching out for the day when I noticed the waitress still standing where she was when she questioned me. She had tears in her eyes as she explained she was heartbroken to hear that of me. I was touched by her caring ways. People like that, I have always appreciated knowing. What I couldn't appreciate was every time Lorraine introduced me as her daughter. Being one to avoid a confrontation, I would just smile and say hello.

To add to my confused life as the year 1997 approached, Ken questioned our daughters, "Want mom and dad to get married?" "What, wait, huh?" I said, as all I heard were two young girls screaming in excitement over their parents getting married. I was dumbfounded over Ken asking them that. "What are you doing?" I questioned him. We were not too far away from splitting up. I guess we both stalled over the whole concept of raising the kids separated. The word marriage was not even mentioned to me. So I was completely shocked when he questioned our girls. The next day we drove to Pelham, New Hampshire where we set a date with the justice of the peace. We then drove to Service Merchandise and decided on the cheaper fifty dollar wedding band rings. Then we went home and waited the two weeks until we were to get married.

A few more disagreements, arguments and not one mention of getting married, I just assumed it was forgotten about, given up on and canceled. I also learned when you assume, it makes an ass out of you. My life was never normal, and it made the events of getting married seem a bit of normalcy. It was a Friday and like every Friday I got out of work and picked up my girls from Ma and Papa's house. I cooked fish all day at work, so I went home and showered. I put comfy sweats on and was sitting on the couch when Ken came home asking, "Why aren't you ready?"

"Ready for what?" I questioned him. That's when he reminded me that we were getting married. I owned work clothes, sweatpants and a pant suit I wore years earlier to a funeral. Wearing a dark colored maroon pant suit I last wore to a funeral, was what I also wore to get married. Ken informed me his brother was meeting us at the office where the justice of the peace was located. I was not breaking my daughter's hearts and telling them I wouldn't marry their father. I actually thought Ken was pulling a joke on me. He could be funny at times and pull a joke off like that. We showed up at the place with seconds to spare, walking in just in time for our six o'clock scheduled time slot to be married.

Ken's brother and his wife were there as our witness. There was no groom's family on one side and there was no bride's family on the other side. No one really knew we were getting married, heck I didn't think we were. We were immediately rushed to stand in position as the woman started her reading. She quickly turned to Ken as she questioned him if he had any vows. He answered her, "No I don't need them." I stared at him as the woman turned to me with the same question and I answered her, "No I do not." Within ten minutes it was over and we were already back in the car heading home. Just like that I was married without vows.

A few months later, Ken and I realized being married wasn't working as we tried to figure something out so we were fair to our daughters. We were still being friends towards each other and I guess we had grown accustomed to the life we had built together. Using the one reason that kept us together, we were still using it to stay together; our kids. But one day it all changed for me and it was Ken's shoulder I leaned on, his hand I held and his empathy I was very grateful for. It was a typical day, my girls were playing, I was reading the newspaper in the kitchen and Ken was watching sports in the living room. My daughters came running out of the playroom and through the kitchen. My whole head spun as I got dizzy and closed my eyes. That's when I saw it; an image, memory, flashback or whatever you label it, it was me on Fletcher Street. I realized in that moment, I was only six years old when my baby sister was born and I felt a mile long stretch of vomit come up as I ran to the bathroom. I threw up, fell to the floor and bawled my eyes out. Screaming an unexplainable pain out before Ken came into the bathroom, shut the door behind him and sat with me.

I puked more, cried more as I realized for the first time just how young I was when my abuse started. What was done to me on Fletcher Street and on Pleasant Street, as the reality of my childhood was so overwhelming. I cried a real lot that day. My daughters noticed and my oldest questioned why I was crying. I explained to her, "Mommy didn't have a good mommy." Ken snapped at me not to tell her that and insisted I say something else instead. He insisted my kids were too young to understand, but I also didn't want to lie to my kids. I decided that day, that I would always be open and honest to my kids in regards to my childhood.

One day, out of the blue, I received a phone call about baby pictures that were found. The baby in the photos were of me and I never saw a baby photo of myself, so I was excited to finally see one. When I lived with Lorraine on Fletcher Street she only had baby pictures of my two oldest brothers on the walls. On Pleasant Street she had those same pictures in the living room with my baby sister's photo added. But I never saw baby pictures of myself. When I questioned Lorraine about them when I was in my young twenties, she informed me, my father's side of the family had them and I really didn't know anyone on my dad's side of the family.

I immediately drove over to Lorraine's house where my baby sister had called me from. I wanted to get a look at those baby photos she insisted were of me. I was almost twenty-eight years old and I never saw a baby picture of myself and seeking my dad's side of the family for baby photos only got confusing for me as I didn't know who I could or should reach out to. I didn't want to explain my childhood to them, I didn't want them to know about my childhood and I didn't want to lie to them about it either.

My baby sister was right, she did find a bunch of baby photos, they were of a cute baby standing and sitting wearing a dress with diapers. The photos had a date on them in the bottom right corner. It was real easy to assume they were of me when I was a baby in 1969. But I knew immediately the baby in the photos was not me. Of course I had to prove the photos were not of me as I immediately told them I was born in December of 1969 and there was no way I was sitting or standing as a fifteen day old baby. Which was the oldest I was as of December 31, 1969. The date on the bottom right of those photos said 1959 not 1969. It was photos of an older sister of ours, whether it was Susan or Pauline, I still don't know.

I don't know if they assumed I would believe those photos were of me or if Lorraine lied to my baby sister about the date on them. But I was getting pissed off as I was just wasting my time and stirring up bad memories I didn't want to remember. My baby sister started to show me other pictures from school and birthdays Lorraine had from Pleasant Street and put in photo albums. "I don't want to see those," I yelled at her and Lorraine. As they continued to look for pictures of myself as a baby. "I want to see a photo before your father came into my childhood," I screamed as I was upset over the whole situation. "Why did you bother?" I yelled as I got ready to leave when Lorraine got all excited. "I found something," she yelled as she waved an envelope in the air, excited to hand it over to me. It was my first communion certificate. I remember that day, I thought to myself along with the day Dave took me shopping with money I received in gift cards from that day also. I questioned Lorraine, "Remember the doll I threw in your face?" Just as I was about to bawl my eyes out and remind her, I noticed something way out of whack with my first communion certificate; my first and last name were spelled wrong. Kathy Melon is what is written. "My name is Cathy Mellen," I yelled. You would think a mother would notice that even back in 1977. "Are you kidding me," I yelled as I so dumbfounded over what I was reading. "My fucking name is spelled wrong," I said over and over again.

Then I noticed she also had my 6th and 8th grade diplomas. "Why do you have these?" I questioned Lorraine. That's when I learned no one of authority knew I was tossed away by my family when I was a kid. The schools mailed my diplomas to Lorraine's because the school system didn't know I was living with other families at those times in my life. How unwanted, unworthy and unloved can one girl feel in her life? Sometimes the downfall of carrying empathy is the sadness you feel over a hurt that will never heal.

I took the school photos, my spelled wrong catholic school certificate and drove home to where that one phone call about baby pictures turned out to be another bout with depression I had to suffer alone because it was my pain to carry. What was the purpose of that phone call? I still didn't see any baby pictures of myself. I was reminded of Fletcher Street, I was reminded of Pleasant Street, I was reminded how I didn't matter and I was reminded I still didn't belong to a family I was trying so hard to belong too.

The lack of stability from my family life made me want for my daughter's the one thing I never had and I was giving them that; a family. Making my marriage work only seemed like the logical thing to do as we both continued to do right for our daughters. I was talking more on the telephone with my oldest brother. Though he claimed not to remember anything I lived through, he always claimed to understand my desire to not want our mother in my life. He seemed to understand when I spoke of the trick questions I faced on a daily basis and he would listen to me when I needed to vent. He would claim to understand my pain but he also claimed not to remember. So the subject would change as we would find other topics to talk about. Like we did one day when he told me of a woman he went out on a date with. He told me the name of the woman and as he continued telling me about her, I was still stuck on the name he said to me. I didn't hear anything he was saying as I shouted, "What's her name?" He then said her name again as I laughed at the fact my oldest brother on Lorraine's side of my family was dating my older sister on my dad's side of my family. My brother's first reaction was, "No fucking way." After he made a phone call to her, it wasn't long before he drove me over to see my sister who I hadn't seen since shortly after my dad died in 1983. Needless to say they didn't date again.

I was super excited to reconnect with her and it wasn't long before I was meeting my two older brothers from my dad's side. My dad also had a daughter who was adopted in Oklahoma where she was born. He told me about her shortly before he passed away. I forgot about it for years but remembered shortly after reconnecting with those three siblings. It was overwhelming at first as there were many questions I tried to dodge in regards to my childhood. I was hoping to reconnect with my stepmother and godfather also, but none of them had contact with them. One day I tested my own memory as I sat by the telephone and pretended I was calling my dad. I was trying to remember his phone number and I remembered it, so I called it. After a few rings a woman answered the phone and I hung up. I don't know why, it was an instant reaction. Before I could call the number back, it was calling me. The lady had caller ID. I answered the phone, "Hello." A woman's crackling voice said, "Catherine?" Then I could hear her tears through her words as she explained her caller ID identified my number with my name. I never changed my phone bill after I married so it was still under my maiden name.

After many minutes of talking on the phone with her, I was soon driving to the elderly complex she lived at in the acre section of Lowell, not far from where she lived when my dad was alive. We hugged, we cried, we talked and we hugged more. When out of the blue I noticed something resting on her shelf and I blurted the question, "How do you have a picture of my daughter?" I was confused and she was confused also. I got up and grabbed the small photo in a frame from the shelf it was resting on. With the clean spot around the dust, I knew the photo had been resting on the shelf for a long time. When I showed the photo to her with a very confused look on my face, she started laughing, "That's you," she responded. A good look at the photo and it was me, before that monster came into my childhood, before my birth mother gave me the childhood she gave me, before the horrible memories, before the horror and before the pain I lived my life remembering. I looked so happy in the photo and boy did my youngest daughter look like a mini me.

It wasn't long before I had my stepmother, godfather and their family at my house. I had my siblings from my dad's side and their family at my house also. Then a letter I received in the mail from a girl in Oklahoma looking for her father and other siblings, meant it wasn't long before I had my older sister from Oklahoma at my house. Then came the reunions with my dad's and stepmother's side of the family and other relatives from my dad's side of the family. The most popular question I was asked was, "How's your mother?" Despite that question, I was so super excited to be reconnected with my dad's side of the family. I got answers to many questions I always wondered about and they were always including me as if there was never any lost time between us. They were always inviting me places, always visiting me at my home and even planning weekend games of softball at any empty local baseball field in the city. I never got into details of my childhood with my siblings on my dad's side, but I also didn't lie to them as I would just say, "I didn't have a good childhood."

On the outside it looked like I had the perfect marriage and home life and on the outside I guess I did. But inside the house, as much as we tried to make our marriage work for the sake of our daughters, it never did. The more we tried to make it work, the more we held anger and resentment towards each other. Working, kids and a busy life made it easy to live under the same roof with a man you don't speak with. Days sometimes weeks would go by without us saying a word to each other. I soon got an invitation in the mail for the wedding of my oldest brother on my dad's side.

I was excited that I would be attending with Ken, but the animosity inside my house between him and I only grew. On the day of the wedding, I had a sitter for my kids, shopped for a nice outfit and was all ready to leave. When out of the blue I hear, "I cancelled the sitter," Ken informed me. "What, why?" I questioned him. We got into a huge argument before he decided to degrade me for believing in my, "New found family," he said as he belittled me about the family I was now a part of.

"Where were they when you needed them?" "Think they cared about you?" "They never looked for you before," he went on with more insulting words. I never made it to the wedding that day and I was so bummed as I was too busy crying and feeling ashamed of the life I lived. My brother was upset I didn't go to his wedding as I was upset with myself for not going. It was the start of me isolating myself from everyone. I wanted nothing to do with anyone except my kids, my home and my work. I wanted to be left alone; no siblings, no husband and no family except my daughter's. Ken and I finally decided it was time to go our separate ways. We just weren't sure how to go about it.

Kneeling over in massive stomach pains one day, I was seen by my doctor on an emergency visit. I was told with all the stress at home, I was experiencing stress pains. After a few routine tests, I was told I had an ulcer which is also caused by stress. I was given medication and a follow up appointment. The pains continued, only now I was puking anytime I brushed my teeth. I changed toothpaste but it continued for days as I awaited my next follow up appointment. By now Ken had nothing but pure hate for me as I hated him also and we both couldn't wait to end our living arrangements along with our friendship. We definitely did not have a healthy loving marriage and it wasn't healthy for our daughters to be subjected to our arguments, animosity and hate for each other.

Arriving at my follow up appointment, I informed the doctor of my pain still happening and the toothpaste puking. He thought it was strange as he questioned me when I last had sex. It had been only one time about three or four months earlier when I wanted to make it work with Ken. But I was getting normal menstrual periods every month so being pregnant was out of the question. My doctor decided to rub my belly with a microphone device as a noise came out of its speakers. I heard the noise it was making and I quickly whacked the device out of the doctors hands. I sat up and blurted, "What the fuck was that?" I knew what it was but I had to hear it from the doctor. "You're pregnant," he said to me. It was the heartbeat we were hearing and I was almost four months pregnant. Instead of getting divorced, we were having another baby.

I was in a marriage heading for divorce instead having a baby. Ken laughed when I told him I was pregnant. He questioned me, "Who's the father?" I laughed back as I answered him, "Umm you are." He was certain it had been at least three or four months since he and I last had sex. I told him he was correct as I told him, "I'm almost four months pregnant." He was as shocked as I was, but we dealt with it. Ken's mother almost fell off her chair when she found out I was pregnant. Acquaintances questioned me, "Is your husband the father?" Our friends wondered, "How?" As most knew we were heading for a divorce rather than a pregnancy. I worked part time, got fat and like my two pregnancies before, Ken did not come to one appointment with me.

I was so mad at myself for ruining the relationship with my dad's side of the family. I was so ashamed of them knowing what I lived through when I was younger. A part of me wanted them to know, I wanted them to know how Lorraine allowed me to live, I wanted them to know but I was too ashamed, embarrassed and humiliated to tell them.

Here today gone tomorrow, a motto I was all too familiar with. I was blaming myself for everything, my childhood, my marriage, my family was everything I deserved. The only good thing in my life was my children and knowing I'll see my loved ones in heaven again.

I had a rough last month of pregnancy as all four of my wisdom teeth decided they wanted out. With emergency medical technicians on each side of me, I had to have two removed just days before going into labor. I am an example that wisdom teeth do hurt more than labor. All I wanted was more ice for my teeth while I was in labor and pushing my baby out. My two remaining wisdom teeth hurt me to the core. But on July 7, 1999, I gave birth to a healthy, happy beautiful baby boy. My daughters were very happy to have a baby brother and Ken was proud to have a son. I had a saying since I was a teen, "Every little brother should be called Adam." The name Adam was a name I always loved. So it made sense that's what his name would be but Ken had no part of it. "I'm not naming him Adam," he yelled. Our arguing got so bad hospital officials threatened to keep my son in the hospital longer if we didn't agree and stop the arguing. For days the woman with the birth certificate would show up at my hospital room only to find Ken and I still arguing over what we should name our son. I then agreed to naming my son after his father. I had to wait a few weeks after giving birth before I could have my remaining wisdom teeth pulled, a very painful few weeks. I soon got to enjoy myself again, pain free of all toothaches.

After my son was born a part of me wanted the family I made for my children to work. I wanted my children to grow up with both parents under one roof. Everyday I thought about Jon and the promises we made back in 1987. I was always blessed, thankful and grateful to have had a friend like him, but I still needed his friendship and I missed him so very much. Then I would remind myself, 'How lucky I am to share an amazing bond as I do with Jon.' In life or heaven, he was, he is and he always will be my guardian angel.

I slowly headed back down the road of depression as I realized my childhood was a secret, my bond with Jon was a secret and all the writing I had done in my life were all stuffed in a closed nightstand drawer being a secret. Though Ken knew I missed Jon, we didn't talk much about Jon anymore, we really didn't talk much about anything anymore.

That was when I opened the drawer back up, the one that held my poetry, my journals and my life. I started writing again sometimes on a daily basis. In my journals or in a poem, either way the writing I was doing was also reminding me of the strength I've carried my whole life. It reminded me of what I deserved, that I mattered and it reminded me to be happy again.

To a few I was becoming a bitch, to others I was dwelling in the past and to everyone else in my everyday life; I was being strong, independent, courageous and hell bent on being acknowledged, heard, respected and supported. Even if it meant losing everything I worked so hard for; my family. After all the fights and arguments with Ken, after all the lies and lack of acknowledgement from Lorraine, after all the belittling and lack of support from my siblings, I finally gave in and fought back for my right to matter. We were all adults now and I deserved their support. I was emotionally torn when it came to ruining my children's family as the first birthday for my son was also the last birthday any of my children would have with both parents present.

Maybe it was me being back to writing again as I would write and feel this empowering voice inside telling myself, 'You deserve their support, you deserve to be happy, you deserve to be acknowledged.' I would cry and question myself for days, 'How could they?' 'Why would they?' The more I remembered the more I wrote. The more I wrote the more I remembered. Every night I went to bed with more questions and every morning I woke up a step closer to knowing my worth. Knowing I mattered even if I didn't matter to the ones I loved. Knowing I am deserving of being loved, of being supported and of being acknowledged. Everyday I was getting a step closer to being a survivor and not a victim.

I didn't just wake up one day and decide I wanted answers, respect, support, acknowledgement and accountability. It ate at me for weeks, months and years. After crossing all my T's and dotting all my I's, I needed one more trip down to my local library, I just had to be sure. I always remembered the horrible abuse I endured from my abuser Dave. A part of me wanted evidence that I wasn't the only one. I wanted evidence that there were others. I just needed the proof. So I attempted one more time in an effort to find some closure for myself. Another search through old newspapers from June of 1980 - July 1981 left me leaving the library with this huge clot of vomit resting in a hollow hole in my stomach. 'There were no other girls and I was his only victim,' I told myself. A part of me was horrified, mad, angry, jealous and still wanting to seek that support from my family. I attempted with my oldest brother first, we were talking over the phone when I questioned him about my childhood on Fletcher Street and Pleasant Street. But like my questions throughout the years before he informed me, "I don't remember that." I attempted with my other older brother when he came home from the military. I asked him to read my journal, the first journal I wrote in.

I offered him the opportunity to read it so he could remember and maybe acknowledge, support and be there for me. Just a day or two later, he handed me back my journal informing me, "I don't want to read that." I was so hurt as I stood there with my journal in my hand. "Ok then," was all I could say. I quickly turned my need for answers, respect, acknowledgement, support and accountability onto Ken. I wasn't getting it from the people I wanted it from, which were my older brothers and Lorraine. I wasn't getting it by standing up for myself, I wasn't getting it by staying in silence, I wasn't getting it by being ashamed, embarrassed or humiliated if I spoke up. So I got it from the one I knew had two choices to do, either give me the answers, respect, acknowledgement, support and accountability I deserved or divorce him.

By the summer of 2000 friends stopped coming to the house or inviting us to their homes because the animosity Ken and I had towards each other shined brighter than a diamond ring. We had been living the same cycle for ten years that some just assumed it was how we should stay. It didn't make sense to me anymore. We teach our kids to be happy, respectful, loving and caring. No way I was going to lie to my children about their parents' friendship. Soon it was the start of the school year for my daughters along with the animosity in the home growing more each day. I quickly made it a living hell for my soon to be ex-husband. I would put check marks on the calendar marking every fight, argument and talk-less days we shared. Some months every day on the calendar had a check mark on it. I would chase him out every room he walked out of while we argued. His animosity towards me only got worse as the months went on. He would puff his chest out towards me, pushing me into walls and punching holes in the wall beside where my head rested. He insisted I couldn't make it on my own, he insisted I couldn't support my kids and he insisted I could never get rid of him. Only this time we were married and one thing I knew for certain, I could now get rid of him legally.

Just a few months after my son's first birthday I was ending my relationship with my children's father for the same reason I always stayed, for my children. As we figured out a way to move and separate ourselves from each other, there was also Christmas coming up soon. As parents we decided to wait until after the holidays to disrupt our daughters and son with the break up of their parents marriage. I stayed upstairs in the home and Ken moved into the cellar, a routine that would explode into a nasty fight. We can pack as many suitcases as we want, but nothing prepares us for the trip life takes us on. All we can do is hold tight and take it one day at a time.

In November I was out Christmas shopping at Ames department store on Bridge Street when I was unexpectedly slapped with reality. It was the first time since I last saw Jon that I actually ran into someone we, he and I knew. In all these years I had not run into anyone who knew about Jon's death, but there was his sister shopping in the same store as me.

As the new year started so didn't my new life. I got my niece to babysit and made plans with my neighbors to go out dancing at a local bar. Ken decided last minute to came out with us and within minutes of leaving our home, we were arguing. I did my best to avoid him by dancing and having a good time. But by the time we got home that night, our niece, our kids and the neighbors all heard us arguing. We were loud, the loudest we had ever been. Then he said something that shut me right up. He made a comment about me always talking about the dead guys I had sex with. I knew he was referring to Jon but what did he mean by guys? "What guys?" I questioned him. He answered me, "Your other dead friend Mark." I was so boiled red, steam coming out of my ears screaming mad. "Ten years we've been together and you think I fucked Mark?" I screamed at him. "Mark was my brother," I continued to scream. I couldn't believe I managed to have three beautiful children with a man who never listened to a word I said. I told him so many times how his animosity, puffed out chest and evil looks were causing me to have nightmares, memories, flashbacks and feeling unsafe in my own home. The loud noise in the house finally went quiet around three in the morning.

Kids woke me up when they awoke which was only a few hours of sleep for me. I called my oldest brother to let him know that I may need some help as Ken was moving out. I was on the phone with him telling him of the fight a few hours earlier when a mirror hanging on my dining room wall showed an image of a man hiding behind my curio cabinet. I screamed bloody murder, dropped the phone then realized it was Ken. He scared the shit out of me but I was glad it wasn't a stranger. I picked the phone up off the kitchen floor and asked my brother to call the police. I quickly hung up the phone as Ken and I argued. He argued I had to leave the home, I argued he was the one to leave.

I called the police to question how long until they arrived and they notified me no call was made to them because my brother didn't call. Within minutes after the phone call I made, police were at my Fulton Street home and within minutes of police showing up, my other older brother came upstairs from the cellar. I was a bit confused, so I questioned him, "How long have you been down in the cellar?" He told me, "Since this morning." I was so mad, I shoved him and yelled at him, "Be a fucking brother." But he left, Ken left, the police left and I started my first day as a single mom.

I was upset my oldest brother didn't call the police for me and upset my other older brother was in my cellar that whole time and did nothing. He claimed it was between a husband and wife. It obviously didn't matter that the wife was his sister. I was being supported by my soon to be ex mother/father in-law whose support, love and friendship never changed despite their bingo partner being my birth mother or their son being my soon to be ex-husband. I had my neighbors whose support, love and friendship showed me friends are the family we do create for ourselves. Everyone else figured, "You put up with it this long, so why change?" But people who saw us everyday like my neighbors and ex in-laws, they were proud of me. My coworkers didn't even know when I got married, they only knew I was getting a divorce because the struggle was weighing on me.

I wasn't expecting all the animosity and fighting from Ken. I wasn't expecting the 'poof' not one sibling is in my life again and I wasn't expecting Lorraine to be telling people I was a drug user. Ken was telling people I left him for my dead friend Jon and my siblings were telling him I was delusional about my childhood. I began doubting myself, afraid of the future as a single mother and wanting to grab my two older brothers by their shoulders and scream, "What the fuck." After getting home from work one day, I was making supper, my girls were fighting with each other and my son was banging every pot and pan out of the kitchen cabinets. I just closed my eyes and said, "Please tell me I'm doing right." I looked out my kitchen window and said, "That's for you up there." Guess it was a prayer I was sending. Moments later all the banging my son was making and all the screaming my girls were making went silent as all I heard coming from my radio resting on top of my refrigerator was Lee Ann Womack singing, 'I hope you dance.' I got goosebumps as I heard the lyrics, 'If you get the choice to sit it out or dance.' I looked out my window and said, "Well played." Coincidence, ironic or a message from heaven? I'll take the message loud and clear.

I was overwhelmed with all I was going through, hearing that song on the radio at first made me smile. But it wasn't long before I was mad at Jon for making me miss him all these years alone. I was twenty-three years old when I learned he died and I visited him every year, but I was thirty-one years old when I finally went to his gravesite. He was laid to rest not far from that stone wall I would sometimes sit on and write in my journals. He was always close by and so I was mad at him again. I'd leave a whole dozen of roses at his grave at a time, it was my way of pissing him off. I went over to my dad's cemetery which is less than a five minute ride away from where Jon is. I figured I might as well see where my dad's gravesite was. I walked into the office at St Patrick's cemetery and I questioned the clerk about my dad's whereabouts. The man looked up my dad's name and responded to me, "There's this hill," and I cut him off. I said, "Thank you I know where it is." St. Patrick›s cemetery is a very flat level area with one hill and a huge tree where since I was a teen, I would sit under and write in my journal or do poetry. My dad was always close by also. Coincidence, ironic or a message from heaven? I'll take the message loud and clear. I then went to St Michael's church just up the street from my Fulton Street home, where on numerous occasions I spoke with Father Mario. He was very empathetic, sincere and interested in my journal. Which I left in his care for a few days. Father Mario and I talked more and I then knew I owed Jon an apology for being mad at him. I understand he was no longer here on earth, but I could still be mad at him and owe him an apology whether he was alive or not. Besides only in my life can the events that followed make actual sense.

On my next day off from work, my girls were in school and my in-laws watched my son while I took a trip to the cemetery. As I approached Jon's gravesite there was a note in a plastic bag taped with duct tape to his monument. It was a letter to me from Jon's family, I remember looking up to the sky and telling Jon, "I'm going to kick your ass when I see you again." It's weird how no matter how much I miss him, think of things he did or said, remember him or cry over him, I always knew I would see him again. Jon's sister put her phone number in the letter, I went home that night and called her. We talked and talked until making plans for me to visit the following weekend.

Ironically there was one bright star in the sky the night I drove over to Jon's sister's house. I also took my diary with me. I made a promise to Jon and I figured the best way was for her to read my diary. I found out Jon's motorcycle accident happened on October 15th and he passed two days later on the 17th, how I never knew, I don't know. I wasn't prepared for the poem she showed me that Jon had written before he died. The poem almost knocked me off my feet, but it was also one of the best experiences I have ever experienced in my life. I realized my journals were about me and though I wrote of Jon and myself, I just never went into full detail about Jon and the secret he shared with me. That night I went home and started one, it took a few months to complete and when I was done, I showed it to Father Mario who gave me his blessing.

I instantly hit it off with Jon's sister, her kids, his mom, dad, sister, brother and more. We were having sleepovers, drinking nights, cookouts, crying, hugging, laughing and always hanging out. I made so many fun memories with them. As the months were going by, the animosity and fights started to slow down with Ken and I as we adjusted to our new lives without each other. The phone calls to or from my oldest brother were few to none and because I pushed Lorraine out of my life, I didn't see my other older brother or baby sister anymore either. My kids were seeing them though, when they were visiting with their dad, he would take them over my siblings house. I was a bit upset about it but their excuse was that Ken was their friend also. Which is fine, I get it but how much am I supposed to let by in my life? My childhood, my birth mother, my voice, my dignity, my dad and now my family's lack of support as I went through my divorce? *You never think you can make it through something until you find yourself making it through.*

I wasn't letting the rumors said about me bother me. I had enough secrets, lies and rumors from my own family about my childhood. I didn't care about rumors from Ken. Before I realized how I was going to support three kids, almost five months had already gone by. Kids ate everyday, cable was paid, rent was paid by my ex as his brother and wife were the landlords. The kids were not affected financially from our split. In fact they were more spoiled because of it. I was proud of myself and looking forward to a fun summer with the girls having no school. I stayed working my thirty hours a week and figured I'd stay that way until after summer. Then I'd request extra hours or get a part time job for Christmas shopping. But there it was, that thing called life and its unexpected paths.

As if my life couldn't get anymore complicated. It started out as a normal day at work. My boss of seven years came out back where I was cooking to inform me of his daughter and husband coming to join the team. I worked side by side with both for breakfast, ordering and scheduling the cooks hours. They had no complaints about me. They loved my cleanliness, my friendliness and they loved my eagerness to help. They loved my rotation, my cooking and always being on time. I started on a Monday with them and by Thursday I left work early because it was a slower day. I was able to run home for a quick shower before getting my kids at their grandparents and school. I got out of the shower and walked around my kitchen in my towel. I sat at the breakfast nook and smoked a cigarette, I went upstairs to my room and I got dressed, I walked back downstairs and cleaned up from the morning mess. Then I heard the front door open and in came three strangers I had never seen before. "Who the fuck are you?" I yelled as I grabbed my phone to call the police. "Who are you?" an older woman said in a startling way. "We just purchased this house today," she continued. "What, wait, huh?" I said in total shock.

They gave me three weeks to move out as they had plans for the home. There was nothing I could do. My ex brother/sister in-law sold the house without telling me. Ken and his brother didn't return any of my calls and it was only the beginning of a rough start to a simple divorce.

The next day, I worked my normal Friday hours. At the end of my shift, my boss's son in-law came in the back door and handed me my paycheck. "There's two checks there, one with three weeks paid vacation, sick days and a severance pay," he said to me. I laughed at what he said assuming he was being funny. I opened the envelope with my paycheck and there were two checks, but I still thought it was a joke. I went to punch my time card out but he quickly grabbed it from my hand. "You don't need that, you've been fired," he said to me. I immediately demanded a reason causing other employees to get upset over me being fired. Before I knew it, my Irish came out and I called him and his wife every swear word my vocabulary knew. I couldn't believe I got blindsided on my home and I got blindsided from my job. Well at least I had plenty of time to pack. I took a week off from looking for a new job as my children and I worked on packing our home into boxes so we could put it in a storage facility. I went out job hunting my second week out of work. I went through the help wanted section of the newspaper, found a few places hiring and filled out applications. Two days later I had my first interview. The only thing it was cooking nights, something I didn't want but the pay was good. As I was driving home from the interview, I drove by a diner with a cooks wanted sign in their window, so I stopped in. They knew my last name because they knew my dad when he was younger. I was also hired on the spot.

I wasn't starting for another week as I had a lot of moving to do along with figuring out where my children and I were going to live. Needless to say I did not take the night cooking job and it would end up being a good thing. How many people can say they love their job? I am one of the few, but yes I would end up loving my job at the Four Sister's Owl Diner and they loved me. But first thing first, I had to find a place to live.

The most conversation I had with Ken was over the phone and only pertaining to our children. Even that came with animosity, fighting and hanging up on each other. He nor his brother would talk to me about the house being sold. My daughters were upset about moving but they were troopers as we packed our belongings into boxes. My son just wanted a box to play with, he packed the kitchen pot and pans about twenty times a day as he kept himself busy. I divided up our belongings pretty fairly and Ken scheduled a day to pick them up.

Ken had a computer system he left at the house for our daughters and was taking it back. He called to explain what wires and phone lines to unplug from where. After writing it all down, I hung up the phone and attempted to start unplugging everything when I thought, 'The world wide web.' The computer was under a year old and a good reason why Ken wanted it back. I then sat at the computer and did a search for missing or murdered girls in Lowell, Mass from June 1980-July 1981. Deep down I knew there were others before me because my abuser told me and a part of me knew I was not his last victim either. *We search for validation until we turn the belittling onto ourselves, just to make it easier for everyone else.* Gosh, did it take forever for a computer in 2001 to get going. The phone line, dial up and the welcome to AOL bell ring. A part of me was relieved when there were no search matches on the screen, but a part of me was bummed because I was once again on my own. I ran into my bathroom so my kids didn't see me bawl my eyes out. I thought about how my life was no different from when I was a kid, I had no family, no home and no job. So I did what I always did since 1981, I looked at the positive in things. I had three kids, a bunch of friends, money in the bank and I just rented a storage unit for all my stuff.

As usual life went on, as did another dose of being an outcast, unwanted and unworthy when it came to my family. My oldest brother owned his home up the road from me. So I called to question him if my kid's and I could stay there with him until I got a place. "For a few weeks tops," I assured him. I mean family helps family out, right? My oldest brother told me he had my other older brother, baby sister, her kids and Lorraine living there already and there was no room for me or my kids. I hung the phone up and cried. Not because I couldn't stay there, not because I was separating from my kid's father and not because I had no clue what I was going to do, I cried because it hurt that he didn't care. There I was thirty-one years old with no support from family again.

It took me, my kids and our friends a whole week of everyday moving boxes and furniture to my rented storage unit facility. I moved into my friend's computer room where my three kids and I squeezed into. Their father moved into a three bedroom with a roommate and took me to court for full custody. I was served the day after I moved out and I started my new job a few days afterwards. Because I was/still am a good mom, I did not lose custody of my kids. But because I lived in such small quarters, I dropped the kids off at Ken's every night for bedtime. I got them after school, after work or at eight the next morning when there was no school. Ken and I would go back to court once a month until I got my own place. I was so busy with my kids, the move, the new job, the divorce, the lack of family and staying strong. It was a few weeks before it all hit me emotionally. I missed putting my kids to bed, I wanted my siblings in my life and I wanted to be a sibling.

It wasn't easy saving money as I had a storage unit to pay, I had room and board, food and the regular weekly necessities. At one of the court dates, the judge let me know a theory of his, "You carry a baby for nine months, remember it takes nine months to start over in life," he said to me Then he postponed court for another month. I was standing up for myself and the result was no different than when I ran to my friends house back when I was a kid. That result was having no support from family. I was making the best of my situation because that is what I always did.

Even though the phone calls to my siblings were no longer a thing, I still called to inform them of my children's birthday parties. My daughters are in May and August while my son is in July. I assumed no one came to my daughter's party in May because we were still in the process of moving and I was fighting a lot with Ken. When I called my siblings about my son's birthday party, we talked and I hung up the phone believing I'd see them at my son's party. Not one sibling came to my son's second birthday party. It was like I was on Butler Avenue standing on the sidewalk wondering why my family was living behind the closed door I was looking at. Only this time I was living in my friends computer room wondering why my siblings weren't there for me as I went through my divorce, the moving and now my son's birthday party. I was hurt, but not as hurt as I was about to be.

I was actually embarrassed and hurt but at the same time I was insulted and ashamed to speak about why my siblings weren't in my life. How do I explain it? "Well it started on Fletcher Street," "Well it started on Pleasant Street," "Well it started in their present day lack of support." I had courage to say I mattered, but I had shame to shut me up. It seemed for every hurt I buried, I was hit with another backstab from my own family. It was my new normal day, I got out of work, picked my kids up, then I went home to my friends house where we would hang out until driving them to their dad's for bedtime. My friends couldn't believe the knives in my back as it seemed they just kept piling on. My daughter's were figuring out their dad's roommate was more than a roommate. They also informed me of their brother's birthday party their dad had for him, then they told me who attended. They didn't go to the birthday party I had for my son, but my siblings went to the birthday party Ken had for my son. It was an emotional ouch that hurt, but my life was so busy it was easier to push the hurt away. It was easier to hold the tears until I was alone. It was easier to move on, get over it, stop dwelling and not bring it up when they weren't in my life. *But everything buried in the world of PTSD and C-PTSD always comes back to the surface. No matter how many times we bury it.*

I continued doing what I needed to do so I could get myself into my own apartment again. Some days I laughed and some days I cried. I was mad at my siblings but I didn't give them the satisfaction of knowing I was hurt. My friends took me to a local baseball field in the early morning hours and had me sit at the pitchers mound. Then they told me to scream all the hurt and knives in my back out of me and that is what I did. I screamed my lungs out, I cried and my friends never left my side.

They didn't tell me to stop dwelling, they didn't tease me for bringing it up and they didn't blame me for not getting over it. They didn't judge me, ridicule me, insult me or shame me. They told me I mattered and they were right, I did matter and I wanted my siblings in my life. So I went to the source; my birth mother. I called her a few days later and I explained I wanted to make it better with my siblings, with her and with myself. I told her all we had to do was talk to my older brothers and baby sister about my childhood. I wanted Lorraine to tell them all the truth but she hung the phone up on me. My mistake for thinking she would agree.

I was beginning to emotionally torment myself when it came to belonging to a family that I never mattered to. I kept telling myself just one more time at a try to belong, all the while belittling my own feelings, my own hurt and the fact that I also mattered. Standing up for myself was something I thought had to be done one time. You speak your mind, your hurt, your pain and your peace, then you move on. It was not that easy. Just when I thought I was handling things ok, I was also back in the routine of meeting new people, new trick questions and more explaining to do. The friends I was living with had family, her husband had family, I had new coworkers, a new boss and new customers at work, all with the same questions, "What part of Lowell you from? What school did you go to? How many siblings do you have? Remember when you were a kid?"

Some days I did all I could to hold the tears in until I left my job. I loved working there and the people were great, I was just living a long life already lived I guess. I felt emotionally drained, at the time I didn't know I suffered from depression, C-PTSD or PTSD. I just thought I had a bad childhood, bad memories and bad luck. Other days I'd get happy meals at McDonald's for my kids and we would go hang out at the storage unit. The kids would climb over the packed unit filled with boxes and containers of what was once our home. Soon my girls were back in school and my only thought was to get my own place by Christmas. As weeks went bye, I started to realize it may not be until after the new year. Just as I was about to go on a poor pity me train ride, always doubting myself, doubting my ability to care, doubting my strength, my courage, it all changed in one day.

September 11, 2001 started out as any new normal day. I was now working alone in the back kitchen of the diner, making the lunch menu and daily lunch specials. The radio was on as it was everyday I worked and I heard the urgent news update about a plane crash, but I wasn't sure I heard it correct. My boss came into the kitchen and I told him what I thought I heard. He also assumed I heard it wrong until another urgent news update announced a second plane had crashed. The busy hopping diner suddenly became a ghost town. Everyone was glued to the radio, television and internet. All wanting updates, how to help, how to donate and all asking why? I don't think the world had a dry eye when the reality of September 11th and all the lives lost became clear.

A Strangers Hero

An act of terrorism, a foreign man's will.
What he did the day the world stood still.
No act of evil could ever compare.
As we heard the news terrorism was here.
The planes had crashed so many lives lost.
Their souls not forgotten no matter the cost.
Strangers came together and friendships were bound.
Assuring families, loved ones would be found.
As days went by, it just got worse.
But hearts of strangers was our only source.
Believing in faith and through God's will.
We all came together the day the world stood still.
September 11, 2001 Forever in our hearts.

As the holidays approached, I knew I wouldn't have an apartment in time for Christmas. One day in work I recognized the family who now owned the home I lived in on Fulton Avenue and I informed my boss. He knew them and told me they buy homes, remodel them and sell them for more than what they paid. I was so mad, they gave me a few weeks to move from that home because they lost their home due to a fire. That's what they told me and I believed them because they gave me no reason to doubt it. My boss was upset and within minutes the lady who I met unexpectedly on Fulton Avenue was in the back kitchen of the diner asking me how to spell my name as she wrote me a check for falsely making me move out of the home. It was enough for a down deposit on an apartment and I immediately started looking for one. Christmas season is a tough time to look for an apartment so rather than stress over it, my kids and I just made the best of it. I had my kids overnight on Christmas eve and for Christmas morning. I spent the rest of the day with my friends and their kids.

I knew my siblings were at my birth mothers, because they were there every Christmas, so I called to wish everyone a Merry Christmas. It was loud there and I made the comment, "It's loud there." Lorraine then told me it was because my kids just showed up and the other kids got excited. 'Wait, what, huh,' I said to myself. Then I questioned, "My kids just showed up?" I yelled into the phone as I was dumbfounded once again. Why were my siblings interacting with Ken and not with me? Another day and another unanswered question.

I didn't think I had any more room for another knife in my back. I actually thought they were stacking up in piles. I went over it again in my head, I thought about it for weeks and I couldn't make sense of my siblings love for me. I respected the fact my older siblings were probably too young to remember what happened to me on Fletcher and Pleasant Street. Something I would remind myself on a daily basis as it was the only sense I could make of it. I did respect my siblings and I respected my siblings didn't want to talk about my childhood. I respected it didn't affect them at all, but I did not respect that as adults those siblings were once again not there for me.

My kids and I made the best of our time while I lived at my friends home. But Ken showing up at my family's house with my kids was something I couldn't wrap my head around. Why was he at my family's home and I wasn't? Luckily with school vacation and working extra hours at the diner, I stayed busy for the week as Christmas came late for me. The day after Christmas I got a phone call from a rental agent who had a four bedroom duplex available and he thought of me. We made arrangements to meet at the property a few days later on Friday. I was happy at first but the reality of paying a monthly rent on my own scared me. It was still so easy to push my pain, hurt and tears to the side as the reality of September 11th was still a fresh wound over three months later. In a world so full of hate, it's sad it takes a tragedy for us to unite.

I was spending my free time reading about the victims, the survivor's, the heroes and the families left behind. I'd cry for them and they were total strangers to me, but I didn't have a bit of empathy for my own self. Two days after Christmas I got a phone call at work to report to a housing agency for an appointment. I left work for about an hour as my boss eagerly told me go. I went back to work with a housing voucher to help single parents with rent. That was a lot of stress taken off my shoulders. The next day after work, I went to check out the four bedroom apartment and meet the homeowner. I left the apartment and drove straight to my bank, I got the security payment for the apartment and I signed the lease. I got the apartment even though I had to wait until late January to move in. I was excited, my kids were excited, along with my friends being excited for me and my kids.

I was ending the year the same way I started the year, with positive new beginnings. As tough as my life has always been, my dad once told me, "No matter what you do, always make an honest paycheck." That's what I was doing and I couldn't wait to be in a home with my kids again.

2002 would bring on a valentine's day divorce and the start of an emotional, mental train wreck over my absent relationship with my siblings. One that would continue for another twelve years.

Moving Forward on a Path Called Life

No snow, cold or slow dragging day could ruin the fact I was about to move into my own apartment with my kids. The landlord gave me the keys early so I could go in and clean the place. My friends and I slowly moved boxes from the storage unit across the city to my new apartment. I didn't keep contact with my siblings while I lived with my friends for seven months and moving into my apartment was no different. By the end of January, I was fully moved into my new apartment at 103 Powell Street located in the highland section of Lowell.

My kids and I were so busy unpacking boxes, setting up bedrooms, hanging pictures, rearranging the living room ten different ways until we decided on the first selection. We were meeting our new neighbors and having friends over everyday. Whether they were my friends, my kids friends or both. I was working early morning hours, driving my kids to their Ma and Papa's before six in the morning, then heading off to work from there. It was overwhelming to say the least, I went through mixed emotions as at first I was super proud of myself then I was super petrified of failing. That's when I would take a deep breath, close my eyes and remind myself, 'I got this.' I knew I could do it because I survived my childhood. Suddenly any ounce of strength I talked myself into having was quickly diminished into pounds of sadness, why's and a pain so intense the tears fell like buckets. I spent my life trying to forget what I was using as my strength; my childhood. As much as I tried to understand my life, the more confusing it made me. It kept making me remember how much my two older siblings did know of my childhood and of Lorraine being so cruel, but I didn't want to remember that. So I kept myself busy with my kids, friends and work.

I started the first week of February 2002 with a postponed court date for my divorce. We all showed up but the case before us would take longer than expected and the judge postponed my date for the following week. I was a bit aggravated because I lost a days pay and it was an hour drive to the Concord, Massachusetts courthouse where my divorce case was being heard. There was nothing I could do or say about it, I'd have to inform my boss of another day I'd need out of work. I just didn't realize how much of a laugh I would get out of it when I realized what the date was postponed to. I laughed so hard I actually had happy tears falling from my face. The judge postponed my date to be divorced to February 14th. I still get a chuckle that I was divorced on Valentine's day. Makes being married without vows more appropriate.

We had a new routine, every Saturday night my kids went to their dad's and I went out for some karaoke with my friends. Though the lack of communication went on for years between Ken and I, but it was not the case when it came to the three siblings I wanted in my life. *It's the longing which gets us, the longing to belong, the longing for family, the longing for answers, the longing for love, support, and the tight bond a family holds.*

I was constantly a busy person working on my feet all day at work, doing something with my kids or visiting friends. My favorite time of the day was when my kids were in bed while I sat on my enclosed porch drinking a hot cup of tea. I began to keep track of how it didn't matter what I did or didn't do, everyday and yes every single day there was always a reminder of the horror I once lived through. I don't ever remember my life without it being broken. I thought there was something wrong with me, I wanted to forget my childhood but I wasn't. Everyday I was thankful for all I had even though I really didn't have much, I had all I needed. I was content, happy and stable. But I also wondered if I had a normal childhood would I want gold? Diamonds? Another husband? Because I didn't want any of that. I was never allowing another person an opportunity to make me feel uncomfortable in my own home again. I had walls stacked so high and the word trust was impossible when so many knives still twirled in my back. I stood my ground, I spoke my truth to the degree where I didn't insult anyone. And my life went on as I argued with myself over and over again because I couldn't understand why I had such a distant relationship with my siblings.

By late spring, I was back to communicating with my oldest sibling over the phone. It started with a long time no speak or a happy birthday call, either way by the time my daughter's birthday came in May, all three of my siblings showed up to her pizza birthday party. As they did for my son's and other daughters birthdays over the summer. Putting my feelings, my self worth and dignity to the side as I also invited Lorraine. I didn't rekindle or have a relationship with her but I tried my hardest to put any resentment I had to the side. I was still feeling what I always did when I was around my siblings; the odd man out. As much as I loved seeing my siblings by the end of the day, I always wished I had a better relationship with them. Between them, life and society, it was hard some days to be strong. Some days I deserved a gold medal for the tears I held in when they should have poured out. Some nights I cried so hard as I sat on my porch. I loved my life but I hated my family life. I wanted them to accept me as a survivor, not the victim they assumed. But how can they accept me as a survivor if they can't remember, talk about or believe a life I lived?

Soon the holidays were upon us and I got lucky on that one in the divorce. I had my kids every Christmas eve and morning until noon time, then they went with their dad and his family. Ken no longer visited my siblings on Christmas since our divorce was final. I got a phone call and was invited to my baby sister's on the first Christmas in my apartment. My kids were already at their dad's and I questioned if Lorraine was going to be there. I was informed she was and I declined the invite.

I didn't want to subject myself to being reminded of the outcast I was. I made the best of each Christmas day though. One year I went to Mohegan Sun for a day of gambling in Connecticut. I went to the movies one Christmas. I went to do Karaoke another. Got real drunk on free drinks one Christmas, stayed home and watched movies on another and every year I was at work for six in the morning on December 26th. Those Christmas day invites and phone calls soon stopped.

I was known as the sister who hated her baby sister's father, who couldn't stand her own mother and I was the sister who had issues. But to my friends I was myself; a happy, fun to be around person. At work one day, a waitress came into the kitchen and informed me, "You have visitors." I looked at her weird, "Really who?" I questioned her thinking maybe it was one of my ex in-laws. She responded, "He says he's your brother." After a month of feeling sorry for myself and picking my heavy heart off the ground, I was having a great day at work when suddenly my day was like nails down a chalkboard. Having a sibling say they were at the diner I worked at was not a common thing for me. I didn't know who it was, it could have been a brother from my dad's side, my birth mothers side or one I hadn't met yet. I walked out to the dining area and saw my older brother with company and I was mad. I was insulted and I couldn't help how I felt. It was an instant reaction as I made a nasty comment about what a sibling is. His company was very insulted and immediately sat up to leave. I realized I insulted the company he was with, I was about to make a waitress lose a tip, I was about to make customers walk out and I instantly went into apologetic mode. I apologized for being rude, for insulting them and I apologized for feeling hurt.

I was always apologizing for being me. I was so used to no one wanting to hear me that by the time I realized I deserved to be heard, I was in my mid thirties and always apologizing for wanting to be heard. I now knew who I could trust and those were the people I stuck with. When I was with my friends, it was always about making fun memories. Many knew my family due to being in my life or passing through, but most never knew the whole story; where it began for me on Fletcher Street. So many times a simple question like, "What did you get your mother for mother's day?" Would trigger days of sadness for me.

Though we didn't celebrate Christmas together, my siblings were now showing up to my kids birthday parties every summer. I went to their kids birthday parties and sometimes my oldest brother had cookouts I would attend with my kids. What I didn't understand was he always understood I didn't want our mother in my life, but he never cared why. I couldn't understand why I couldn't let go of the resentment I felt.

Maybe I was jealous? Why was she an ok mother to them but not me? Why did I have a wall so high when it came to them? As much as I wanted them in my life, I felt I could be myself when they weren't around as life continued to throw me hints of that very fact.

There was a 40th birthday party for my oldest brother held at my baby sister's home. I knew I would be seeing Lorraine but I sucked it up. I also knew there would be other people there so I could easily avoid her which is what I did. My kids played with their cousins and I chatted with the few people I did know at the party. It was held inside and when it came time to open his gifts, we all gathered into one large open room. I leaned against a curio cabinet that rested against the wall. I wanted to make sure I was resting on the wooden part of the curio cabinet and not the glass part, so I turned around to take a look. There, inside the curio cabinet was a photo of my baby sister's father, the monster who terrorized my childhood. I instantly moved away from the curio cabinet. I went to the bathroom where I panicked, I was breathing heavy and I had a bucket of tears about to pour out. I couldn't do it, I got my oldest daughter and told her I wanted to leave. She could tell I was about to cry and without hesitation she gathered her brother and sister. I didn't want to make a scene, so I left without saying bye.

My older brother came outside and questioned why I was leaving. It was too late, I was in tears. I told him about the photo I saw in the curio cabinet being displayed as if he was a good man. I yelled at him, "Does she even know what her father did to me?" But it didn't matter, I got in my car and drove home to the place where I felt safe, loved and wanted. There was nothing I could do, I was stuck and all I could do was deal with it alone. It's hard to imagine there are others out there with the same hurting pain as the one you carry. There is this hole in my heart, I had since I was a kid. Some days I felt it more than others and even as an adult, there was not a thing I could do about it, except to deal with it. Seeing the photo of my baby sister's father was not emotionally or mentally good for me. I sunk into a depression as the days and weeks went on. I tried ignoring it for days, but it built up until one night I was sitting on my porch with my hot cup of tea when it hit me. "Don't they care?" I blurted out so I could hear myself say what I kept questioning myself. "Don't they care what I lived through?" "Do they even care at all?" I continued to question myself. The tears just poured out as I felt this pain no open wound could ever compare. They were my family, wasn't I theirs? I had a birth mother who would only argue with me when I talked about it, I had two older brothers who claim not to remember and a baby sister who would never believe her father was the monster he was. Where does that leave me? Do they know how cruel it was towards me? It was belittling, gas lighting, hurtful and it was cruel. But it was my problem, my pain.

Everyday there was always something from my childhood reminding me of the huge hole I carried.. I was too jumpy, I said sorry too much, I had trust issues or I scared too easily. The trick questions I faced everyday, the silence I stayed everyday and the pain I felt everyday of my life. I was always reminded by my friends, coworkers and people in my everyday life of how strong and independent I was and how I was a survivor.

I was told I was head smart, street smart and deserved better from my family, but none of it mattered to me because I wanted my family to know how strong and independent I was. I wanted them to know how I survived all I did without their support or how I accepted their apology they never gave. All that mattered to me was their acknowledgement, their acceptance of me as I am and not the person they made me out to be.

With my taxes one year I decided to buy a computer system for the home. That way my kids had it for school and I had it to play some arcade games I would download. It wasn't long before I was using google to look up murdered or missing girls from June 1980-July 1981. I still needed that closure and I tried reaching and grabbing for it many times. I just didn't realize I was trying, reaching and grabbing from the wrong hands. I knew there were girls before me and I knew there were girl's after me. Maybe it was survivor's guilt I was carrying with me? Maybe it was lack of acknowledgement from my family? I would look at people and know they could never truly understand what I lived through. Then I would get frustrated that it would take for me to die and my journals to get read for the truth to be told. 'Why?' I asked myself that question a million times during the years I lived in the highlands with my kids. My google search came up empty again.

I canceled numerous nights out with friends and coworkers because I was too depressed to explain why I was depressed. Most times, I just wanted to be left alone. How am I supposed to move on, get over it, forgive or forget when it's a part of me? I get it didn't happen to my siblings but the thing is, it happened to me and I was punished, abandoned, ridiculed, mocked and laughed at because I was horrifically raped, sexually and physically abused. It was like a joke to my siblings but again it was my problem, my pain.

I was soon invited to the wedding of my oldest brother. I dreaded seeing Lorraine but I was looking forward to seeing my siblings as I always was. They were my family and I wanted to be accepted by them. I knew if they got to know me then they would see all I ever wanted was their support. When the morning of the wedding came I got a phone call from my baby sister. She was informing me her older brother from her father's side was in town and wanted to see me. I had not seen him since the late 1970s but I just wanted to know, "Why is he here in Massachusetts?" I questioned my baby sister. She responded, "He's here for the wedding." I could feel my stomach turn in knots, but I agreed to meet up with him before the wedding even though I knew it wouldn't be good for my emotional self being. He came to my house and he told me I was never around when he visited. He told me about cookouts and reunions where my two older brothers and baby sister were at, but I wasn't. I told him the monster his father was but he didn't seem interested and left quickly for the wedding. I gathered my kids and we headed to the outdoor venue where the wedding was taking place. I questioned myself as I drove there, 'How do they keep in better touch with our baby sister's brother than they do their own sister?' It was suffocating me, trying to belong as who I was and not what they saw me as. I was slowly realizing I was only tormenting myself.

I would tell myself, 'Just one more time.' It really bothered me to know my baby sister's older brother from her father's side was at my oldest brother's wedding. I didn't stay long and left before the wedding was over. A girl can only hold in the tears for so long. I was hurt and I couldn't help how I felt, feeling like an outcast in what is supposed to be my family.

I guess it was piling up on me, I would think of the times I lived on Fletcher Street, Pleasant Street, Butler Avenue, Lawrence Street and into my adulthood. I would think about all the times I was shunned away, belittled and insulted. I would think of the photo I saw at my baby sister's house and then I'd cry it out. Most times it really hurt to do so. I knew if I wanted to be a part of their lives, then I had to forgive, forget and get over it as my family expected me to. I was always fine with that as long as I got the acknowledgement and support I deserved. They never could give that, yet I was the bad one for knowing what I deserved.

Thank God for many aspects in our lives. I had my kids, a job I loved and friends who loved me like family. I loved to be happy, writing poetry and faith. I would look at Jon's poem then his picture until finally closing my eyes and keeping our memories alive. I loved the vivid memories I have of Jon. As years went by, my children lost their beloved Papa on June 19, 2006. They were also losing friends to gun violence, drugs, health and unexpectedly losing a lifelong friend. One was my friend's seven year old nephew who passed away after a long battle with cancer. On the morning of the funeral, I stopped at Dunkin Donuts where I got three coffees and munchkins. My ex in-laws were watching my son while I attended the funeral. They always liked my company so I showed up early and stayed for coffee while chatting with both my ex in-laws.

Despite all the heartache in life we still must keep going. It's what I did and some days I seemed to only co-exist, but I kept going. I dated a few guys but I loved being single and raising my kids that way, something my ex father in-law said to me many years earlier. I helped my ex mother in-law get a job at the Lowell Sun newspaper. She was a stay at home housewife and mom her whole life but with Papa gone she was lonely. She was super nervous so I drove her to work her first week and picked her up after work also. Soon she was driving herself to work and ended up reconnecting with old friends from her school days. Then in 2008 my oldest daughter graduated from high school and I was so proud of her. There were so many good times living on Powell Street. We had food fights, water balloon fights, birthday parties, dinner every night, sleep overs, Christmas, hanging outside in the driveway and more. We definitely deserved the good moments. As another year went by, the birthday parties for my siblings kids were on days my kids were with their dad making for another year of barely speaking with any of my siblings. Then life changed drastically for my children and I.

The third year anniversary of our beloved Papa was a bit tougher that year as it was also the seventeenth birthday of my daughter's lifelong friend who passed away months earlier. My children and I talked about how it was ok to cry, to talk about it and to feel sad. We hugged, we cried and we prepared ourselves for our day of heartaches. I hugged my kids a little tighter that morning when I left for work. It was a day in my children's life that is filled with so much sorrow and there was not a thing I could do to ease their pain. Nothing could ever prepare my children and I for the events that would take place that very afternoon on June 19, 2009. It was the last day of school for the city of Lowell school kids. I got out of work, picked my youngest daughter and her friend up from my house, then drove to get my son from school across town. I dropped my daughter and her friend off with other friends they were going to the cemetery with. I gave her my child support debit card to buy some flowers, then I drove home with my son and his friend who was sleeping over. It was about a fifteen minute ride to my house and as I pulled into my driveway, my daughter was calling me on her cell phone. I answered it saying, "Miss me already?" A lady's voice responded how the phone she was on fell out of a truck that was flipped onto a tree in the Merrimack River. I responded, "Oh ok thank you." My son questioned who called me as we started to head into our apartment. I looked at him and said, "Some lady who said..." I paused a bit confused and quickly called my daughter's phone back. Again I heard the lady's voice when she answered it and I questioned her if she just called me. She responded, "Yes."

The look on my face made my son know there was something wrong. I ran red lights, stop sign's and drove like a mad woman across town. I then had to drive on sidewalks because traffic was backed up, when I realized the traffic was backed up due to a car accident, there was no stopping me. That was my daughter in that accident and I was getting there. I hit a state sign and went right through the police roadblock as I kept driving. Then I panicked when I realized my son and his friend were in the car. I pulled the car over, getting my son and his friend out, and we ran as fast as we could to the accident scene. I saw a motorcycle laying on the road and the bottom side of a SUV on the opposite side of the guardrail where the Merrimack River is. Before my son and I could get any closer, a woman drove over and told me to get in. She informed me all the kids have been taken to the hospital. Two ambulances did fly by me when I was running so my son, his friend and I got into her vehicle. Within minutes I saw my oldest daughter stuck in the traffic. She was with her cousin and we made eye contact, she jumped out of the car she was in and ran over to the one I was in.

We drove as fast as we could to Lowell General hospital where my daughter was being transported to. Along the way we saw an ambulance on the side of the road with an emergency vehicle behind it. I almost jumped out of the moving car as we drove by, but they assured me my daughter was already at the hospital. We arrived and quickly the hospital waiting room was filling up with my ex husband and his family, his wife and her family, my kids friends and they had a lot of friends.

I went to call my friend and as I did, I looked around the waiting room saying to myself, 'Figures.' Meaning it figures I once again had no family. It had been almost two hours since the accident and we were all losing our patience until finally a doctor came out and requested the parents into a room. "No I'm not going," I said as the horror of being told my daughter didn't make it scared the shit out of me. I demanded they tell me and they informed me my daughter was alive and wanted to talk in private. Ken, my daughter's stepmother, my other daughter and I went into the room. We were informed the ambulance on the side of the road we saw did in fact have my daughter in it. They pulled over and performed a surgery on my daughter right there via telephone with a surgeon at the hospital. Technology at it finest, had that not been available my daughter would not have survived. We were informed of another surgery as soon as she got to the hospital, we were informed of her condition and how she was being transported to Boston in the next med flight and we were informed we could go see her but only one parent can be with her for the transport to Boston.

We were in a very tiny room as the doctor spoke to us but for some reason the small room seemed to stretch a mile long as I listened to the doctor talk of my daughter's injuries. Just about every bone from her waist to her face was broken. From her tiny nose in five places to her spine which severed in the crash, leaving my daughter paralyzed. She was covered in purple dry blood, her face was unrecognizable, her clothes sliced along the side from nurses, doctors or emergency medical technicians. I was speechless, I was blank, I was living this reality fog. Everything was happening so fast yet moving in slow motion. A nurse informed me I had a sister in-law out in the waiting room but was confused. "I don't have a sister in law," I said, but I did, it was my oldest brother's wife and his son. They came to the hospital, I remember seeing them quickly and feeling really cool that I had family there also. We were being rushed out as the med flight got cancelled due to the weather and we were transported by ambulance instead. It was little before seven o'clock when we hit Storrow Drive in Boston Massachusetts and like dominoes the cars pulled over. We were in Mass General hospital's parking lot within eighteen minutes from when we left Lowell. I was escorted quickly out of the ambulance, my hand placed on my daughter's stretcher she was being transported on and we all ran. We ran into the hospital and into a room where I was squished into a corner by the number of medical professionals tending to my daughter. I just watched all these people work on her when it hit me what the doctor said to me back in Lowell, she said my daughter was paralyzed. I was helpless as I looked at my daughter and though she was unconscious, I swear she looked right at me and waved her finger to me saying, "Mom what are they doing I only broke my pinky," and then I fainted.

I awoke outside of my daughter's room and I was so embarrassed I had fainted. They were working on my daughter and I go faint. I fainted because it was a pinky promise that I made with my friend Jon back in 1987 and I fainted because it hit me what the doctor told me back in Lowell; that my daughter was paralyzed.

I didn't have time to think about pinky promises, I had to get back to my daughter and that's exactly what I did. I don't know how much time went by before we were taken to another room, only this time I could not go in with her. They were performing an MRI on her. A doctor informed me of getting a priest as my daughter had a 125% chance of not surviving out of the MRI. I looked at the doctor and blurted out, "Are you nuts, do you know how many angels she has with her?" I questioned the man. The doctor stood before me with a quickly confused look on his face. "Well they better be in there with her right now," he firmly argued back at me and I returned the argument, "They are." The doctor continued asking me questions about my daughter. I questioned him about the motorcycle driver. "How is the other driver?" I questioned the doctor. He informed me he did not know but would question around.

I was then taken into a room with Ken and his wife. We were told our daughter was put in a medically induced coma until she can have surgery in seventy-two hours. Those hours felt like a year had gone by. I was a zombie, I was helpless, I was empty and I was lost. It wasn't until midnight when I screamed, "Where's my son?" I panicked but my oldest daughter assured me he went with his aunt on his dad's side back in Lowell.

I questioned about the motorcycle driver again to a nurse and she assured me she would find out. As the hours went by, I had to sign papers for blood transfusions and await the arrival of a plastic surgeon from California to fly in. My daughter was a sixteen year old female with facial injuries as she suffered almost two hundred stitches under one eye, over a hundred stitches above the other eye and they lost count after one thousand, seven hundred and seventy-nine stitches on the side of her face. (Yes you read that right!) As the night went to morning and morning into day, I was in the same predicament as I was back in Lowell; Ken and his family, their stepmother and her family, my daughter's friends and figures, no family for me.

My daughter still had broken glass all over her from the accident but we could not touch her. She was on a motion bed that moved a lot with many wires and beeping sounds. Another twenty-four hours went by before the nurse I questioned about the motorcycle driver, had approached me to let me know how the driver was doing. First she questioned me if I ever lost someone in a motorcycle accident. I informed her that I had lost someone I love dearly in a motorcycle accident and I questioned why she was asking me that. She then informed me, "Well they were with you, because there was no other drivers involved in your daughter's accident." I was certain, "But I saw the motorcycle laying next to the firetruck," I responded to the nurse who shook her head. "Sorry your daughter was involved in a single car crash," she said with a heart warming smile. Again I was helpless, speechless and beside myself. When a child is rushed to the hospital as much of the time, love and care they give to the child, they also give it to the parents or guardian and I am so grateful for that. I had no clue we were being watched, followed or looked after by anyone in the hospital.

Even though Ken and I had so much animosity towards each other for many years as I kept taking him to court for child support, I just assumed it was behind us as we dealt with this horrific ordeal we were dealing with. My heart broke for Ken as I was reminded it was also father's day weekend. I just assumed my daughter had three parents and I assumed we were going through this together. I followed Ken and his wife everywhere they went. I went out for a cigarette when they did, I walked to the cafeteria when they did, I sat in waiting area when they did, I cried with them, got bad news with them, was lost, empty and beside myself with them. I just didn't realize they didn't want me there with them.

Not even forty-eight hours after my daughter's accident, I found myself sitting in the pediatric waiting room surrounded by Ken's family. I had my ex-brother in-law on one side of me and my ex-sister in-law on the other side of me. They were talking to me with a paper and pen in their hand as they were trying to explain logic to me by saying, "We just want to help you." They wanted me to sign my name on a piece of paper that would give them all rights and say of my daughter's care in the hospital. They wanted me to sign off on being my daughter's guardian. They wanted me to sign my daughter's care off to them, all the while insisting I sign my name. When out or nowhere, a woman who worked for the hospital came into the waiting area and she squished herself right next to me as she grabbed the pen and paper right from their hands. She knew exactly what they were doing. With all I was going through, they managed to draw up papers and try to trick me into signing my rights to my daughter away. I was beside myself and instantly got up to stand where Ken and his wife were standing. Every time they moved, I moved with them. I followed them every time they tried sneaking away because to me, we were going through this together.

As I tried to make sense of all that was going on around me, all I could do was cry. Every phone call I got from a friend, coworker or my daughter's friends, all I did was break down into tears. Then I was told some nurses were bothered when they saw on camera how I was not wanted or supported by my daughter's father. Nurses saw I did not have family there supporting me. "No I have family," I told them as I thanked them for looking out for me. It was embarrassing to mention the lack of family I really did have. I walked back into the waiting area and looked around, nope no family of mine was there. A part of me went sad, then mad, before finally reminding myself, 'Figures.'

There were so many times in my life when I didn't have family there for me that I was now dealing with moments like this in one word, 'Figures.' Instead of dealing with the emotions of having no family around me, I headed for the elevators in an attempt to go outside for a cigarette. When I got off the elevator on the ground floor, there were people walking one way and people walking the other way. People rushing, working, worrying and then there was my baby sister walking with Lorraine. I was so mad I instantly insulted her, "What the fuck is she doing here?" I yelled. I was so mad at my baby sister for bringing that cruel cold hearted woman to see my daughter. I stormed away from them heading towards the outside of the hospital before turning around.

I headed back upstairs to be with my baby sister and Lorraine. I felt bad for being rude to them when they only came to see my daughter. They were not there for me, they were there for my daughter, so I took them to see her. Only thing I did not do was prepare them for what they would see. They both gasped in horror as they saw my daughter's badly injured face. What wasn't covered in bandages was covered in black and blue bruises. They only stayed a few minutes and I walked out with them as I headed for that cigarette I was first heading out for. It wasn't long until my daughter was visited by my older brother and his wife. They said a prayer over her bed and stayed a few minutes before leaving.

As doctors prepared my daughter for her eight hour life threatening surgery, Ken and I were allowed to escort her down to the basement floor where the surgery was taking place. They had us put on a face mask and hospital gowns over our clothes while telling us to kiss our daughter before we left. Even though she was our daughter, Ken still stayed as far away from me as he could. We headed back to the fourth floor pediatric waiting area and awaited the call from the doctors. There I was in the same predicament; Ken and his wife along with their family, my daughter's friends and a figures, no relatives in my blood line there. We finally got the call they were on their way up and my daughter survived the surgery. I was constantly on the phone with my ex mother in-law updating her with my daughter's condition. My oldest daughter would pick her up and drive her to Boston so she could be there with us. The accident happened on the anniversary of her husband's death and it was not an easy thing for her to go through being alone at home. I did not mind when she was at the hospital for my daughter. Because even though she was Ken's mother and even though he was remarried, she was still one of my best friends. She may have been my kids grandmother, but she was also there for me. Only problem was the staff at the hospital assumed she was my family, they assumed she was my mother.

Ken, his wife and I on numerous occasions were taken into a room where we had a conference meeting with all doctors who were treating our daughter. The meetings were about her continued care and the outcome that was to be. A few days after the surgery when I was walking to my daughter's room with my ex mother in-law, we were stopped and escorted into a private room because doctors wanted to talk to me.

My ex mother in-law and I sat at a big round wooden table as we listened to what they wanted to tell us. They were not saying nice things about how I was being treated by Ken and I had to quickly stop them from speaking. "Please don't talk bad about my ex husband in front of his mother," I said to the medical professionals when suddenly not one mouth was closed. All mouths just opened in confusion with a few of them at the same time questioning my ex mother in-law, "You're his mother?" The confusion set in as the doctors were dumbfounded to learn the lady who sat with me the most was my ex mother in-law and not my mother. The atmosphere in the room quickly changed as I defended all what doctors were saying. "No I have family," I said. "No I'm not being treated wrong," I continued in a defensive tone as I had excuses for everyone except my own reality.

I questioned a nurse one day about the large board on wheels behind all the machines which were hooked up to my daughter. "That's a circuit board," she answered. I lost it and broke down crying. There were so many wires I had to go through just to give my daughter a kiss on the cheek. I couldn't sit on the side of her bed because one side was machines and circuit boards while the other side was wires. A nurse gave me a sandwich one day and told me to eat. "You haven't ate anything in days," she said as she reminded I was being watched by staff at the hospital. She grabbed me by my shoulders, "You've been in shock," she said to me as she sat with me and explained my body had been in shock for the past nine days. "Nine days," I yelled at her and suddenly I was confused. "What day is today?" I questioned the nurse who answered me, "The 28th of June." I was confused and dazed over realizing nine days have gone bye. "Stop being stubborn," the nurse said to me as she explained how they knew I did not have support from family. They also knew I did not have support from my daughter's father or stepmother. All she explained did make sense to me and I realized I had been in shock. I decided to go outside for a cigarette as I took in all the nurse had said to me. As soon as I walked out of the intensive care area and into the hallway, there was Ken and his wife getting on the elevator. I kicked into action and grabbed the elevator door before it closed. Assuming they were heading outside I said, "I could use a cigarette." But they were heading down to the cafeteria. "Oh sounds good," I said as I talked and talked to the two people who just wanted me to go away.

I followed them to the cafeteria, got my food and waited for them, but they were taking to long. So I paid for my food and got us a booth. I walked back into the cafeteria to inform them of the booth I got. There were many times when all they found were two seated tables in the cafeteria, but I found an empty booth with enough room for all three of us. I saw them pay and then I saw them walk in the opposite section of the cafeteria. When out of nowhere I felt a whack upside my head. No it wasn't a real whack but it sure felt like one. All I could hear was my ex father in-law saying, "Durrrrr." Right there in the cafeteria I got a dope slap from heaven. Everything the nurse explained to me, I totally ignored once I left the intensive care area. I then went outside for that cigarette.

My main focus was my daughter in the intensive care unit, my other daughter and my son back in Lowell. Along with learning about every injury my daughter suffered, I was praised by the doctors and nurses for my continued support and help I was being. I was supported by every doctor, nurse, janitor and even parents of other patients. And then I finally saw it, it took a dope slap from heaven but I finally saw it. I finally understood what the doctors and nurses were trying to tell me, I gave them the ok, "Yes you may step in as my family," I said to Dr. Whalen. My daughter's heart would race fast when visitors were in the room so with the approval of doctors, I put a stop to all visitors in order to help my daughter heal under less stress.

Being outside one day, I saw my oldest brother and his wife walking towards me. Assuming they were there for my daughter, I immediately informed them of the no visitor rule. But he informed me, "We're here for you." Then he said something that I still wonder to this day of why he said it. "After all you've been through," he said to me. It was my instant reaction to question him, "You remember?" But he shrugged it off, "What no," he said followed by, "How is she doing?" The conversation quickly went to my daughter's health and condition. We then walked across the street and ate at a pizzeria pub, while they ate. My brother tried getting me to talk either about my kids, my job or even the menu at the pub. All I could think about as I sat across from them was my daughter over in the intensive care unit and what did my brother mean by, "After all you've been through." Not going through my divorce because he wasn't around. Not my teen years because he wasn't around. Wait, he remembers my childhood? But I was too emotional over my daughter, but he was here with his wife, but it wasn't the time or place. Too many buts on my plate to deal with it. I then rushed the dinner, thanked them for coming and headed back to my daughter.

Things got better for me at the hospital, having the support from every doctor and nurse helped keep me in a strong state of mind and stay focused on my daughter's care. I learned more about her injuries and I watched as miracles happened. I never felt so surrounded by angels as I did on the fourth floor of the pediatric intensive care unit. I never doubted my daughter's recovery and knew I would one day bring her home. I was given a discharge date of March 2010, that's when doctors believed it would be before I could bring my daughter home as I had a lot to still learn about her future care.

As my daughter awoke from her medical induced coma, her painful agony was only beginning. Medical procedures after medical procedures, sponge baths, first hair wash since accident and just transferring her caused her to scream in pain. She was finally being discharged out of the intensive care unit and into regular patient care as we awaited an empty room at Spaulding Rehabilitation Hospital just down the road from Mass General. My daughter was moved to the 18th floor and allowed a visit from her closest friend only. I prepared her for my daughter's bruised face but it didn't stop my daughter's friend from fainting the minute she saw her.

The next morning I received a phone call from the insurance agent for the driver of my daughter's accident. He was calling about my daughter and instead he got me in a full blown mental breakdown. That poor man stayed on the phone with me and listened, cried and prayed with me. He didn't hang up until I cried it out. The next day we got my daughter ready for her transfer over to Spaulding. I went and decorated her new room with a bunch of her stuff from home. Then I returned to the hospital for the ride with my daughter. Once we were inside the ambulance my daughter made a comment about the song playing. It was, The Climb by Miley Cyrus. It was a short ride as the ambulance pulled into the parking area of Spaulding. They wheeled my daughter into the parking area as I heard the song coming through speakers in the parking lot.

Inside the building the same song played, inside the elevators the song still played, down halls, through doors until finally at what would be my daughter's home for the next ten months, her hospital room. The music continued to play as we realized the hospital was playing it for my daughter.

They welcomed her with such an inspirational song. *Inspiration comes in so many forms, how lucky we are when we find them all.*

My daughter's first day of visitors at Spaulding was out of control. Over a hundred visitors before the hospital put a stop to the visiting. It was one heck of an emotional summer. I saw miracles, I saw inspiration, I saw support and I saw a tough sixteen year old. She was so determined to heal and go home. Doctors at Spaulding didn't take shit at all and like at Mass General; the doctors, nurses, janitors and parents of other patients all supported me.

As we got into a routine, I was able to drive home and spend time with my son. Only problem was I never drove on the highway or in Boston. I followed my oldest daughter to Boston one day and a few days later I headed back to Lowell. Easier said than done when you have a cluster of *what the fucks* going through your mind. *Wtf* I never drove on a highway. *Wtf* I want my kid home. *Wtf* I miss my other two kids at home. *Wtf* can't their father be more supportive? *Wtf* can't this be a nightmare? *Wtf* can't I wake up from this? *Wtf* exit do I take? And before I knew it, I'm lost.

My highway experience continued...

*Left Spaulding one day and almost two hours later I was lost in North Reading where a police officer escorted this crying lady towards her way home.

*Left Spaulding and kept missing my exit as I continued to drive on and off exit ramps. My daughter called to see when I'd be back from Lowell. I was crying as I told her I could still see Spaulding. She yelled that I had been gone for three hours.

*My first ride into Boston not following my daughter, resulted in me missing the Spaulding exit, over a bridge, through a tunnel and on to Logan International Airport.

*Another time I got to Burlington and panicked as I thought I was lost so I turned around. Played this out about five times until I realized I had to go through Burlington to get to Boston.

My oldest daughter would sleep over at Spaulding along with her cousin, giving me time with my son. He didn't see his sister until August when I had him spend the day with us. I didn't want him seeing his sister until her bruising faded. Spaulding had a list of requirements that must be completed in time for discharge. My daughter had her list and I also had one. I was required to take four weeks of classes to learn about spinal cord injury as my first question was, "What's an SCI?" "Spinal cord injury," the doctor answered me and told me to start studying.

With my daughters busy schedule of therapy and appointments, I was studying all I could in the early morning hours. I would walk outside of the parking lot and walk the parkway of the Charles River. I found serenity when I sat there. I was able to collect my thoughts better. I was able to remind myself that my daughter was alive and for that I was grateful.

My daughter never once said, "Why me?" She had her bad days, therapy she didn't want to do or wanted to sleep later. We cried a lot and we made the best of our stay. As the first four weeks went by, I was able to make a list of every doctor and nurse who cared for my daughter. I wrote a summary of all my daughter's injuries, her care and the outlook on each injury. I also completed my four weeks of classes and training. I was congratulated by the doctors and that's when I surprised them again. I questioned if I was allowed to retake the classes. They were puzzled as they told me I passed the training with flying colors. That's when I said, "My daughter didn't." Then I reminded them it was her who was injured. They all smiled at me and agreed. Soon I was retaking the classes, only this time with my daughter.

I experienced so much over the summer of 2009. Doctors and nurses loved my eagerness to be a constant involvement in my daughter's daily care. I was invited to help perform a spinal tap on my daughter, an emotional experience indeed. They explained every x-ray image as they were being taken. I was given free nursing, physical, occupational and emotional classes related to caring for my daughter. I was given books, advice, lessons and a first hand look into the lives of doctors, nurses and emergency medical technicians. I basically went to nursing school, free of charge.

Due to living on the second floor, I knew we had to move in order to bring my daughter home. Being out of work since my daughter's accident, Spaulding set me up with all the state funded help there was available. I suddenly found myself on food stamps, welfare and housing. My daughter got on social security and I just wanted to be home with all three of my kids. Housing called me one day to inform me of an available three bedroom handicap accessible apartment and I took it. Moving my daughter out of her room at Spaulding started one week before we even knew she was being discharged. I would pack up things and carry them down to my car. Nurses were catching me and stocking me up with medical supplies. Back at home my oldest daughter did most of the packing. It was hard for all of us to move out of the home we had for over seven years, but it was to bring my daughter and their sister home. It took two days and two Honda's, but my daughter, friends and I moved our home on the second floor in the highlands to the ground floor in downtown Lowell. Downtown, the place I guess I never really left. My job was located downtown, my whole teenage life was spent downtown and I was about to bring my daughter home, to downtown. It took many trips back and forth from Boston to Lowell with my car and trunk stuffed with my daughter's belongings. I blew the doctors expectations of my daughter's care, instead of the original ten month discharge date of March 2010, I left Spaulding Rehabilitation hospital on August 28th 2009 with my daughter. She was finally coming home.

Strength isn't measured by the pounds you can lift. Strength is the determination to never give up.

We were now living in a ground floor apartment in one of Lowell's old mills. A building which once employed hundreds of mill workers in the 1800s. Amazing the history inside the walls of renovated old mill buildings. At times I felt like I was right where I was supposed to be. One morning I was sitting outside in my tiny fenced in terrace, drinking a coffee and reading the newspaper when my mind wandered. 'I'm taking care of someone paralyzed,' I thought to myself as tears poured like buckets. My son was at school, my daughter was sleeping and I decided to take a ride to the cemetery. I got to the cemetery, I fell to my knees, crying and sitting behind his stone where I missed and talked to Jon. Driving home my toe throbbed and I told myself, 'Not a good idea to wear sandals.' Yes, I broke my big toe.

Being home with my kids was so overwhelming. Financially it was killing me, emotionally it was draining me and physically it was weakening me. But I kept going with appointments, tutoring, therapy, kids needing rides and calls to 911. The unexpected hospital stays and many scares as my daughter continued to fight all the setbacks related to her injuries. Let's not forget laundry, dinner and food shopping. Sometimes I felt like someone shoved the energizer bunny up my ass as I just kept going and going. My work raised money and in September my daughter was an honoree at a very large motorcycle ride benefit. Another very amazing, extremely emotional and overwhelming feeling of support from so many who showed their love, their empathy and their friendship for my daughter. So many people praised me but I just brushed it off as I assumed I was doing what a mother was supposed to do; everything my own mother didn't. I was back to talking to my oldest brother on a regular basis again. He became a huge help when he made the back door steps into a ramp so my daughter could stroll outside. He used zip ties, bungee cords and belts so he was able to give her a ride on his motorcycle, something she really wanted. I appreciated all his help and it wasn't long before I was reaching out to my baby sister, other brother and yes, even Lorraine.

It was hard for my ex mother in-law as she was very close to my kids and I. She was as lost as I was that summer of 2009 and when I couldn't be there for her, her bingo friend and my birth mother Lorraine was. I invited Lorraine to my house shortly after the new year. She came into my apartment like we were best friends. She was laughing, joking and acting as if there were no problems in our relationship. I didn't mean to be rude but I wanted to know, "How can you act like my childhood never happened?" I questioned her. Her smiling, happy mood instantly changed as she told me what she always told me, "Jesus Christ Cathy how do you still even remember?" I answered her, "Just looking at you reminds me."

She grabbed her coat and walked out of my apartment telling me, "I don't deserve this bullshit." I yelled down the hall, "You don't deserve this bullshit?" "No I don't deserve it," I continued yelling before slamming my door and regretting I invited her over. Now on top of everything I was dealing with everyday, I had to pause to cry and be depressed over a childhood I was still trying to forget. My ex mother in-law supported me and my decision to separate myself from Lorraine. "She's a good friend, I just don't approve of her motherly ways," she would tell me. I knew what days not to visit my ex in-law and I always respected her for giving me the heads up all the time.

My son didn't always take the bus to school, as some mornings I would drive him. We would stop at Dunkin Donuts and visit with my ex mother in-law for a few. One night she called me to make sure I was stopping by in the morning. "I need to tell you something," she said to me and I assured her I would stop by. The next morning I grabbed us a coffee, dropped my son off at school with a donut and a frozen fruit drink. Once I was at my ex in-laws house, she was overly excited, flustered and overwhelmed with what she wanted to tell me. I wasn't sitting down when she started to question me, "Your friends nephew, your friends nephew who died?" She continued saying as she tried to remember his name. "Matty," I answered. "Yes," she responded anxiously and excitedly. "Calm down your going to give yourself a heart attack," I said as I insisted she sit down and drink some coffee. I was giggling a bit over her excitement, like she was a little kid in a candy store.

After collecting her breath, drinking some coffee and calming herself down, she questioned me about my friend's seven-year old nephew who passed away a few years prior. "When did your friend's nephew pass away?" she questioned me. I thought for a minute then told her, "He's forever seven so it was March 2007." Then I questioned her, "Why?" She got a bit hyper as she continued, "Ok did you go to his funeral?" she questioned me in a matter of fact manner. I answered her, "Durr yes," I laughed as I reminded her how Papa and her watched my son while I went. She got more excited as she jumped up, "What did you bring here in the morning with you?" she questioned me as her voice tone flustered. "Ma what's wrong?" I questioned her as I could tell something was bothering her. She repeated her question, "What did you bring here that morning with you?" "Three coffees and my son," I answered her as she started to cry. I questioned her again, "Ma what is wrong?" But she didn't answer as she grabbed tissues, blowing her nose and making me cry also. I started talking about that morning in March 2007. "Remember Papa telling me Matty was up in heaven playing baseball?" I questioned my ex mother in-law. I always remembered him saying that to me that morning, for some reason it made me feel warm inside as I left to attend my friend's nephews funeral. I assumed my ex mother in-law was crying because she was missing her husband. But she continued with her questions, "You are positive me and Franny watched KJ?" (Franny was what she called her husband and KJ was my son)

"I am one hundred percent positive your losing your mind," I told her as I was and still am one hundred percent positive my ex father in-law was there the morning I went to my friend's nephews funeral in March of 2007. Then my ex mother in-law asked me a question that I could not answer, "How is that possible when Franny passed in 2006?" Every hair on my body stood as I just stared at my ex mother in-law until we hugged and cried. She was right, my ex father in-law died in June of 2006 and my friend's nephew died in March of 2007. To this day I will tell you both my ex in-laws watched my son that morning in 2007. How, I don't know but they were both there. I couldn't make sense of it, was it signs from heaven? I mean how else did I survive my childhood? I have been protected by angels since I could remember and it still didn't change the fact that I could not make sense of it. I went into a quick depression and I exhausted myself in trying to make everyone else happy. I buried myself in writing. I visited the cemetery more and I took time for myself to get a moment of peace everyday.

I continued to keep in touch with my siblings, whether it was through a quick phone call or a comment on a Facebook status. As spring turned to summer I was still in the same scenario of hoping to make it work with my siblings. My older brother invited me to a cookout where Lorraine would not be. So my daughter and I decided to go and many members of his wife's family were there as we were introduced to them. But then in came Lorraine, I tried keeping my cool, I tried sitting there as if we were a happy family, I tried but I couldn't. I told my daughter I wanted to leave and she didn't hesitate, so we left. I was also invited to a cookout at my oldest brother's house and I was once again told Lorraine would not be there, but that was not the case. By the end of summer, I realized no matter what I was invited to by my siblings, I would have to tolerate seeing Lorraine. Only thing is, it's what I have been doing my whole life and I decided I wasn't doing it anymore. I had too much on my plate to pretend my childhood, my pain, my horror and their lack of acknowledgement never happened. I couldn't do it anymore and I accepted, respected and was proud of myself for doing so. Even if the three siblings I wanted it all from for so long never saw it. Boy I thought I cried a lot in my life, the tears just fell, poured and soaked through every word or emotion I heard and felt. I cried over commercials, I cried over cartoons, I cried seeing other people crying. I cried wondering where all the tears came from that I've cried.

My oldest daughter made me a grandmother the same day my youngest daughter prepared for another major surgery. My granddaughter was of course the apple of her aunt's, her uncle's and my eye. Like the heartache matched with the month of June's tragedies in my kids' lives, it wasn't long until my heartaches, matched with the one day in October was here. The day my dad and Jon passed away on. I walked around with a heavy heart, a black hole in my stomach, a confusion of question marks in my head and buckets holding my tears. I cried more than I did any other October. I knew I had to do what I have always been doing; keep moving on.

My daughter was in and out of hospital stays and before I could stuff a turkey, it was the holiday season. My ex mother in-law spent Thanksgiving with my kids and I at our home. She came out driving with us to look at Christmas lights and on Christmas eve she came over for dinner and to hang out for awhile. As the year 2011 came upon us, I concentrated my life and my time on people who I knew loved me and not people who claimed to. I was still learning my lessons as Facebook was reconnecting me with many friends from the 1980s and suddenly I had a social life.

Before I knew it, I was out meeting up with old friends at a bar, a fundraiser or a nearby Dunkin Donuts. Of course reconnecting with all these friends from so long ago came with the questions and with questions came depression and more tears. I would stare at my Facebook friends list and count how many knew me from Pleasant Street or when I was a young teen. I would stare at my laptop screen just wanting to scream at it. I got a private message from a girl who I knew back in the 1980s and also knew my oldest brother from the 1980s. But she had just found out in 2010 that we were each other's sibling. I was seeing photos and status shared of my siblings and Lorraine at restaurants or dinners at each other's houses. Only now I was learning to accept it was not my fault. I was learning to not let it bother me when it came to my siblings. I was learning it was their loss not mine.

In July of 2011, there was a wedding on my children's fathers' side of the family. My children were going and the morning of the wedding my ex-mother in-law called for me to pick her up. She wanted to come hangs out with us for the day. She wasn't feeling well, and she was having some stomach problems which she was being treated for by her doctor. She stayed all day at my house, we played cribbage, watched a movie, she took a nap on my couch, and I dropped her, my son and daughter off at the reception where the wedding was taking place. Later that night, I returned to pick up my daughter and son. My ex-mother in-law was getting a ride home from someone else at the wedding. The next morning my phone rang a little after seven, it was my ex-mother in-law. She told me she didn't realize how early it was and how she was up all-night thinking of all the fun she had at the wedding and hanging with me all day. She also complained of pain in her side but brushed it off as a needed bowel movement. I offered to pick her up, send my oldest daughter, call 911 or her son, but she insisted she would be fine and told me she would call me back in a few hours. After a few hours went by and I didn't hear from her, I called her back. There was no answer and I assumed she was sleeping. By late morning I was panicking, I called again and there was still no answer. I kept calling her, leaving voicemail messages, hanging up, calling back until I called my ex-husband. He also got no answer but insisted she was probably busy. So, I called my ex-brother in-law, "Please check on your mom?" I questioned him as soon as he answered the phone.

All the animosity we had towards each other from the hospital in 2009 was quickly moved to the side as my ex-brother in-law took my out of the blue phone call to heart. Not only did he fly to his mother's house, but he also called 911 for a wellness check. Gosh that woman was like a mother to me. Within the next hour of that phone call to my ex-brother in-law, I had my heart ripped out when I heard the words, "She's gone." There was no warning, my ex-mother in-law had passed away unexpectedly. Soon all of my ex-mother in-laws grandchildren were at my house. I made sure all the kids ate as I cooked and made beds for all the ones who spent the night.

I didn't realize the integrity I carried until the morning of her funeral. I was told Lorraine was disrespected and brushed off by my ex-in-laws. As the funeral home prepared to leave for the church, she needed a ride to the church and cemetery. I understood they saw Lorraine as the ex-wife's mother. But I saw her as my ex-mother in-laws' friend and they should have respected that, but they didn't. So, for my ex-mother in-law, I allowed Lorraine in my car for the ride to the funeral mass. It was a quiet ride from the church to the cemetery except for memories of Ma we would talk of. It killed me losing my ex-mother in-law, she was one of my best friends as another downpour of tears left my eyes. Once the service was over my daughter and son left with my oldest daughter for the after party at my ex-brother in-laws.

I was left with driving Lorraine back to her car at the funeral home. Gosh the things I did or tried to do to prove I was a good person to this lady. I tried to make conversation with her as I thanked her for being a good friend to my ex-mother in-law. Then I tried being a human with her as I told her how I wanted a mother. "Don't you think I want a mother?" I questioned her but she said not a word. "I want my siblings in my life," I said to her and still she said nothing, so I bit my tongue for the rest of the ride. I thought maybe she was thinking of what to say. I thought maybe she would finally agree that it was time to talk, but once at the funeral home she hopped out of my car and proceeded to her car. I jumped out of my car and ran over to her. I begged her, "Please let's finally talk?" But she quickly changed it into an argument and so I told her, "You have two choices." She turned to listen to what I had to say. "One, tell my baby sister the truth about her father or two, get the fuck out of my life." She turned around and walked away. It was her choice, her decision and she walked away.

My ex-mother in-law was now laid to rest with her husband. I was blessed with twenty years of memories and friendship that just seemed to end so abruptly. My children and I lost a big piece of ourselves when we lost her. We would reminisce on fun times we had with her and how much we missed her. Within one month of her passing, we noticed the radio station oldies 103 went off the air. We would joke how she took it to heaven with her as that was her one and only radio station she ever listened to. But it was the events of Halloween 2011 that made us question ourselves, "Is Ma behind this?"

For twenty years I would help my in-laws decorate their front yard for Halloween and Christmas. I would also help them take the decorations down when the holiday was over. Even after my divorce from their son, after my ex-father in-law passed away and after my daughter's car accident left her paralyzed, we helped my ex mother in-law decorate for Halloween every year. She passed away in July of 2011 and her house, which she raised her children and lived in for forty years was cleaned out by September 2011. Her yard was being decorated for Halloween one last time by everyone except my children and I in October 2011. "Mom," my daughter screamed from her bedroom. With tears in her eyes, she showed me her Facebook newsfeed. It was a video of her father's family decorating my ex-in-laws yard for one last time. I was pissed off and there wasn't a damn thing I could do about it because I was the ex-wife. I felt the steam coming from my ears as I thought about how mad my ex-mother in-law would be, but there wasn't a damn thing I could do. Gosh did we dread our first Halloween without her, it was her favorite holiday. Ma and Papa spent many years making their own creatures, graveyards, tombstones and scare things placed throughout their front yard. The crowd of kids in costumes multiplied, the candy supply tripled, and my ex-mother in-law loved every minute of it.

As Halloween 2011 approached, my kids were making other plans to stay busy on that day and I never once drove by to see how they decorated my ex-in-laws yard. I didn't have the heart to drive by it. With my teenage daughter being recently paralyzed, not having a weekly paycheck anymore, the shit support from my kid's father, my dad and Jon's anniversary of their passing, my family history, memories from my childhood, my ex-mother in-law passing away and my first Halloween without her. My plate was getting heavier and heavier with every heartache I carried.

Like the radio station oldies 103 going off the air, some things leave you wondering. Days before Halloween, a snowstorm swept through the Massachusetts area. Dumping many inches of heavy wet snow, downed power lines and loss of electricity throughout many parts of Massachusetts. Many went days without electricity resulting for the first time in history; the cancellation of Halloween. The 2011 Halloween Nor'easter, as it was called. When my children and I first heard on the news about Halloween being cancelled, we laughed. We looked up to the sky and said, "Well played Ma, well played." As electricity was slowly restored to homes and businesses, a new date for trick or treating was made available. I could see the hurt in my kids' eyes as they thought of my ex-in-laws home being displayed for Halloween without them. When out of the blue, I hear my kids laughing in hysterics over a phone call they received. The house was sold, and everything had to be out of the front yard before Halloween would be celebrated. I looked up to the sky and said, "Well played Ma, well played." I'm glad to say the last Halloween at that home in 2010 was celebrated the way it was for over twenty years, with my kids and me. As the holidays came, we were missing my ex-mother in-law bigtime, but we kept the faith knowing, a part of her is always with us.

The year 2012 started off with trips to see the Boston Bruins. Being out of work, I was able to drive my daughter to the Ristuccia Arena in Wilmington, Massachusetts, where the Boston Bruins did their hockey practice. A town my baby sister lived in. My daughter worked her way to not only meet but also pose for photos with old, new, and legendary Boston Bruins hockey players. Of course, she posted it on Facebook, and it wasn't long until my baby sister started to meet us there with her sons. They lived close by to the arena and it became a weekly thing, for a couple of weeks. I think my baby sister and I had a million questions we wanted to ask each other but we didn't. We talked about the weather, our kids' fathers and our kids, of course. Until one day while at hockey practice, we decided to meet back at my house for coffee.

Once at my house, I sat at my kitchen table where my sister was sitting, and she questioned me. It happened so fast, I mean I waited over thirty years for it, but when it happened it caught me off guard. My baby sister questioned me, "What happened on Pleasant Street?" After a brief pause, "I've waited thirty years for this," I answered her. "I have to tell it from the beginning," I continued, "It started long before Pleasant Street," I went on trembling but ready to tell my baby sister about her monstrous father. "It started on Fletcher Street," I continued. Taking deep breaths as I made sure I spoke slowly, so I didn't fuck it up. "Your father started raping and abusing me," I continued before being cut off. "What did you just say?" I quickly questioned my baby sister. "What did you just say?" I repeated louder as I heard her say what I thought she said, "I don't believe you."

It was like that claw machine where you put money in and try to win a stuffed animal with the mechanical claw, only it was my insides being gutted out in one big swipe. She didn't give me a chance to talk, she just cut me off with, "I don't believe you." I was instantly devastated, I started to hyperventilate, and I dropped to my knees bawling my eyes out as I was beyond hurt. It was like I had a razor burn slice through the heart. My friend Tammy who I have known since 1982 decided to surprise me with a visit. Talk about perfect timing. She came to the back door and immediately let herself in. "What's wrong?" she quickly questioned me and all I could tell her was, "She doesn't believe me," "She finally asked me and she doesn't believe me," I continued until I just let out a loud scream and cried my eyes out. I heard Tammy say, "I think you better go." I never heard my baby sister leave, I never heard the door close, I just remember looking up and she was gone. I had so many questions, why did she bother to ask me? Why did she bother to bring it up? Why didn't she give me a chance to answer? Why doesn't she believe me? One of my biggest burdens I ever carried in my life was telling my baby sister about her father. I always hoped, prayed, wished, and begged it would have been my oldest brothers or Lorraine to tell her the truth about her monster father, but they never did.

As summer became fall, I realized I was back to the no contact with those same three siblings. It was then that I realized out of all the siblings I do have, I don't have a relationship with any of them. They either have different fathers or on my dad's side, a different mother. I don't blame them for our lack of relationship, and I don't blame myself.

I don't remember what provoked the phone call but after reconnecting on Facebook, I was soon on the phone with my oldest brother from my dad's side. The one whose wedding I blew off all those years ago. To this day that phone call is the sincerest conversation I ever had with a blood related relative. He listened to my reason for why I missed his wedding all those years prior. I listened to his reason for why he was so mad that I didn't go. We accepted each other's apology and we talked more. Then he did something I still talk about to this day, he praised me for being strong, for being independent and for having a caring heart. He told me to be proud of myself and that he was also proud of me. I truly appreciated it.

Another birthday, Christmas and as the year 2013 began, I looked around and saw once again the only blood relatives in my life were my children and granddaughter. I also had friendships that are twenty, thirty or forty plus years long as everywhere I went, I made friends and I kept friends. No matter how positive I made my day, I always went to bed wondering why didn't my birth family care?

I would soon be tagged in a Facebook status that caught me off guard. It was my baby sister announcing her engagement to her boyfriend. I congratulated her, got an invite to the wedding and nothing else. No involvement in the wedding, no invite to a wedding shower, no bachelorette party, nothing. But I also wasn't involved in anything when it came to my three siblings, so I took it for what it was. At times I felt like I was dropped off in the middle of the ocean and left to swim back, one tough task at a time. People were constantly praising me for my strength, for being a great mom and for being a good person. But at the end of the day, it was always just my kids and me.

After approaching me with the hopes of living with my other daughter in their own apartment, I then spent the next ten months training and teaching my daughter all about her medical needs, doctors and supply companies. My daughter was a bit overwhelmed as she didn't realize all I did behind the scenes. We soon began the hunt of looking for a handicap accessible apartment for my daughters and a two-bedroom apartment for my son and I. I really believed it would be a slam dunk search and we would be packing up soon to move. But that was not the case as rent prices had skyrocketed in the city of Lowell and finding an available handicap accessible apartment was near impossible. I didn't know what to do. I was stuck, I was helpless in giving my daughter what she wanted and what she deserved, her independence.

Playing on Facebook one day, I received a private message from my old work, The Four Sisters Owl Diner. They decided to send me a message to see if I'd be interested in working again. I admit I was excited, scared, eager and overwhelmed. It was over four years since I last held a spatula or stood behind a grill, but I did it. With the help, empathy and compassion from my old boss, coworkers and old customers, it made my day easy as I transitioned from a full-time nurse to the eight hour a day cook I once was. I worked just one day and went home so full of completion and heartache. It was extremely emotional as I missed being a full-time cook.

In August, I realized I was living in what my daughters were looking for, a handicap accessible apartment. My son also approached me about his thoughts of living with his dad for his high school years. After having a normal conversation with my ex-husband, we agreed that in September our son would move into his dads on a full-time basis. That was a lot to take in as I concluded my son was moving in with his dad, my daughters were moving in together and I was moving out of my own home so my daughters could have the apartment and experience to themselves. I didn't know what was wrong with me. Why did I hurt so much? Why did I walk with buckets of tears behind my eyes? Why was life so confusing? Why was I dealing with this alone? How do I live without living with my children? How did my life change so fast? Then my old coworker called informing me they wanted me back working regularly at the diner again.

On September 1st my son moved into his dad's and my oldest daughter moved in with my youngest daughter and I went back to work, one day a week at first. My daughter's nursing program laid me off so I could collect unemployment and my children's dad continued to pay me child support as I transitioned back into the workforce. In October I moved into my own one-bedroom apartment. Moving into my own place and having a Facebook invitation to my baby sister's wedding made me want to reach out to her and my two older brothers. So, I reached out to them either by phone call, text message or message through Facebook. I informed them of my move and invited them individually to visit me at my new apartment.

As overwhelmed I was with not having my kids living with me anymore, I was also proud at how independent I raised my kids to be and I was proud of myself for how far I had come in life. Then I waited for my siblings to visit me. A visit that would never come from not just one of them, but all three never came to my apartment. I would see Facebook status of them being at a restaurant close by, at a friend's house or at each other's homes. I would see Facebook photos of a cousin's reunion they shared together but failed to invite me. Another cousin on Facebook invited me to a fundraiser for his wife who passed away unexpectedly. I went with a friend but walked in to see my three siblings sitting together. I went over and said hello but feeling like an outcast, I sat away from them and left the fundraiser early.

I would remind myself, I have more than I had when I was a kid. Who cares if I didn't have support of a family, I never had it before from them, so why should they start now?

As the year 2014 came around, child support payments stopped, unemployment payments stopped, and I started picking up more days at the diner. Though my son was now living with his father, I still saw him every day. Hanging out at my daughter's and getting the rest I needed when I was home in my own apartment was my life now. After being sent a Facebook message requesting my home address, I was soon sent an official invitation to my baby sister's wedding. (I did give them my address before, but?) She had a bridal shower as I saw the pictures on Facebook, but I was never invited.

I don't know if there was any Jack and Jill, a bachelorette party or get together to celebrate their upcoming wedding because I was never invited if there was. On the day of the wedding, I worked until noontime. My oldest daughter drove her sister and brother, I picked up my longtime friend and we drove to the address where the wedding was taking place. Lorraine was shocked I was there; my two older brothers made a mockery out of me, and their longtime friend praised me for being me. The home was beautiful where the wedding was being held. It was an outdoor wedding, and the weather was perfect for the celebration. A beautiful bride she was, and I cried a few happy tears. Even though we weren't in each other's lives like she was with our older brothers, I was still very happy for her. Her wedding was perfect. Afterwards there were a lot of photos being taken and my name was called. The bride wanted photos of her family, so we all lined up. Her husband, kids, Lorraine, older brothers, nephews, my kids and of course myself.

I didn't want to stand next to Lorraine, so I waited for everyone to get situated and I took a stand at the end of the line next to my two older brothers. Right as the photo was about to be taken, they made a quick dash to the other side of the line. Leaving me with no choice but to stand next to Lorraine or cause a scene, so I stood there and let the quick one-minute photo session be over. I was not going to make a mockery out of her wedding, and I pretended it didn't bother me as I walked under the tent where the wedding party was preparing for a toast, some food and a good time. I only knew about three of my baby sister's friends. I did not know many people at the wedding at all.

I sat at the table where my kids, nephews, older brothers and one of their friends were sitting at. I was really hungry and ate my plate clean. I was about to go up for seconds when I noticed Lorraine was sitting at a big round table all by herself. I immediately questioned my older brothers, "Why is the bride's mother eating at a table by herself?" They both looked over at her, laughed and went back to eating as one of them said to me, "Because you're here." All the food I ate suddenly rested in the pit of my stomach as I was quickly reminded that I do not matter to them. Instead of vomiting all I wanted into his face, I instead got up and walked over to where the bride's mother was sitting. "Why is the bride's mother sitting over here alone?" I questioned her immediately as I approached her, and her answer still rings so loud and clear to this day. Lorraine's answer to my question was what my oldest brother had told me just moments earlier, "Because you're there." My eyes widened over her response as I quickly turned around and disposed of my plate, grabbed my purse and walked back over to Lorraine. "I'm not sitting there anymore, go sit with the bride's family," I said to her. I then walked out of the tent area and smoked a cigarette as I collected my thoughts. I kept telling myself, 'Don't let it bother you.'

I was thinking of sneaking off when the bride and groom came over for a group photo on a set of stairs that was outside the tent area. I didn't stand near Lorraine or my brothers for that photo, but my baby sister did get a picture of me with my two older brothers, the first photo of its kind. As I waited for the wedding photos to be over, I decided it was best to say bye before I left.

While waiting on the bride and groom, I noticed Lorraine was again standing alone. So I walked over to her and said, "Hey can we talk?" But she walked away. I assumed she didn't hear me. She was walking slowly in circles around the display of flowers. So, I tried to make conversation,

"Flowers smell so nice," I said. She nodded her head and I said, "Beautiful flowers." She then responded, "They are beautiful." I was determined to make conversation with her. "Look can we finally get together one day to talk?" I questioned her in a soft tone. She then turned her head, looked at me and said, "Nope." She quickly walked away, and I did the same thing, I walked away in the opposite direction. My kids stayed a little later to hang out with their cousins they rarely see. I said goodbye to the groom and bride, once again inviting them to my apartment when they had a chance.

I dropped my friend off at her home and I went home where I cried, got mad, got sad, angry, depressed, isolated and felt ashamed, worthless, unloved and unwanted all over again. What did I ever do to make her hate me so much? She kept me from my father's family out of spite. She kept me from her family out of silence. She only ever wanted me to be silenced and I could never understand why. There was nothing I could do; they were what I had to call family and they sucked.

I don't know why I continued to subject myself to the ridicule, humiliation, and embarrassment. Those two older brothers and baby sister had wives and a husband who only knew me by what they were told about me. I was feeling like I was back in 1985 when Lorraine told me the man she was moving in with didn't like me even though he didn't know me. I told myself over and over to not let it bother me, but it did, no matter how many times I told myself. Deep down it hurt, but now it was more of a disappointing kind of hurt. I was disappointed in my two older brothers for never remembering and not wanting to talk about what they should have all these years; me. No matter how many times I would remind myself of how wrong they were for treating me like they did, their digs of pain continued. Through Facebook, I found out I had another sibling, another child Lorraine failed to raise. I did my own research and found him on my own. Through Facebook, I found out about my baby sister's 40th birthday party. I was never invited, yet I was invited to her wedding.

In October I agreed with my boss to be put on payroll. Which meant getting my first real paycheck in many years. I was only working as a fill-in, so I got paid cash when I worked. That is until October when I woke up for work the Friday, I was to receive my first paycheck. As the day went on, my knees got wobbly, and my gut went hollow when my boss handed me my paycheck. Even though it was a part time paycheck, it was still a paycheck. I opened it from it's envelope and the first thing I see is the date; October 17, 2014.

Suddenly a warm smile went over me, through me and all around me. I quickly realized that I also should be proud of myself for all I've survived. I knew my life was never about what I've been through, it's about what I survived and that made distancing myself to save myself more rewarding and understanding. By the last week of December, I made an agreement with my boss to become a full-time employee beginning in January. I picked up more days at work as the holidays made for very busy time at the diner. I was excited over the thought of getting a full-time paycheck every week. They say when things happen, they usually happened in threes. I've seen it happen, doesn't mean it will always happen, right?

December 31, 2014... I got out of work and drove to the store for the newspaper, milk and two lottery tickets. I picked up a plate of Chinese food and went home. I took a shower, heated my food up and ate while reading the newspaper. Made myself a coffee, then I remembered the scratch tickets I had, so I scratched them. The first one was a twenty-dollar winner, the second one was a five-hundred-dollar winner.

January 1, 2015... I got out of work and drove to the store which sold me the winning tickets. I cashed them in, got two more scratch tickets, the newspaper and went home. I scratched the tickets as soon as I got inside my home. The first one was a loser, the second one was a five-thousand-dollar winner. I rubbed my eyes a few times, took a picture of it and zoomed in at it. I never won that much in my life, and I was so excited.

January 2, 2015... I got out of work, and it was a Friday. I was on my way home to shower and then go do some shopping at Walmart for a few things I needed. I had to drive through downtown and over the Bridge Street bridge to get over to my side of the city. I came to a red light as I was crossing the bridge, so I braked and waited behind a car which was also stopped. It was a long red light at a major intersection with the VFW highway. I was looking out my driver's side window at the bright sun shining over the icy cold Merrimack River. I thought about what I'd be spending my full-time paychecks on, some new clothes, shoes, trips. I saw a white car drive by in the lane next to me, then it all went dark.

With no brakes, no warning and driving fifty-eight miles per hour, a man crashed so hard into my car, his jeep landed partially on the roof of my car. Crushing my trunk, backseat, totaling my car and pretty much being the needle in the haystack that knocked this strong independent Irish girl, right down to the ground.

It all happened so fast, the Bridge Street bridge was closed to one lane of traffic as fire trucks, ambulances and police vehicles filled the street of broken car parts. I hurt but the adrenaline started to take effect when they attempted to get me into an ambulance, I looked over the bridge and saw Route 110 where my daughter's accident was just a few years earlier. I panicked, I was having an anxiety attack and I kept thinking I was at my daughter's accident scene all over again. A trip to an emergency room, physical therapy and a surgeon was now my future. The results from an MRI performed on me put a stop to my physical therapy as the surgeon informed me of my injuries before signing me off to a pain management center.

Just two weeks after that man crashed his jeep into my car, I was informed of my permanent injuries. "Injuries, you mean more than one?" I questioned the doctor as he informed me I suffered a rotated cervical spine, damaged facet joints, irreversible ligament, tendon, muscle and nerve damage. It would be only the beginning as more injuries were found. I was given medications, cortisone shots and a very painful medial branch block. My neck felt like it was on fire, swollen and painful. The back of my head felt like a crackling pain all through my skull. One side of my head felt like it was ongoing with electrical sharp zaps while the other side of my head was an ongoing ringing bell with hard throbs and spasms. The top of my head was heavy pressure and migraine headaches. I couldn't drive and I couldn't rid the pain I was feeling. I couldn't clean my house, shower, sleep, cook, walk, run and I couldn't have my granddaughter sleep overs anymore. Admitting I was permanently injured was not something I believed I had to admit. I tried exercise at home, but I only put myself in worse pain. I tried rest, but it only made me weaker and bored with boredom. By April, I was losing weight and living with so many painful injuries as my list continued to grow; occipital nerve damage, damage from my Axis-1 to C-5 on my left and C-2 to C-5 on my right, ten percent loss of sensation on left side of my neck, weakened left arm, tinnitus, insomnia, and vertigo. I was sleeping a few hours a week and anything I did only caused me more pain. Everything from my neck up hurt and it hurt twenty-four hours a day, every day.

My life got so chaotic as I was filling forms for my health insurance, forms for state aid, forms for social security disability benefits and by the time I got all the forms done completely, it was time to do it all over again. My doctor, my pain doctor, lawyer for my car accident and my social security lawyer all had to sign forms for insurance, state aid and food stamps. I felt so hopeless, helpless and completely drained. I was sitting on my couch one day crying over the severe head pains I was feeling; throbbing, spasms and jolts hurting all through my head and neck as I held my head in my arms. Kneeling over and begging for it all to go away.

"Please go away," I kept saying as I rocked back and forth on my couch. My hands were on my head as I closed my eyes and there I was so vividly, running down the stairs inside of Pleasant Street. I was wearing brown grananimals corduroy pants with matching red, brown and a white striped shirt and I was chasing my mother out the door. I could see, hear, and feel the atmosphere of 1980 Pleasant Street. I always remembered running to my friend's house that Saturday morning because that was the day my abuser never touched me again. It became a motto in my life, whenever the emotions of my childhood got the best of me, I would remind myself that my abuser Dave Umpleby never touched me again. I knew exactly what the memory that flashed through me was, because it was a memory I remembered but also a memory I spent my life pushing out of my head. I instantly sat straight up, hurting my neck even more in the process. I gasped for air as I was horrified with a feeling of being scared which I had not felt since I was a kid. I couldn't understand why I was remembering it so vividly.

Why was this memory flashing through my brain, my eyes and my emotions? It mortified me as I saw the memory as if I was reliving it. The feeling, the sounds, the smell, it knocked the wind out of me as I tried to make sense of it all. It was a horrifying, traumatic memory but I also knew it was just a memory. I held my head and neck as I rocked back and forth crying over the pain I was feeling. I reminded myself, 'I'm safe.' I reminded myself, 'It's only a memory.' I cried feeling the fear I haven't felt in decades.

They say repressed memories are memories that have been unconsciously blocked due to the memories being associated with a high level of trauma. What they don't tell you is repressed memories feel like being dragged for miles and miles as your open flesh scratches along the hot tar road. Leaving just enough skin for you to feel every ounce of burning pain.

I was feeling cheated once again. My life was always about, I ran to my friend's house in 1980 when I was ten years old, I lived there and there, then returned to my mother until I lived there, there and there, then it was 1983 and I reconnected with my dad who passed away just five months later. It was easier to explain it that way rather than thinking of all the sadness, hurt and pain that is associated with remembering that time of my life. So yes, I felt cheated because I remembered so much. I felt everything my young self felt that Saturday morning when I chased Lorraine down the stairs and out the front door. I was now forty-five years old, and I was reliving my ten-year old self, at least I thought I was ten years old.

It was midafternoon when I experienced my first repressed memory and by the time, I got off my couch from that memory, it was already after ten o'clock. I hyperventilated and panicked for over five hours due that one memory. I decided I needed a hot shower as food was not in my appetite at all. I felt so weak with a thousand-pound weight resting in the pit of my stomach. I felt unsafe and unwanted as I did that same Saturday morning all those decades earlier. I walked straight from the sofa to my bathroom. Crying over how empty it felt to be me.

As I was rinsing the shampoo out of my hair, my eyes closed when the water and shampoo ran down my face. That's when I saw the hockey sticks, I was peeking from, I saw the playroom in the attic of Pleasant Street and I saw my abuser as I also heard him, "Oooooh Cathy." I drank a mouthful of shower water while I gasped for air as I once did so often when I was a child. All I could do was cry, my head and neck hurt from my injuries and now I was being hit with these real life-like memories. They were as if I was reliving the scene, the smell, the feeling, the still shot images on continuous replay as I tasted the horror I once lived. *It's feeling your ribs slam against the bandaged torn sealed scars of your heart as you gasp for a breath that is really a knife, slicing the pain wide open.*

Then I yelled, "What the fuck." It didn't solve anything, but I got out of the shower. I sat on my couch until almost five in the morning, sitting in a towel with my jammies still in my hand as they were when I got out of the shower hours earlier. I was trying to understand why I was remembering these memories.

I was at a loss, my eyes gazed at my floor for hours before doing the same to my walls. Over and over again I replayed my life and questioned myself, 'Why the fuck am I remembering this shit?' I didn't need to be reminded of my childhood or my family's lack of emotional support because I already knew it, I was living it. I was now seeing my doctor monthly and my pain doctor on a weekly basis. In May I endured my first radio-frequency ablation and I finally admitted to my doctor that I needed to speak to someone about my childhood. She scheduled my first appointment with a medical professional behind a closed door. Only problem, there was a three-month grace period. My appointment was scheduled for August, and I had to go through another anniversary of my daughter's accident, anniversary of my ex-mother in-law passing and a whole summer of feeling like I got dragged by a truck.

I could not escape the horrible images, sounds, still shots and feelings from Pleasant Street. I'd stay awake so I didn't have nightmares. I'd leave every light on at nighttime. I'd watch a movie only to have a simple word send my thoughts roaming. All I could see, hear and feel was that Saturday morning on Pleasant Street. I'm chasing my mother down the stairs, I'm dodging her whacks as she's outside, I'm seeing her car drive away, I'm seeing the front door as I'm sitting on the sidewalk outside of Pleasant Street. I'm peeking through hockey sticks, my abuser in his green Shaw Print uniform, his words, his voice, "Ohhhhh Caaaathy," he hollered throughout the attic that morning. His grunts, huffs and anger just kept coming every day, repeatedly in horrifying life-like memories.

No matter how busy I was, how busy I kept myself or how busy my loved ones kept me, I was slowly becoming an emotional train wreck. I drained all I was able to save since returning to work. I was unable to pay my rent until a friend offered to lend me enough money to pay my rent for a few months. I was then able to concentrate on finding relief in dealing with my physical pain all while trying to rid the horrible memories I kept seeing.

I would hear the huffs, grunts and laughs as if my abuser was standing right there behind me. When I fell asleep, I would awake to hear him in my ear so clearly and terrifyingly. I cried over everything, I woke up crying and I fell asleep crying. I cried when I ate, and I cried because I was crying. I was so lost, confused, and empty. *Like a metal fist punched its way down my throat and ripped my insides out piece by piece.*

I was sitting in my lawyer's office one day, bawling my eyes out over all I was dealing with. My painful injuries, unable to work, bills piling up, repressed memories, painful procedures on my neck, the stress, exhaustion, and pain. He tried to praise me, I cried. He tried to inform me of all going on with my case, I cried. He explained the Massachusetts laws for a car accident, I cried. Then he said to me, "You're an emotional train wreck," and I stopped crying. *"Just keep writing so you don't become an emotional train wreck."* My friend Jon said that to me decades ago and there I was in my lawyer's office, I was a complete physical, emotional, and mental mess.

I left my lawyers office and went straight to Walmart where I got myself some new books to write in. Only problem was with my head and neck injuries, it hurt to write. The one thing which kept my sanity my whole life was writing, and I was now unable to do that. I would rip the page out, throw the book against the wall and try it all over again another day. I was in too much pain to visit my daughter's, too much pain to see my son and too much pain to socialize with my friends. All while relying on them to drive me to my doctor appointments, laundry and food shopping.

I was staying in bed for days and walking in circles during the night. I was scared, a scared I had not felt in over thirty years. The more I tried to forget, the more the horrible huffs, grunts and evil laughs I heard. The more I tried to forget, the more nightmares I had and the more I smelled the atmosphere of Pleasant Street. I was waiting for my permanent injuries to heal as I was very stubborn and refused to believe I was permanently injured. All those classes of self-defense I took were no use to me now. I was once this strong independent, take no shit kind of girl and now I was a weak, injured train wreck in the making kind of girl. I was slowly giving up as my injuries and repressed memories began to quickly take over my life.

It was all I was seeing, hearing and feeling; the atmosphere and emotions I felt on Pleasant Street. I'm outside of Pleasant Street, my mother's hand opening my bedroom door, I'm hiding behind hockey sticks in the attic as I'm crying and quietly begging, "Not again." My abuser's huffs, grunts and his evil laugh were every day and every night. No matter how much I tried, begged and prayed for it to go away, it was there. As I awaited my August appointment, the repressed memories only got worse. I was so emotionally drained and never imagined my life could be harder than it was when I was a kid, but there I was, and my life was about to only get more complicated.

I found myself one night, waking up as I walked into my bedroom door. I was trying to grab the door and hide behind it, but it wasn't my adult self, and it wasn't my bedroom door. It was my child self running to Lorraine's bedroom door on Pleasant Street. Even though I was sleeping in sweatpants and a t-shirt, I could feel a nightgown I was wearing when I was a kid. I could feel the atmosphere of Lorraine and Dave's bedroom and I could feel him as if he was standing right there next to me and it was horrifying. I could smell, hear, and feel my abusers heavy breathing as if it was clear as day. I stood at my doorway for a bit wondering how I got from my bed to the doorway. "Did I really just run and scream in my own bedroom?" I questioned myself out loud, I did, and I was scared. It was more of a mortifying, horrific, petrified kind of scared. 'I'm safe,' I reminded myself repeatedly, but it didn't shake the emotions I was feeling. I must have stood at my door looking all around my room for hours as I reminded myself, 'I'm safe.' Then I fell to my floor, I leaned against my bedroom door and bawled my eyes out. Tissue after tissue, nose blow after nose blow, I cried so hard and I was crying either for what I was feeling or for the little girl I once was, it only made me cry more. I felt so cold, disgusted, and nauseated over the horrible memories I once lived.

I never imagined I'd find myself talking to a medical professional behind a closed door and I couldn't wait for my August appointment to arrive. I knew I needed to get to that appointment, I was ready to talk because I was mad that I was dealing with the horrifying memories while dealing with excruciating pain from my injuries. I was mad because I was dealing with what I ran from my whole life, my childhood.

The horrifying memories continued; my abuser's hand over my face until I fell asleep, waking up on Fletcher Street on top of their bed and he's kneeled over me, his rants as I'm hiding behind hockey sticks, his laugh, his taunts, the tears I tasted and the pain I felt. A replay of the horror I once endured was all flashing in my head, my eyes and my life. Every day it was horrifying, horrific still shot images and life-like videos of me watching my child self. Then I was denied my social security disability insurance because I was too young. That was the excuse I was given. I had to reapply and wait many more months to find out if I'll be approved.

I tried pushing those repressed memories out of my head, my mind, and my life but they just kept coming. I endured another radiofrequency on my cervical spine and finally it was my August appointment. I explained my repressed memories and I explained my reasons why I had to start from the beginning. With a quick history of my birth parents, I then began to tell my life story from the beginning, where it all started on Fletcher Street.

Due to the graphic nature of my life, I had to go up the ladder of medical professionals to speak with someone behind a closed door, to see where I belonged. I was quickly seen by a therapist, a psychiatrist, a psychologist and counselors. Because I was cleared of having no drug, alcohol, suicidal or mental disorder and because I didn't want a medication or prescription, they didn't really know what to do with the strong Irish girl standing in front of them.

I always believed that no pill, no drug, no drink and no love song could ever erase or take away the pain that was instilled in me at such a young age. The medical professionals didn't give up on me and I was meeting with a counselor on a weekly basis. Not being able to work or move like I once did was quickly breaking down a girl who spent her whole life keeping herself strong in a world, I could have so easily crashed in. Though talking with a medical professional was helpful, at times it felt so emotionally draining. As I continued being dragged down by my recurring repressed memories, another one was added as I found myself standing in the kitchen of where my birth mother lived in 1985.

I was standing in her kitchen wearing my corduroy Levi jeans, I had a confused look on my face as I felt the wind from my mother's hand while she fanned it in the air letting me know, "All those pictures will be all over the newspaper." It's all I saw, still shot images of photos, my abuser Dave's photos. I saw his drawer open with bundles of photos wrapped in elastic. I saw me in the tub crying as photos from his polaroid camera developed along the sink and on top of the toilet. I saw him showing me pictures of myself on Fletcher Street. I saw myself waking up to see photos scattered all over Lorraine's bureau.

I saw the kitchen of her Lawrence Street apartment, the washing machine, sink, wooden table and chairs. The cabinets, the backdoor and doorway into the living room. I saw Lorraine's face, I saw my look of hurt, disappointment and confusion as I wondered, 'Why does she hate me so much?' Then I saw the photos again. "Oh my God the photos," I jumped up from my bed and screamed when that memory flashed through my head. "What the fuck," I screamed my next shout out to the walls of my bedroom. My stomach bounced up and down as I slowly started to hyperventilate, have a panic attack, an anxiety overload, a mortified nightmare, meltdown or all the above. A gut-wrenching emptiness as it all sinks in. Tears filled up and poured down my face as I felt so sad for that little girl, the little girl I kept seeing, the little girl who was me.

My emotional train wreck life continued. I felt the emptiness I buried so deep within myself. I buried memories of the cruelty Lorraine had towards me. I buried memories of why she abandoned me, why she didn't stop the abuse, why she didn't protect me, and I buried questions of why she gave me the childhood she allowed me to grow into. It was a reality into the lack of everything I have received from my birth family and a painful truth.

By December, I was spending hours a day in bed hurting and crying. Just days before my birthday, I finally let myself cry for everything I lived through when I was young. I was finally feeling empathy for the little girl I once was. With only a few weeks left of 2015, I could never imagine the horror and the reality I was about to relive. It was all the move on, get over it, forget, forgive, stop dwelling and it wasn't that bad, all laughing at me saying, "We're back." *No matter how many times I thought I faced the reality of my childhood, I once again find myself facing it again.*

With the many years of abuse, I did remember I was shocked, devastated and mortified to know there were even more memories I had no choice but to remember. The flashbacks continued with all the hurt, pain and fear as if I was back on Pleasant Street reliving the life I once lived, reliving the horror. As the memories continued, I continued to find out the reason why I was experiencing them. They were all memories I was remembering, so I knew they couldn't be repressed memories. Just because I hadn't thought about them in over thirty-five years, they were still memories I was remembering. No matter how many layers of clothes or makeup you wear, you can't dress up an emotional train wreck.

The memories continued; I'm in the attic behind hockey sticks, being taunted to come out from hiding, knocks on the bedroom door, my brothers laughing as they try convincing me to jump off the back porch rooftop. Hearing the words, "You know the drill." The hurt and fear as he poked underneath my oldest brother's bed, more knocking on that bedroom door, huge hole in the cellar wall, the pile of rocks on the cellar floor, being told, "Try it out, your arms will be here when you're found."

I'm in bed on Pleasant Street unable to move, homework being delivered, my ribs are broken, those damn knocks on the door again, hiding behind hockey sticks again, more knocks on the door. Fletcher Street, Pleasant Street, Lawrence Street, Pleasant Street, Butler Avenue and back to Pleasant Street. I just wanted it all to stop. It didn't matter I turned a year older, it didn't matter it was the Christmas holiday season. The horrible memories continued.

In all my years with my kids, I always started my Christmas shopping in September or October. But there I was just six days before Christmas, and I had not done any shopping at all. I pulled myself together and my friend took me out shopping. I was impressed with all the sales going on just a week before Christmas. I drained my bank account so I could buy gifts for my kids and granddaughter. I guess I was trying to mask my rundown train wreck look. My kids and I talked about my repressed memories as they were concerned about me. That's when my family relations made sense to them, as I was always honest with my kids about my childhood.

I just wanted the pain to stop, the memories to stop, the sounds, images and life-like still shots of my childhood, but they just continued coming at me in waves. I would hear my mother's cruel words, I would see myself asking her to come with me to the police station. I saw nude photos of myself in newspapers. Being told Dave was in jail. "A jail for child pigs," she said. I saw myself hiding behind those hockey sticks over and over, the cookout at Lorraine's sister's house and those knocks on that bedroom door again. The bruises all over my stomach, my badly beaten face, my brothers not calling the police.

The horrifying memories just continued consuming my mornings, my days, my nights and my life. What mostly got me out of bed was to grab another box of tissues or to use the bathroom. Anything I did provoked a memory. I'd open my refrigerator door and see the snack cabinet on Fletcher Street as a hand goes over my mouth. I'd finish drinking a bottled water and see my abuser crushing his beer can. At the grocery store, I'd grab an item off a shelf and see myself being slammed onto the attic floor. I'd fold laundry and see myself hiding under beds, behind chairs, in a dryer and under the outside porch. Places I hid sometimes for hours at a time when I was a kid. It hurt to accept what I was remembering and to say it out loud would prove to be an unbearable experience I didn't want to face.

Questions filled my head a million times a day. How can this be true? How could they make me suffer this alone? "No, no, no," I'd say repeatedly. Then came the memory of toys on top of me as I hid inside the toy box in the attic playroom on Pleasant Street. The suffocating rush of wind as I gasped for a breath while I'm being yanked out by my throat. That was the day I remembered the last attack I suffered by the hands of my abuser Dave Umpleby. Deep breaths and keeping calm was no match for the panic attack I suffered as that memory became so crystal clear to me. "Oh my God," I yelled. "I begged them to call the police," I said out loud. "They knew," I continued to yell. "They always knew," I continued as I bawled my eyes out. That was the day I knew for a fact, for over thirty years, I had buried all the memories of my family's knowledge of the abuse I had endured.'

The repressed memories were reminding me about my family and my last year living on Pleasant Street. The memories were reminding me about the last attack I suffered and about my older siblings who pulled my abuser away from me so he would stop stomping on my child size body. It was just the beginning of a horrifying reality as more and more of the year 1981, 1982 and the degrading of my fifteen year old soul in 1985 start to emerge in horrifying repressed memories over the course of almost two years. It took nightmares to make reality out of memories I only wanted to forget. I was dealing with the reality of all my family did know from back then and how hurt I was to realize, remember and face the reality about the caring, loving, safe family, I never had.

I was always proud of myself for getting away from Pleasant Street, yet I had to stay proud in silence. No one wanted to hear about a bad childhood never mind a horrific one. The first time I spoke openly, comfortably, without fear, shame, humiliation or embarrassment about my childhood abuse, was also the last time I stayed silent. It was more than the weight of the world off my shoulders, it was over a thousand memories of my young child self finally being heard.

I am no longer ashamed, embarrassed or humiliated by what happened to me in my childhood. I now realize I was only a kid. Sometimes the memories get overwhelming with images of things that monster did to me and I puke. "My God I'm that girl," I'd say out loud as I sickly shake my head in disbelief. I get that people, family and society don't want to hear the reality of childhood sexual abuse, but that is so unfair to the child who suffers the sexual abuse. I get that people, family and society don't want to hear how cruel family can be to a family member, but that was something I also didn't want to believe. I wanted to believe my family loved me, I mean we were all adults now, they had to love me, right?

I hate the childhood I was given; I got a few lifetime friends from it but I did not get family. Family don't do what my family did to me. That monster was not done with me when I ran that morning, nor was he done with his monstrous ways. Not thinking there was more to my repressed memories, I began my search for answers, a search that would become a horrifying reality I now live.

A Search for Answers and The Horrifying Reality

After seeing the memory of being pulled out of the toy box on Pleasant Street, all the memories came back in rewind, fast forward and still shot image form. So many horrifying emotions, fear and tears. Feeling scared, holding my breath, chasing Lorraine outside, running out my bedroom and into my abuser, being blocked by him or hearing him counting. I'm in my oldest brother's bedroom, under his bed, I'm standing in the middle of the playroom, I'm tossed off my abusers work boot and my older brothers pulling him away. Every memory from my last year living with my family on Pleasant Street, I was suddenly remembering. I was remembering the exact reason why I ran that Saturday morning on Pleasant Street, because I was fucking scared, I was petrified of my abuser, and no one gave two shits about me in that house. That is why I had no choice but to run to save myself.

I drilled in my head for decades all that mattered was that monster never touched me again. Burying all memory of the cruelty I received from my family. I hated the reality my nightmarish memories were reminding me. The pain I felt hurt me right down to my soul. *A gasping breath of shock as all you blow out is the swarm of bees stinging its way through your mouth of pain.*

I was living with twenty-four hours a day of non-stop head and neck pain. Seven months of traumatizing memories that would continue for another twelve months. My car accident lawyer called me one day to check up on me and ended up being a friend instead. He told me two scenarios of a strong-willed, well-liked person. Both were great stories but when he was done, I realized he was referring to me. I was the strong-willed, well-liked person he was talking about. That phone call made me open my eyes and I reminded myself, 'You survived your childhood you can survive this,' and that is what I chose to do.

I closed that wound in my heart back up, prepared for another radiofrequency on my cervical spine and took time to remember all I spent my whole life trying to forget. I tried writing in a journal again, but it was too much on my injuries, so I started typing instead. It was easier to walk away from the typewriter than it was to rip up another page of writing. I soon found myself reaching out to people who once took me in and reaching out to Lorraine's other children including the two brothers I once lived with. I reached out to the friends from Agawam Street, friends from Pleasant Street and friends from my teen years. Aside from the lack of remembrance from my siblings, everyone I talked to remembered. They remembered me and my cruel family, except of course those two older brothers.

I typed my life out in three-month intervals, starting at age five-years old in 1975. I was physically here but I was mentally lost on the cellar floor of Pleasant Street. My childhood was so confusing as I tried to put my schools in order. For over thirty years I assumed my school field trip to the cranberry bog was from the Moody School in 6th grade 1980. For over thirty years I believed I went to the Moody School for 6th grade, but I would soon find out I didn't.

The horrible memories continued, pain doctor appointments continued, and the horrifying reality started to become crystal clear. "They knew," I said a hundred times a day. Lorraine always knew, but my two older siblings also knew about the beating I suffered in the attic, my screams while being in that bedroom and begging them to call the police. One was going to call when he got to his friend Chris's house and the other said, "You don't call cops on family."

I was hurt, I was sad, I was angry, I was empty, and I was lost. I called my friend whose house I ran to that Saturday morning on Pleasant Street, and I questioned her, "Does your mom remember that Saturday morning on Pleasant Street?" She quickly answered me, "Oh my God yes." I fell down to my floor and I bawled my eyes out. I now accepted the reality of why I ran that morning, because I was petrified of being put in that cellar wall. I felt every emotion I felt when I was a kid. I just cried and cried until I had enough tears that I started to use them to lift me up.

After days of crying, I also remembered more about that hole dug into the cellar wall, what was put in there, why it was dug and when it was dug. I drew a map of what the cellar on Pleasant Street looked like, where the hole was dug, where I was tied by a chain, and I sent it in a text message to my two older brothers asking what they remembered of my childhood. After being ignored for days, my oldest brother called, but claimed not to remember anything. I informed him of my memoir I was typing and how I remembered everything. He became curious about my memoir and made plans to come see me at my apartment, the one I've been living in for three years already. Needless to say, I was very excited over my oldest brother coming to see me. It would end up being an eye-opening journey that led to answers for the so many questions of why they always wanted me silenced.

I wouldn't wish it on my worst enemy, I wouldn't wish it on the most hated person in the world and I sure as hell wouldn't let someone I love, who loves me, a friend, coworker or a stranger deal with it alone. Especially if they turned to me for help, for closure, for an ear to listen, a shoulder to lean on or a hand to hold. As I started to see the reality of my childhood and how unwanted I was treated, I also began to feel so insulted that my birth family made me live through it all alone. Gosh did the reality of that hurt right to the core of my every being. It's what my friend Jon told me back in 1991, I was fighting for a family I never really had. Twenty-four years after Jon died, his words still have big impacts in my life. As much as I didn't want to believe it, it was true.

I didn't deserve this, and I knew it. But finally, my oldest brother was coming to see me at my apartment and it made me happy. At the time my friend was visiting from Florida and was present when my oldest brother came to visit. "I don't remember that" he said to everything. I was crying as I told him I was going to the police so they can retrieve the photos and film from that cellar wall. I cried to him, "He raped me." I cried to him about the last attack I suffered in the attic. I cried to him about when it started on Fletcher Street, "Your first day at karate," I said. I cried to him about reaching out to other people who took me in when I was a kid. I cried to him about my pain, my horror and my life. All he could say was, "I don't remember that." Then he questioned me, "How do you even remember what Fletcher Street looked like?" Out of all I said to him that day, that was the question he had for me. I answered him as I stood up and did a diagram of what our Fletcher Street apartment looked like. His eyes widened as he looked surprised I remembered and just as quickly he got up to leave. I asked him to please proofread my memoir once its done and he said he would. I asked him to please visit me again and he said he would. I asked him to please keep in touch and he said he would. I asked him to please talk with our other brother and baby sister and he said he would. I was so happy my oldest brother visited me.

I turned to my friend and I gave her a huge hug of happiness. "I'm so glad he came to see me," I said to her. But she had the saddest face I've ever seen on her as she told me, "No honey, I'm sorry." As tears filled her eyes, she hugged me and explained to me what she witnessed out of his visit. "He was only here to see what you remembered," she said to me. I looked at her strangely and told her, "No he wasn't." By the look on her face I knew she was right. Within minutes, my overly happy self was shot back down to reality as I realized my friend was right. No matter how much I tried to make myself not think about it, the hurt was there. I kept telling myself, 'They can't be that cruel.' I kept reminding myself, 'Get over it.' I kept reminding myself, 'Just forget about it.' My friend soon went back to Florida and I continued experiencing many horrible memories.

It was months and months of days, hours, minutes and seconds of still shots images and memories. Sounds of huffs, grunts and voices. Smelling the clothes and atmosphere as if I was taken back in time. Feeling every emotion of the pain, fear and terror I was very familiar with. They wouldn't stop, no matter how many times I kept myself from sleeping. No matter how many times I forced my eyes to stay open. No matter how busy I kept myself, the horrifying memories kept coming back.

From Fletcher Street, as I was sick to my stomach while so much flashed through my head. Waking up on Lorraine's bed while my abuser was on top of me and his threats of being killed. The nude pictures of myself, the double reel film I was forced to watch, pornography of my five and six year old self. The hundreds and hundreds of times I told Lorraine and the pain I always felt.

From Pleasant Street, as these memories kicked the shit out of me, turned me into an emotional train wreck and knocked me down as I tried to understand why I was seeing, feeling and smelling everything from my childhood. Crying, hyperventilating and begging it to stop. Having broken ribs, feeling ashamed and feeling worthless. My beaten face and my abusers work boots. His taunts, his threats, his grunts, his huffs and his voice.

From Butler Avenue, as I'm standing outside on a sidewalk so heartbroken. The cruelty and living with the neighbors. Finding out what was put in the hole dug into the cellar wall on Pleasant Street and being dead to my own mother.

From Lawrence Street, as I found out my abuser never went to jail and asking Lorraine to take me to the police. Her hands waving in the air as she tells me the nude photos of myself will be all over newspapers. Her degrading of my teenage soul. The horrifying memories continued. I will admit to this day it still hurts like a fresh wound meeting an old one and all that's left in the wake of a handshake are the shreds of false hope I chased for over twenty years

As I kept experiencing my traumatizing, horrific repressed memories, I reminded myself constantly of the older brothers I lived with as a child. We were adults now and they still shun me away. So I asked myself, where the heck does that leave me? Don't they get it? I remember everything now. I remembered the sign one brother hung outside on the street pole, stating in black marker a sexual gesture with my name. Know why that was done? Because a knock on Dave and Lorraine's bedroom door caused the door to open a little. Afterwards I was teased because I knew my brother was getting me help. I knew my abuser was caught and he knew he was caught, but he also taunted me that my brother wasn't getting me help. My abuser was right, my brother didn't get help that day, he wrote a sign stating, 'Cathy gives head.' I also remembered my other brother who released my hands from the stair banister as I screamed, "He's raping me."

In March 2016, after many days and nights of thinking about it, I decided to go to the police to report what Dave and Lorraine allowed to be buried in that cellar wall. All the humiliation, shame and embarrassment I carried for over thirty years was too heavy and it wasn't mine to carry anymore. It belongs to Lorraine, Dave and it belongs to the siblings who fail to remember, talk about or believe the survivor I am. For over thirty years I blamed myself for missing out on so much with my siblings. The repressed memories helped me see it was them who missed out on so much with me.

I continuously replayed my oldest brother's visit to my apartment and all I talked with him. I thought about the question he asked me about my memory of Fletcher Street. Of all I said to him that day, his only question to me was what did I remember of the apartment itself. I had to muster up the strength and courage before I got myself to the police, which took a few weeks. I had the map I drew of the cellar on Pleasant Street and I remembered that my oldest brother stayed on Pleasant Street with Dave until school was out. But I was confused because our mother moved in springtime 1982 and I ran in 1980, so where was I in 1981?

I just assumed I stayed at my friend's house from 1980 to 1982. Then I'd say out loud, "No can't be." Then I'd think to myself, 'If I ran in 1980 and Lorraine moved in 1982 and I was returned in 1982, where was I in 1981?' I knew I stayed with Sandi's family the first time for one year, not two years. Trying to figure it out was so mind boggling and confusing. Going over it again and again in my head, 'I ran in June of 1980 and Lorraine moved in 1982,' 'I went back to her in 1982 so where was I in 1981?' "Uuurgh," I would yell as I hated the confusion it caused me. I didn't want to think of the pain I was feeling from my injuries in the car accident. I didn't want to think of the memories I was being forced to remember, but there I was dealing with it all.

I went back to typing my life story but I was stuck on the year 1979. I typed about camping at Wyman's Beach in 1979 but I also knew we camped another year there. Which would have made it 1980, but I ran in June of 1980. So how could that be? It made my brain hurt with all the questions and memories it had going on inside. You could take a metal fist with spikes, cover it in liquid acid and punch it into my heart. Twisting until the acid dissolves every moving organ in me and it still wouldn't compare to the pain I felt being part of a family I was never really a part of.

Throughout all the reaching out to people from my past, I was also finding out about more children Lorraine had and never raised. This time it was her first born, a son. I creeped his Facebook page and he is a spitting image of another brother.

Within three weeks of my oldest brother visiting me at my apartment, I called my friend up and questioned her for the ride to the police station. I walked in and up to the Plexiglas window. "I'd like to pay someone to go into my childhood home," I said to the officer on the other side of the window and of course I started to cry. The officer had me take a seat as I waited until a uniformed officer sat next to me with a pad of paper. "Start from the beginning," he said to me. I told the officer about the abuse, film and photos from 346 Fletcher Street. I told the officer about the abuse, film and photos from 121 Pleasant Street. I told the officer about all Lorraine said to me on Butler Avenue.

I was anxious, I was nervous, I was embarrassed, but I was telling my story. "Please help me get those films and photos out of the cellar wall?" I pleaded with the officer. He wrote everything down and told me a detective would call me. I went home and smiled a smile of proudness. I then fell onto the middle of my living room floor and bawled my eyes out as so many memories from my childhood were leaving me with hashtag smiley faces on them. It was like the kid in me was finally being heard. Days later a female detective called me and we spoke about the photos, film and abuse I endured, then she passed it to the district attorney's office.

I went back to typing, but I was once again stuck on that one year of my life. It really tested my patience trying to figure out what happened to me in 1981. My hands were in the air as I couldn't make sense of it, so I made myself a check list.

I knew we moved to Pleasant Street in 1977 after making my first communion in May and making my baby sister's first birthday in August, be celebrated at our new apartment which was Pleasant Street.

I knew I went away to summer camp the following summer in 1978.

I knew we camped at Wyman's Beach in 1979.

I knew I ran in 1980.

I knew I was returned to my family on Butler Avenue in 1982.

I knew my dad passed away in 1983.

I knew we camped two summers at Wyman's Beach.

I knew one of my checks was wrong, but I have an impeccable memory, I always have. I was wrong somewhere but I had to put it on the back burner as I dealt with issues in my life. More procedures and more needles in my skull and neck, more nerve medications and before I knew it, another month went by and rent was due. I was already three months behind on my rent. Being out of work for over a year due to the car accident and awaiting social security approval, my landlord was impressed I paid rent as long as I did. He allowed me to stay as I awaited another decision on my social security application. I tried getting assistance for my rent but

I needed an eviction notice. I didn't have one because my landlord, like myself assumed the social security administration would come through for me.

Two more months went by with still no decision from social security. It was now over six months since I applied for food stamps and cash assistance, which meant it was time to reapply for benefits. It may sound easy but I was dealing with intense everyday pain, reliving a horrifying nightmare everyday and I no longer drove a car due to my injuries. I didn't mind the paperwork, but I hated bothering my doctors to fill out papers on just about everything I was applying for.

While applying for assistance with my rent, I was turned away from one agency because I had a car accident settlement coming. Massachusetts has a three-year cap. I explained it could be another two years before that happened, but I was turned away. I was turned away from another agency because I didn't live at the homeless shelter. I explained I was trying not to go homeless, but I was turned away. I was turned away from another agency because I didn't have a mental health condition. I explained that I do have post traumatic stress disorder and anxiety from my childhood. The woman left me alone in the interview room while she went to get more information pertaining to getting me some help. When she returned to the room she came with another woman who said, "I'm sorry we can't help you," she bluntly told me. I pleaded with both woman, "I'll be homeless in a month." It didn't matter as I was informed, "I'm sorry." As they stood there shaking their heads. I was so furious I got up, thanked them for wasting my time and I walked out of the building. I didn't serve in our military, I wasn't in an abusive relationship, I didn't use drugs or drink alcohol and I wasn't suicidal. So many people have it so much worse than me. I can't go around claiming mental health issues when all my problems stem from my childhood, right? I was once again gas lighting myself.

After talking with my landlord, he agreed to let me stay another month in hopes I'd be approved for my social security benefits by then. My hands were in the air as there was nothing I could do. Procedures on my neck and needles in my head continued. Weekly meetings with my counselor continued and soon I was grabbing boxes from local stores so I could start packing. Where would I store all my stuff? I didn't get enough money a month to pay for a storage unit.

My friend's son was getting his own place, my daughter needed a bureau and suddenly all my furniture went to places needed. All I had were boxes filled with my life. I moved boxes to my daughter's, my friend's and her brother's house. June 1, 2016 was the first time since I was a teenager that I became homeless. I didn't go to Lowell's homeless shelter but like when I was a teenager, I moved into a room at my friend's parents house.

It was emotionally hard on me but I knew I had to focus on the positive of my situation. I had more than when I was a kid, I was able to stay at my friend's parents house and I knew my social security would be here soon. Aside from my physical and emotional pain, my whole body felt so stuck, like I kept stepping in sticky glue with every step I took. My insides felt so blank with a heavy mountain of pain weighing me down. It was hard wiping the tears, fears and horrifying memories away every time I left my room. I didn't want my friend's elderly parents to see me like that. Some days I did good at hiding all my hurt but other days, they knew I was dealing with a lot. As I said before you can't dress up an emotional train wreck. Every step I took, I felt myself sinking more and more into a sinkhole of shame, secrets and silence just screaming to be heard. Because I was now considered homeless, the social security administration agreed to rush my case. It made me feel good and any negativity I carried, I quickly turned it back to a positive. I knew by the end of summer I would be back in my own apartment again.

I spent a lot of my mornings, days and nights typing my life story. I was still trying to make sense of the missing year of my life. I was certain it had to be a year after I left Pleasant Street in 1980. I looked through my first written journal, I wrote in it that I was ten-years old when I ran from Pleasant Street. It was confusing and frustrating not knowing my whereabouts for a whole year of my life. The repressed memories I was still experiencing. The reality of knowing for a fact what my two older siblings and Lorraine did know, made me feel like I was experiencing a slow, painful, gut wrenching, heart breaking death.

As physically and emotionally miserable that I was, I made the best out of my 2016 summer. In August, I finally received the big white envelope in the mail from the social security administration. I was nervous and anxious to open it, I went up to my rented room and opened the letter. I was denied again because I was young and had working legs. I called my lawyer and within days, I was in his office appealing the decision. Because my case was rushed they used my records from my first denial decision and denied me again based on that. I was so mad at the state of Massachusetts. My friend drove me around the city to get papers signed, filled out and returned so my case could be rushed again. Within a week, I was informed they would review my case in October 2016. It was only a few more months, so I sucked it up like a buttercup. I cried when everyone was sleeping and I typed all day long.

In September, I underwent another radio-frequency and by October, I agreed to start injections in my neck called Dysport injections. A bunch of tiny needles being jabbed in my neck and head every ninety days for a year. My first dose was scheduled for November. I continued seeing my counselor weekly and I continued reaping the backlash of being a statistic in a world full of abused children who grew up. I continued to type, whether it be my poetry; my life story, my memories or my thoughts, I kept typing. One day while typing, I went back to the first half of my life story I had typed months earlier. I tried to figure out that missing year of my life again. I was sitting on my bed, typewriter between my legs and I was trying to remember. Looking straight ahead was a stack of boxes and bins I had stored there when I moved in.

'Photo albums,' marked one of the boxes, I kind of smiled as it was a box I never unpacked. From my divorce in 2001, it stayed on a shelf in a closet. When I moved to Powell Street, when I moved in 2009 and when I moved in 2013, on a closet shelf it went. There I was in 2016 unpacking the box and under a few photo albums was a large yellow envelope. I knew exactly what was in it, my first communion certificate with my name spelled wrong, school photos of me from age five to my 6th grade class photo, report cards, along with my 6th and 8th grade diplomas. Like a tidal wave drowning me in slow motion, images of my first repressed memory mixing with all the horrifying memories, came together and finally rested peacefully in its own completed jigsaw puzzle. That one envelope answered all the doubt, shame and questions I needed to know, leaving me gasping for air.

It's like being sucked in by a riptide with no water, just a mountain wave of salt and sand smacking your face as you're dragged into what seems like the center of the earth. How could anyone ever understand how hurt I was, how empty I was, how cheated I felt? I had no choice but to remember everything from Pleasant Street as the memories just kept coming. Pulling my diplomas, school photos, report cards and first communion certificate out of that yellow envelope was like a ball of vomit in my stomach. I always remembered missing my 6th grade graduation because I was left at my mother's cousin's house the day I ran from Pleasant Street. So I grabbed a piece of paper and wrote down all the schools I went to from first grade to eighth grade. The Bartlett, Rogers, Oakland, LeBlanc, Moody and Butler schools.

Looking through my report cards, I was able to remember the Oakland and LeBlanc schools were the same school. I went there during the name change which is probably why I assumed it was two different schools. Then I looked at my check list again,

I knew we camped two summers at Wyman's Beach. I remember it clearly, I always have. Chipmunk Trail is where we stayed the second summer.

My dad passed away one year after my short stay on Butler Avenue. I remember it clearly, I always have. My dad passed away October 17, 1983.

I missed my 6th grade graduation because I was abandoned at Lorraine's cousins house.

'Wait my diploma,' I quickly thought to myself as I grabbed it and in slow motion my eyes looked at the date on my diploma at least a hundred times. My 6th grade graduation was in 1981. My confusion crumbled, my doubts cleared up, my shame burned, my questions finally answered like the ocean floor speeding in a flash of light and crashing upon my face, the flashbacks came in tidal waves; the toy box in the attic I'm pulled from, the sign hung on the outside pole, Barker Avenue, Lawrence Street, Lorraine's hands waving in the air until finally stopping at the memory of me running down the back stairs on Lawrence Street. I was fifteen-years old when Lorraine managed to degrade what was left of my teenage soul after I questioned her to accompany me to the police department so I could report my abuser Dave Umpleby. They can claim lack of memory all they want, but I remember it all now.

I cried and hyperventilated as I realized it wasn't a year after I left Pleasant Street that was missing from my life, it was a whole year of more horrifying traumatizing sexual and inhumane cruelty abuse that was the missing year of my life. I ran in 1981 not 1980 like I assumed for over thirty years and even as adults, my family allowed me to believe it. Not only were my repressed memories reminding me of my last year living with my family on Pleasant Street, they were reminding me of the horrifying game Dave started with me, reminding me of all Lorraine said to me about the hole dug in that cellar wall and what was put in there. They were reminding me of my conversations with Lorraine on Lawrence Street and all her degrading comments to steer me away from going to the police. No matter how many words you put together, there is no describing the loving, caring, safe family you never had.

Tissue after tissue as I cleaned my face, cleared my eyes and brushed my hair so I could head downstairs for some supper. As I moved my typewriter from my bed, I saw my laptop resting on top of one of my packed boxes I used as a table. "No," I cried out loud as I gasped for air. "No, please let there be no one," I begged in a voice out loud. I then grabbed my laptop, opened it and turned it on. As a bowl of vomit rested in the pit of my stomach, I typed in, Murdered/Missing girls in Lowell Massachusetts June 1981-July 1982. Then I pressed the enter button. My laptop screen lit up with names, photos and unsolved murders from 1981 to 1982 along with a 1974 unsolved murder and a 1993 unsolved murder, all from my hometown of Lowell Massachusetts. I just wanted to bang my head into the wall of my room but with my neck injury, I decided against it. It felt like my head was going to explode, I couldn't face it, I couldn't continue reading the screen on my laptop, I couldn't take it all in as it was just too much to bare.

I questioned myself over and over, 'How could they claim to love me?' It's all that went through my head about my birth mother Lorraine and my two older brothers. I cried as my mouth stayed open trying to scream but all I got was a taste of that cold cellar floor from 1981 Pleasant Street. Asking myself the same questions only made it worse on me as I continued to question myself, 'Why did they make me suffer this horror alone?' I didn't care about their lack of everything when I was younger, I didn't care about the apology I never received in my twenties and I didn't care about their lack of empathy and support in my thirties. But I reached out to them in 2016, when they were in their late forties to early fifties and they still shunned me, ridiculed me, belittled me and disregarded me as if I was yesterday's trash. They did not care, they will be the first to say they did care, but I am here to say, "No they did not." I was still that emotional train wreck, only now it was like I was plowed into and drove over about a hundred more times by a dump truck. I was so heartbroken, sad and mortified for the little girl I once was. All those years and decades when I thought I faced my childhood and stood up for myself, was me just telling myself that. I was a month shy of my forty-seventh birthday and I finally faced my childhood. I cried for the little girl I once was, I felt sad for the little girl I once was and I finally felt empathy for not only the little girl I once was, but I felt empathy for my mid forty-year old self also.

The pain I felt was in the pit of my stomach, shooting through my heart and out my mouth as it scrapped each memory with a sharp glass of pain. I was hollow, I was lost, I was so damn sad and I remembered everything. It's all that flashed before my eyes and it's all that played in my head; the childhood I spent my whole life trying to forget, the lack of protection I endured, the mortifying fear I endured, the traumatizing horror I endured and the unwanted, unloved feelings I endured. It's all I saw; images of

Fletcher Street, Pleasant Street, Butler Avenue, Lawrence Street and the degrading of my fifteen-year old soul with the words from my own mother.

The next morning, my friend came to my bedroom door with a coffee and the mail. My big white envelope from the social security administration had arrived. I felt a bit positive as I got excited over the thought of being in my own apartment in time for the Christmas holiday, but that was not the case. I was once again denied my social security benefits. This time they agreed I lived in pain but I was strong willed, an author of a memoir and I had two working legs. Another classless excuse from my home state of Massachusetts. My journals and typing to help me understand my repressed memories was used against me. Being strong willed and head smart was used against me. Having two working legs was used against me. The excuses I was given for their decisions were insulting. I quickly went back to the same routine of running around to have forms filled out and papers signed by both my doctor and pain doctor.

Another meeting with my social security lawyer and this time I got good news. Both my doctors were very upset to hear I was denied benefits and both would be writing a narrative for the judge who decides my approval for benefits a fourth time. My lawyer was also upset I didn't get approved which made me feel better about being wrongly denied. He and his office were very sincere and understanding with me. The state of Massachusetts really failed me and there was not a thing I could do about it.

My head continued to hurt, my neck hurt, burned and gave me sharp electric pains. Christmas was coming and I was broke. I had five dollars in my checking account since the year before. It was my first Christmas not being able to spoil my kids in over twenty years, but my kids are so awesome and they didn't care. We had our Christmas eve together, our Christmas morning together and a great breakfast.

Soon after Christmas and with the shock of now knowing that the missing year of my life was another year of horrifying abuse and inhumane cruelty, I realized I was now only experiencing memories. As painful as the memories were, at least I wasn't experiencing anymore repressed memories. With all I had been through in my young life, thinking or remembering my life between 1980 until my dad died in 1983 was always too much confusion for me. Though I always remembered so much, I just forgot how hurt it felt to be me back then. It was always easier to forget my feelings, my worth and my self being because that was all I ever knew. My repressed memories put it all in full circle and deep down it was sad, but one thing I finally knew was that I mattered, even if I didn't matter to those siblings and Lorraine.

I typed the continuing pages in my memoir and as I typed of the day I was dropped off on Pleasant Street in late August 1981, my heart went into my stomach, vomit rested in my throat and tears poured from my eyes. The more research I did, the more sick to my stomach I felt. It was a weekday during the last week of August 1981 when I was dropped off on Pleasant Street, my abuser saw me and charged after me as he was on a drunken rampage to silence me for good. Then I read about Janice Filamond.

Janice Filamond was thirteen-years old when she disappeared in late August 1981. She was a typical teen who had no reason to run away from home. In April 1982, a grim discovery of human remains on the Lowell/Chelmsford line was a family's worst nightmare. Days later the remains were identified as that of thirteen-year old Janice Filamond. Today the case of Janice Filamond remains open and unsolved.

I don't know if my abuser Dave Umpleby is responsible for the disappearance and vicious murder of Janice Filamond, but I am one-hundred percent positive he was capable of committing it. If you have any information about the murder of Janice Filamond please contact the Middlesex County District Attorney Office at (781) 897-8300

Just weeks after the remains of Janice Filamond were identified and a hole in a cellar wall remained, another girl from Lowell Massachusetts would be reported missing.

Brenda Lacombe was just nineteen-years old when she went missing in May 1982. She left her grandmother's apartment in the early morning hours of May 16th to go see a friend.

It wasn't until an anonymous caller made a phone call to Harvard police on the evening of June 4, 1982 that Brenda's missing persons case became a homicide. Brenda's lifeless body was found in a wooded area off Littleton County Road in Harvard, Massachusetts. Police indicate Brenda was most likely not killed where she was found but rather dumped there, possibly up to three weeks prior to being found.

Today the case of Brenda Lacombe remains open and unsolved.

I don't know if my abuser Dave Umpleby is responsible for the disappearance and vicious murder of Brenda Lacombe, but I am one-hundred percent positive he was capable of committing it. If you have any information about the murder of Brenda Lacombe please call the Worcester County DA's Office at (508) 755-8601

These young girl's murders were committed during the year my family remained living on Pleasant Street in 1981-1982 and would be the reason behind my courage to go back to the Lowell Police Department to report my abusers coincidences to multiple unsolved murders.

My abuser was thirty-nine years old when he first came into my life in 1975 and he was forty-five when he last violently assaulted me in 1981. I was not his first victim, I was not his last victim, nor was he done with his monstrous ways. He was an evil predator who tortured his female victims. His reminders throughout the years of girls he killed before me, were not so much as to threaten me, but more of him praising about how he got away with each one.

Dave Umpleby passed away in 2003, but the crimes he committed still remain unsolved. As I researched more about unsolved murders of women (1955-1990s) who were found in a place and manner my abuser praised about, the more horrifying it became. From his time in Maine, Florida and Massachusetts, unsolved murders seemed to follow throughout his life. Including the multiple unsolved murders from Massachusetts.

As the year 2017 was upon us, I was given good news, bad news, opinions, advice and praise. In January, I was informed social security wouldn't be hearing my case again until sometime in 2021. I was devastated and did what my lawyer insisted would get my case heard quicker, I closed out my claim from 2015 and I reapplied for my social security benefits.

In June, I was again denied as it was taken for a first time applying status because I had reapplied.

Life can throw punches that bruise right down to our soul and it's our job to keep going anyways.

I once again appealed social security's decision on their denial. I continued talking about my childhood abuse and I didn't keep anything back when I spoke. I was mad while dealing with my painful injuries, I was also dealing with the horrifying reality that another girl is buried inside that cellar wall on Pleasant Street.

I continued to meet with a counselor on a weekly basis. The more I talked the less ashamed I felt, the more I talked the less embarrassed I was, the more I talked the less silent I stayed and the more I talked, the more my courage grew. I was introduced to an advocate. I didn't feel defeated when I left my meetings with her. I felt like I was healing in a way that I became a survivor rather than the victim I was for over thirty years. She always said I was inspiring, yet she was so inspiring to me with her empathy, support and praise.

In September, I settled my case from my car accident. I received payment in October, found an apartment in November and moved in on the first of December. In that time I was also informed of a June 2018 court date to plead my disability case. My hands were tied and there was nothing I could do but wait another six months to receive what I worked my whole life for should I need it, my social security disability. I carried weights and bricks of hurt as I accepted the reality of my childhood, it wore on me like it was a fashion trend. Lorraine and my siblings could never understand how much their lack of everything has hurt me throughout the years.

I became a grandma for the second time in the first nine days of 2018. I underwent another radio-frequency, more Dysport injections and prepared myself for my June 14th court date for my social security. Just a few days before my court date, I was notified the date had to be postponed until July 18th. Another month and four days away and not a damn thing I could do about it.

I went home where I enjoyed my time with my kids and my granddaughters. I was in my own apartment again and I was happy to be where I was. But I couldn't shake the pain I felt. All I ever did to my birth mother Lorraine and my siblings was wanting the abuse to stop. It will always hurt knowing I was never really a part of their family. At times, it still made me doubt my strength the more I questioned myself. Why didn't I matter to them? Why did Lorraine allow those nude photos and films of her own daughter to exist? Why was Lorraine so scared of police finding out about the hole in the cellar wall? Why does it still bother me? I have empathy, I have a heart and that is so much more than my family ever gave to me.

It was finally July 18th and my day in social security court. The judge immediately informed me of his approval decision and how I should have never been denied in the first place. He talked more, made me cry and like so many others since I ran that day back in 1981, he praised me and he supported me. I've had nothing but positive people in my life since 1981, so why would I want to forget that? I may have just been a kid when I was abused, but that doesn't make it forgivable. I wasn't just smacked around. I was raped, I was brainwashed and I was terrorized for six years of my childhood. It ate at me, why Lorraine was so afraid of me going to the police back in 1985. Why degrade me just to steer me away from going to the police?

Meetings with my advocate continued as I continued to research unsolved murders to my abusers timeline of relationships. I worked the courage up to walk into my hometown police department and in August 2018, I did just that. I walked into the Lowell police department to inform them of my abusers possible connection to the unsolved murders in and around the city of Lowell. I wasn't dripping in sweat, I wasn't anxious and I wasn't scared. I actually knew the detective from when I cooked at the Owl diner. He listened to my story, informed me he had my stuff from 2016 and took my folder with a copy of all the coincidences and timelines my abuser has to unsolved murders. I left the police station so damn proud of myself.

Two weeks later in September, the detective called me. Sometimes the news you hear is like a sharp blade slicing through your soul, this was one of my sometimes. On the phone with the detective, I am told the cellar was full of cobwebs and had the impression no ones been down in that cellar for decades. I was told how they followed my map and the hole in the wall was right where the map showed it would be. But it was hidden behind boards and bricks. I didn't hear much after that and he talked for a bit. I instantly went hollow, sad, angry and so hurt. How could my family let me live this horror alone for so long? It didn't happen overnight, but I soon realized I wasn't angry anymore at my family, I was disappointed in them.

I called the detective a few days later and we talked more. It was too dangerous to investigate the huge hole dug in that cellar wall because the foundation and rocks are dangerously falling apart. We came to the agreement that I would drop off a copy of my memoir to him. Not so he knows what I lived through, but so he knows what my abuser was capable of, so he knows the threats I was feared into about his other victims and so he knows the many coincidences involving him to many unsolved murders. I made copies and highlighted the area's the detective should read.

I am not ashamed of what happened to me when I was a kid anymore and that is a huge step I took that led me into a pool of courage and support. The two things I lived more than half my life thinking I never had. I remembered every tear I cried and fear I felt. I now know it was 1981 and not 1980 when I ran that Saturday morning.

Highlighting parts of my memoir was traumatizing for me and the detective called a few weeks later asking if I forgot about him. I explained it was causing me to have nightmares and he informed me to drop it off as is. A few days later I handed a briefing of my memoir over to the detective and I felt like I was that fifteen-year old girl who was finally being heard. The detective informed me, he and a few other detectives have made numerous trips into that cellar located on Pleasant Street. They tried using flashlights and fishing poles in an attempt to see what is buried inside the deep, well dug out hole in the wall. But the falling rocks and foundation made it too dangerous to proceed at the moment. Dave Umpleby is now listed in the Lowell Police computerized database and though answers won't happen over night, I know one day, they will.

At times it felt like the wind was knocked right out of me, at times I gasped for breathes and at times I cried a horrifying, soul tearing, voiceless scream. The image of the cellar on Pleasant Street with Lorraine standing over a mound of rocks is all I could see no matter what I was looking at. I could feel the fist punch my gut every time as the vomit exited my mouth like a ricocheting rocket returning for another round. It disgusted me, yet it also saddened me for the little girl I once was. For decades I considered myself just another statistic in a world full of abused children. I was finally seeing I mattered and I wasn't just a statistic, I am a survivor.

I am proud of myself for doing what my fifteen year old self tried so hard to do back in 1985, but at the same time, it is a horrifying reality I live everyday. I now leave that aspect of my life to the detectives of the Lowell Police Department. It is not up to me to prove my abuser is responsible for these horrific crimes. It was only up to me, to tell my story and that I have done.

Soon the holidays were here and I just wanted to concentrate on the holidays. I was out Christmas shopping with a friend one Saturday in December and my cell phone started blowing up with calls and text messages. My daughters, my son, their cousins and my friends' kids were all notifying me about a degrading and insulting Facebook post my baby sister put on her Facebook page. She was upset with me for sharing my childhood trauma and family secrets on my blog that I started a year earlier. She claimed I was a delusion druggie with mental issues but after being bombarded with comments from the many who love me, she took the Facebook post down.

Later that night she called me through Facebook and we talked for over four hours before making plans for her to visit me the following day. We talked so much on the phone even though I couldn't understand why she wrote that Facebook post, I was just glad we were talking and I was happier when she visited me. She stayed for seven hours as we talked about my abuser who is also her father, we talked about our mother Lorraine, we talked about our siblings and we talked about the horror I lived for six years of my childhood. I felt like I owed her an explanation for being a lousy big sister. Shit, I didn't even know how to be a baby sister never mind a big one. But there I was for seven hours with my baby sister and this time she believed me. It was like a thousand pound boulder lifted off my shoulders knowing she believed me. Just two days later she began private messaging me through Facebook insisting I was wrong about our older brothers, her father, the years I claim I was abused and about my life. It wasn't long until I messaged her back to stop belittling me. Her messages stopped and the relationships I have always had with my siblings resumed back to what it always was. I may not have had the bonded protection from siblings in my life but for seven hours, I had a sister. I will never understand how long after the horror of my childhood was over, long after my abuser was no longer with Lorraine and long after we were adults, my family protected my abuser and silenced me. I lived over thirty years in shame, secrets and silence as a victim until reality showed me I was a survivor.

The year 2019 was full of emails and phone calls as many relatives and friends of the victims began reaching out to me through social media. I felt bad I was unable to be of any help to them and at the same time, I remind myself that I was just an eleven year old kid at the time.

Due to the graphic details of my childhood sexual rape, I wrote the first years of my abuse 1975-1982 in A Childhood Tragedy Under A Mother's Watch.

I tell my story in hopes I can help others understand the reality of being a statistic in a world full of abused children. I tell my story to unlock the silence of family secrets and to bring awareness towards childhood trauma. I lived my whole childhood as a trophy in a child predators sick world and my abuser was not finished when I ran in 1981. Do I believe my abuser is responsible for many unsolved murders in and around the New England area? My answer is, "Yes I do."

Detectives have a copy of my memoir, those young girl's murders still remain unsolved, hundreds of nude films and photos of my child self still remain buried in a cellar wall. I know one day, it will all be recovered and the city of Lowell will finally have answers about the monstrous predator my birth mother harbored.

As the Coronavirus put a stall in many aspects of our every day lives along with the unsafe foundation on Pleasant Street, retrieving all that is buried inside that cellar wall going into the sidewalk will resume once it is safe to do so. I will never get justice for what happened to me in my childhood, but it would be nice to have the closure of knowing those photos and film are in the hands of the police. As for healing; they say time heals everything, well I'm still waiting.

I will continue to push for the contents buried inside that cellar wall to come out. In the meantime, I continue to manage my life in a productive way. As horrifying as my life story is, I am grateful to be on the other side of my repressed memories. Without them, I would still be blaming myself for my childhood. I have no more questions or doubts when it comes to my childhood or the selective memories of my birth family. When the emotions of my childhood sneak up on me, I call a friend to talk, I let the tears fall and I do not blame myself anymore. I may have survived my childhood, but it doesn't mean I am not still surviving. Some days I still have to remind myself that I am safe, but now I also remind myself that I am not a secret anymore. One of the biggest steps I ever took was accepting it was never about the forgive and forget, it's about the acknowledgement and accountability.

As life goes on, I continue to write daily and as long as time will let it be, one day there will be a part three of my continuing life story. Until then, I look forward to my Spring 2023 release of Understanding Childhood Trauma, Do You Understand It Now? Because I have a lot to say and society has a lot it needs to understand.

If you or someone you know suffers from the daily stigma of childhood trauma and family secrets, please know it is ok to stand up, speak up and shatter the silence. We are not victims anymore, we are survivors.

Thank you for reading me.

An Abused Child

Wrap your arms around me
Give me your tightest hold.
You still wouldn't see my pain
Or the horror that's been told.

No way you could feel, my scars hidden so well.
No way to feel, these open wounds I tell.

A fear greater than evil, a cruelty beyond control.
A voice that's been silenced, through a shattered childhood soul.
Struggling for the strength or the words to a voice.
Society made the decision, silence is the best choice.

Decades go by, so much time lost
I'm telling my truth, no matter the cost.

My story will help others
To find their own strength
Scars to empower
Healing has no length.

Child Abuse is a matter
That shouldn't be taken mild
Even as an adult...
I was still once An Abused Child.

About the Author

Catherine Mellen is an American poet, author and blogger. Born in 1969 Lowell Massachusetts. She wrote her first poem at age fourteen and quickly adapted her love for words. Shamed by the childhood she lived, she became a cook and caterer for nearly three decades. An auto accident at age forty-five, left her disabled and a victim to horrifying repressed memories. In 2018 she started a blog where she shattered her silence on childhood trauma, family secrets and the monstrous predator her birth mother harbored.

Her poetry has been published in numerous poetry journals and she is the author of *A Childhood Tragedy Under A Mother's Watch: Part One 1975-1982 Lowell, Massachusetts*, *Christmas in Poetry Land* and *Survivor's Mind: When Childhood Trauma and Poetry Collide*, which is the poetry behind her lifetime of living in shame, secrets and silence along with the courage, strength and survival she wrote with each poem.

Upcoming releases include:
- American Dream, Tales of a Poet
- Understanding Childhood Trauma, Do You Understand It Now?
- A Promise Made, A Promise Kept… A true story of friendship, clairvoyance, and the undeniable bond of a promise.
- Christmas Stories in Poetry Land
- And many more, follow her on the Amazon or Goodreads app for updates of new releases.
- When Catherine isn't writing, she can be found enjoying her time with her children, granddaughters, and friend's.

Read about my life but don't have any pity, I am a strong Irish girl from an all-American city.

www.ingramcontent.com/pod-product-compliance
Lightning Source LLC
LaVergne TN
LVHW051827080426
835512LV00018B/2758